A Student's Guide to Analysis of Variance

In the investigation of human behaviour, statistical techniques are employed widely in the social sciences. Whilst introductory statistics courses cover essential techniques, the complexities of behaviour demand that more flexible and comprehensive methods are also employed. Analysis of Variance (ANOVA) has become one of the most common of these and it is therefore essential for both student and researcher to have a thorough understanding of it.

A Student's Guide to Analysis of Variance covers a range of statistical techniques associated with ANOVA, including single and multiple factor designs, various follow-up procedures such as *post-hoc* tests, and how to make sense of interactions. Suggestions on the best use of techniques and advice on how to avoid the pitfalls are included, along with guidelines on the writing of formal reports.

Introductory level topics such as standard deviation, standard error and *t*-tests are revised, making this book an invaluable aid to all students for whom ANOVA is a compulsory topic. It will also serve as a useful refresher for the more advanced student and practising researcher.

Maxwell J. Roberts and **Riccardo Russo** are experienced teachers of research methods and statistics. Both are lecturers in psychology at the University of Essex.

A Student's Guide to Analysis of Variance

Maxwell J. Roberts and
Riccardo Russo

Routledge
Taylor & Francis Group

LONDON AND NEW YORK

First published in 1999 by Routledge
11 New Fetter Lane, London, EC4P 4EE

Simultaneously published in the USA and Canada
by Routledge
29 West 35th Street, New York, NY 10001

Routledge is an imprint of the Taylor & Francis Group, an Informa business

Reprinted 2001, 2004, 2006 and 2008 by Routledge
27 Church Road, Hove, East Sussex BN3 2FA
270 Madison Avenue, New York NY 10016

Transferred to digital printing 2011

Typeset in Times by
J&L Composition Ltd, Filey, North Yorkshire
Printed and bound in Great Britain by
the MPG Books Group, Bodmin and King's Lynn

This publication has been produced with paper manufactured to
strict environmental standards and with pulp derived from
sustainable forests.

British Library Cataloguing in Publication Data
A catalogue record for this book is available from the British Library

Library of Congress Cataloging in Publication Data
Roberts, Maxwell, J.
   A student's guide to analysis of variance/Maxwell
J. Roberts and Riccardo Russo
   Includes bibliographical references and index
   1. Analysis of variance,   I. Russo, Riccardo.
   II. Title.
   QA279.R63   1999
    519.5'38–dc21   98–27699

ISBN: 978–0–415–16564–8 (hbk)
ISBN: 978–0–415–16565–5 (pbk)

Max Roberts
  To my parents

Riccardo Russo
  To my parents

Contents

List of figures   x
List of tables   xiii
List of boxes   xv
Preface   xvii
Acknowledgements   xx

1   Introduction   1

2   Averages, measures of dispersal and the *t*-test   9

Summarising data 9
Distribution 10
Variability 13
Testing for differences with the t-test 17
Intuitive statistics 22
Using one- and two-tailed tests 23
A note on statistical power 27

3   Using variance to test hypotheses   30

**4   Calculating *F* ratios for one-factor between-subjects
designs**   41

5   One-factor between-subjects ANOVA: advanced topics   62

ANOVA and the central limit theorem 62
Assumptions underlying ANOVA 69
Dealing with rogue data 75

6   **Following up a one-factor between-subjects ANOVA**   **82**

The meanings of ANOVA outcomes 82
Pairwise comparisons for single-factor designs:
  planned comparisons and post-hoc *testing 84*
Making comparisons between every possible pair of
  means 92
Linear contrast analysis for single-factor designs 98

7   **Calculating *F* ratios for one-factor within-subjects**
   designs   **110**

Sources of error variability 112
Calculating F for a within-subjects design 118
Planned comparisons and post-hoc *testing 128*

8   **An introduction to factorial designs and interactions**   **134**

Outcomes of factorial designs 137
Managing factorial designs 148

9   **Calculating *F* ratios for two-factor between-subjects**
   designs   **153**

Analysing a 2 × 2 between-subjects factorial
  design 156

10   **Following up a two-factor between-subjects ANOVA**   **172**

Some pitfalls in interpreting interactions 191

11   **Interpreting two-factor mixed and within-subjects**
   designs   **194**

12   **Interpreting a three-factor ANOVA**   **211**

13   **Summary and frequently asked questions**   **224**

A summary of follow-up tests for Analysis of
  Variance 224
Frequently asked questions 227

Appendix A: Writing up the results of Analysis of Variance   **233**

Appendix B: Statistical tables   **244**

Notes   258
References   260
Index   261

Figures

2.1 Frequency histograms showing data which are close to a normal distribution (top), a negatively skewed distribution (middle left), a positively skewed distribution (middle right) and a bimodal distribution (bottom)   12

2.2 Frequency histograms showing highly varied data (left) and more uniform data (right)   13

2.3 The component parts of the between-subjects t-test   21

2.4 Comparisons of one- and two-tailed statistical tests   25

3.1 Low within-group variability, and hence low standard error, is important when comparing group means   35

4.1 The location of the within-group variance in a two-group study   45

4.2 The location of the between-group variance in a two-group study   48

5.1 Distributions of data in three experiments showing normal data which conform to the assumptions of ANOVA (left), skewed data that are still analysable by ANOVA (centre) and mixed data that cannot be analysed by ANOVA (right)   71

5.2 Distributions of data which clearly violate the homogeneity of variance assumption   73

5.3 A plausible relationship between the number of problems solved and problem solving skill   76

6.1 The two possible outcomes when using Analysis of Variance to analyse a single-factor design   83

6.2   A linear trend in an experiment with three levels
      (left) and a quadratic trend in an experiment with
      three levels (right)   101
6.3   Two sets of data which fit a linear trend equally
      well   108
8.1   A $2 \times 2 \times 2$ design   138
8.2   Two interaction plots showing the four cell
      means (top) and, for comparison, the four level
      means (bottom) taken from Table 8.3   140
8.3   Interaction plot showing no significant effects   141
8.4   Two interaction plots, each showing one
      significant main effect only   142
8.5   Interaction plot showing two significant main
      effects and no interaction   142
8.6   Simple main effects illustrated   144
8.7   The original expertise study cell means from
      Table 8.3   145
8.8   Three different interactions: all have non-parallel
      lines   146
8.9   The effect of scale on the visual appearance of
      an interaction plot   146
8.10 A 2×3 design showing an interaction despite
      the two simple main effects of factor B being
      identical (upper graph). The interaction is due to
      the three differently significant simple main
      effects of factor A (lower graph)   147
8.11 No effect of background music on memory test
      score (upper graph) but this conceals a
      significant interaction that links performance to
      music preference (lower graph)   149
9.1   A typical 2×2 between-subjects design (top) and
      its two main effects (bottom)   154
9.2   The four simple main effects for a typical 2×2
      between-subjects design   155
9.3   Two illustrations of interaction in relation to the
      simple main effects   155
9.4   An illustration of a less straightforward
      interaction in relation to the simple main effects   156
9.5   The wrong way to calculate an error term for a
      between-subjects factorial design   162

10.1   A predicted outcome (top left) but with an
       unexpected difference (top right), and a predicted
       outcome (bottom left) but one of the actual
       differences is unexpectedly small (bottom right)   172
10.2   Four pairwise comparisons to test the simple
       main effects of a 2×2 ANOVA   174
10.3   The between-group Sum of Squares for a main
       effect is calculated from the sizes of the level
       means in relation to the grand mean (top) but the
       between-group Sum of Squares for a simple main
       effect is calculated from the sizes of the cell means
       in relation to the mean of these cell means only
       (bottom)   175
10.4   Interaction plot showing the location of the
       specific simple main effects of interest for the
       example data   187
10.5   Interaction plot showing the three key significant
       differences   191
10.6   An interaction created by a ceiling effect (top)
       and an interaction concealed by a ceiling effect
       (bottom)   192
11.1   Plot showing the interaction between expertise
       and position type for the example data   198
11.2   Plot showing the interaction between passage
       type and word frequency for the example data   205
12.1   Two interaction plots for recall data showing an
       effect of context for recall memory but not for
       recognition memory   217
12.2   Interaction plot for 9-year-olds showing that
       many errors are made when pronouncing low
       frequency irregular words   221

Tables

2.1	Two experiments which are identical apart from the difference between means	22
2.2	Two experiments which are identical apart from the numbers of subjects	23
2.3	Two experiments which are identical apart from the standard deviations	23
3.1	Examples of between- and within-group variability	36
4.1	ANOVA equations for two- and three-factor between-subjects designs	55
4.2	ANOVA table based on the mnemonic experiment example	56
4.3	ANOVA table summarising the component parts for a between-subjects design	61
6.1	Some examples of weights for testing specific hypotheses	103
7.1–7.5	Various ways in which pairs of subjects with pairs of scores can be different	113
7.6	Data with high between-subject variability	114
7.7	Data with low between-subject variability	114
7.8	Using between-subjects ANOVA on a within-subjects design	116
7.9	Using within-subjects ANOVA on a within-subjects design	118
7.10	Removing between-subject variability	119
7.11	Summary of components for within-subjects ANOVA	127
7.12	Summary ANOVA table for the counting example	128

7.13	Within-subjects ANOVA with correction to p values applied	132
8.1	A 2×2 factorial design	136
8.2	A 2×3 factorial design	137
8.3	Imaginary data for a 2×2 expertise study	138
9.1	Summary table for the components of a 2×2 fully between-subjects design ANOVA	166
9.2	Data from a driving study with non-orthogonal factors	168
9.3	ANOVA table using unweighted means	170
10.1	Summary of procedures for calculating simple main effects for a 2×2 fully between-subjects design	178
10.2	Simple main effects analysis for the example data	186
11.1	Simple main effects analysis for the expertise data	198
11.2	Individual calculations for a 2×2 mixed design ANOVA	200
11.3	Simple main effects analysis for the letter deletion data	205
11.4	Individual calculations for a 2×2 fully within-subjects design ANOVA	207
12.1	Raw data for the memory and context study	214
12.2	Cell and level means for the memory and context study	214
12.3	ANOVA table for the memory and context study	215
12.4	Simple simple main effects table for the memory and context study	215
12.5	Cell means compared by the first simple simple main effect in Table 12.4	216
12.6	Raw data for the word pronunciation study	219
12.7	Cell and level means for the word pronunciation study	219
12.8	ANOVA table for the word pronunciation study	220
12.9	ANOVA table for 7-year-old children	220
12.10	ANOVA table for 9-year-old children	221
12.11	Simple main effects table for 9-year-old children	221
A1	Imaginary data for a reasoning experiment	241
A2	Transformed data for the reasoning experiment	242

Boxes

3.1 An example of a simple between-subjects design
    experiment   31

4.1 The performance of mnemonic and control groups   43

4.2 Calculating the within-group Sum of Squares for
    the mnemonic example   46

4.3 The preferred method for calculating the within-
    group Sum of Squares   47

4.4 Calculating the between-group Sum of Squares for
    the mnemonic example   49

4.5 The preferred method for calculating the between-
    group Sum of Squares   50

4.6 Calculating the degrees of freedom for the
    mnemonic example   54

4.7 Demonstrating basic ratios   59

4.8 Basic ratios for the mnemonic example   61

5.1 Estimating the population variance when the null
    hypothesis is true   66

5.2 Estimating the population variance when the null
    hypothesis is false   68

5.3 An example showing a comparison of variance
    between groups   74

6.1 An example study involving planned comparisons   86

6.2 Making planned comparisons on the example data   89

6.3 Performing a Scheffé test on the example data   91

6.4 Performing the Tukey test (equal numbers of
    subjects per group)   95

6.5 Data for an investigation of the relationship
    between stress level and performance   102

6.6	Calculations of L for various possible predictions from the example data	104
6.7	F tests for the contrasts outlined in Box 6.6	105
7.1	A digit Stroop task and data	120
7.2	Applying the formula to calculate the between-subject Sum of Squares	123
7.3	Using basic ratios to calculate between-subject variance	125
7.4	Computing the components for the counting example	126
7.5	Variances of difference scores	130
9.1	Example data for a 2×2 between-subjects design	157
9.2	Calculating the necessary basic ratios for analysing the example data	160
9.3	Calculating the Sums of Squares discussed so far, using the example data	163
9.4	Calculating the Sums of Squares for the interaction using the example data	164
9.5	Calculating the degrees of freedom for the example data	165
9.6	ANOVA table and interpretation for the example data	166
10.1	Calculating between-group Sums of Squares for the expertise example	177
10.2	Completing the expertise example	179
10.3	Data and preliminary analysis for the anxiety study	184
10.4	Performing the planned comparisons on the selected data	189
11.1	Preliminary analysis for the expertise data	195
11.2	Performing ANOVA on the expertise data	200
11.3	Preliminary analysis for the letter deletion data	203
11.4	Performing ANOVA on the letter deletion data	208
A1	Writing up a single-factor ANOVA	235
A2	Specimen results section for the expertise study in Chapter 11	237
A3	Specimen results section for the letter deletion study in Chapter 11	238
A4	Specimen results section for the transformed data	243

Preface

Analysis of Variance is a statistical test in widespread use in psychology and related disciplines, but whose coverage in otherwise comprehensive introductory texts is usually incomplete. This is particularly the case when techniques for analysing factorial designs are discussed. Books which cover Analysis of Variance comprehensively are usually too advanced for intermediate students, use frightening notation, or do not make clear which knowledge is essential for the successful analysis of undergraduate project work. Faced with this, and having been set the task of teaching intermediate statistics, the first author decided against recommending a book which might not quite go far enough in coverage, or cover too much introductory material, or be too advanced, and prepared his own course handouts instead. These grew in number, and developed with field testing, until they provided quite a comprehensive guide to Analysis of Variance. Gradually, it became apparent that it might be possible to develop a book from them. The second author, meanwhile, was teaching an advanced statistics course to undergraduate and graduate students, using his own handouts, which complemented those of the intermediate level course, and the decision was made to join forces in order to complete the project.

This book is different from other statistics texts because it aims only to cover the essentials of Analysis of Variance. This stems from the philosophy that it is better to teach a few topics well than many topics badly, and that a good understanding of statistics is preferable to learning a set of procedures by rote or how to press the right button on a computer. The main intended audience is undergraduate psychology students who have just completed a course in introductory statistics, but the book will also be a useful refresher for graduate students, and cover useful ground for any researcher in related disciplines who is comparing groups in order to find out whether they differ.

The book is structured so that readers are introduced to topics fairly gently, and we have kept advanced material to a minimum. However, we do assume that all readers have already successfully completed an introductory statistics or research methods course. We have tried to keep the notation under control, and have made full use of figures where appropriate. Before introducing Analysis of Variance, we begin with two revision chapters. Their aim is to identify the key topics in previous teaching and outline their importance. In our experience, this is useful to students for at least two reasons. The long vacation gives ample opportunity to forget material, and introductory courses quite often shower students with a very diverse range of topics, not all of which are relevant to Analysis of Variance (ANOVA). In subsequent chapters, we cover single- and multi-factor ANOVA, and have extensive coverage on the meaning of interaction and how to make sense of factorial designs. Although this book contains many formulae, it is neither a cookbook nor a workbook of exercises. However, we do believe that performing ANOVA on small data sets with small numbers assists the learning of the underlying principles. *Small* is the key word here, and we also believe that there is little to be gained in analysing real data sets by hand. In addition, all of our examples have been devised with our likely readership in mind wherever possible.

Given that we expect most students to perform ANOVA by computer, the reader may be surprised that we have not linked this text to any of the currently available computer packages. There are several reasons for this, not least that it prevents the book from quickly going out of date. In addition, linking the book to a particular package will deter instructors who do not wish to use that package for their teaching purposes, immediately making many pages at best irrelevant and at worst confusing. We are also concerned that a statistics course that is too heavily based on computer exercises can substitute a knowledge of procedures for the understanding of fundamental principles, so that the outcome is highly proficient computer operators rather than competent statisticians. For example, the psychologist who understands why unbalanced factorial design should be analysed by using the unweighted means approach is far more likely to bother to check the values of the unweighted means, as opposed to the weighted means which most computer packages give by default. Similarly, the psychologist who understands why it is usually absurd for a small difference between means to be significant but a large difference from the same experiment to be non-significant is far more likely to spot computer software that performs the Newman–Keuls test incorrectly (to date three such professional packages have been discovered by the authors).

Our coverage of topics is necessarily selective, but we none the less intend any reader, following our suggestions, to be able to analyse data in a way that is acceptable for most undergraduate projects, possibly for publication in a professional journal. Thus, for example, we do not discuss the massive range of *post-hoc* tests available, instead we suggest those which are versatile, have widespread acceptance and do their job perfectly well. Curious readers are referred elsewhere. However, we have covered the important topics of analysing and interpreting factorial designs in detail. These are some of the most frequent experimental designs in psychology, and precisely the designs where readers will require the most help. Overall, our intention is to give confident readers sufficient background to enable them to take their own decisions, while giving less confident readers preferred courses of action if they do not trust their own decision making, although we by no means present our advice in the form of absolute truths.

We have steered clear of advanced material so that this book may be used for a short, self-contained intermediate level course; readers are referred to other texts should the need arise to understand more advanced topics. The exact use of this book depends upon the intended structure of the course. For highly mathematically confident students, it should be possible to squeeze all topics into 12 or even 10 one-hour lectures, especially if the revision material at the beginning is omitted. For less confident students, covering all of the material and combining with additional examples can easily result in a course that occupies an entire academic year.

Finally, a brief note on style. In order to improve the flow of text, we have tried to avoid writing in the third person whenever possible. We have varied style between first and second person and between singular and plural. This is partly deliberate, enabling us to avoid the clumsy 'he or she' and the ungrammatical 'they', plus we believe that a varied style tends to make a text more readable.

Acknowledgements

We would like to thank the people who have read various versions of this manuscript and made suggestions and corrections. These include David Clark-Carter, Margot Roberts, Linda Murdoch, Elizabeth Newton and Christopher Douce. Many improvements were made as a result of their feedback. In addition, staff and students at various universities have brought to our attention numerous corrections and suggestions for the course handouts upon which this book is based. We are very grateful for all the help that we have received from the named sources and others, although, of course, any remaining errors are the authors' alone.

The Studentized Range Statistic tables are based upon those devised by L.H. Harter and are reproduced with the permission of the Institute of Mathematical Statistics.

Chapter 1

Introduction

A book devoted to a single statistical test may seem excessive, but Analysis of Variance is more a collection of data analysis techniques than a single statistical test. In trained hands, they are extremely powerful and can make sense of the most convoluted data sets, but in untrained hands they can occasionally be dangerous. However, we will be starting at the basics and working forwards slowly. Although formulae and worked examples are given, we will keep the numbers of subjects and the scores low, simplifying the worked examples. In the first two chapters, we will begin by revising the most important topics that you were taught on your introductory courses. We will then discuss experimental designs in which a single independent variable can have three or more levels, and then designs with more than one independent variable. Hence, if you have ever been frustrated by being restricted to trying studies with one independent variable and two levels, or have been forced to choose between two alternative independent variables when you would have preferred to try both, then you will find the scope of these more advanced statistical tests to be liberating. However, first we must start with the basics, and to begin with we will recap on some of the key phrases that the remainder of the book will assume you are familiar with.

Experiment

For an experiment, at least two groups of subjects, or the same group of subjects on at least two different occasions, are treated exactly alike in all important ways with one exception – the experimental treatment. Any differences observed in the behaviour between the conditions must have been caused by the difference in the experimental treatments. Typically, the experimental process has five components:

(a) Subjects are allocated randomly to different experimental treatments.
(b) The experimenter is careful to vary only the treatment of interest.
(c) The experimenter measures some aspect of the behaviour of the subjects.
(d) If there are differences between the groups, the experimenter concludes that these differences were caused by the treatment.
(e) The experimenter interprets these results.

Experiments have several advantages over other forms of research. In particular, they are the only way of showing that there is a direct causal relationship between a particular treatment and measured behaviour. As long as the experiment is performed properly, differences must be due to the treatment and nothing else. However, this is not the end of the story. The results may be open to interpretation, they may not generalise to other situations, or they may need to be replicated.

Sometimes you may run a study which appears to be an experiment but is not. For example, males and females are often compared. These studies are not experiments; they are quasi-experiments. The experimenter is not controlling the classification – it is not possible to decide randomly whether a subject will be male or female – and this means that the exact cause of any difference can never be known.

Variables

A variable has the property that it can take different values. In other words, it varies. All psychologists are looking for relationships between variables. In experiments there are two types of variable. The *independent variable* is manipulated by the experimenter. This is also known as the *treatment variable*. Independent variables have at least two different levels; these are the experimental conditions. The *dependent variable* is measured by the experimenter in order to investigate the effects of manipulating the independent variable, hence it *depends* upon the independent variable for its value. Good dependent variables are readily observable, easily expressed as numbers, and measure the behaviour that they are intended to measure (i.e. they are valid). In quasi-experiments, instead of independent variables there are *classification variables*. Subjects are still assigned to groups, but the assignment is out of the control of the experimenter.

Samples and populations

Population refers to everyone. Thus you could talk about the population of UK university students, in which case you would be referring to every current university student in the country. Psychologists like to draw conclusions that apply to everyone, but because they do not have time to test everyone, they test *samples* from populations instead. They then try to decide whether the results they found for the samples apply to the entire populations from which they were drawn.

Experimental design

For a *between-subjects design*, also called an *independent subjects design*, two or more separate, completely independent groups of subjects are tested. Each group is assigned to a different experimental condition. Each subject contributes one single score to the final analysis. These designs have the advantage that you do not need to worry about fatigue or practice effects due to subjects' having to perform lots of different tasks. They have the disadvantage that they are less powerful than the alternative, so that many more subjects are required (see below). It is also possible that, due to bad luck, groups may be assembled that differ even before you test them. In order to avoid this problem, plenty of subjects need to be run, and they must be allocated to groups randomly or as unsystematically as possible, so that it is unlikely that groups are being created that differ.

For a *within-subjects design*, sometimes called a *repeated measures design*, one single group of subjects is tested once with each of the experimental conditions, and there must be at least two of these. Hence, each subject contributes at least two scores to the final analysis. Alternatively, similar subjects such as identical twins can be given one task each, but are then analysed as matched pairs using a within-subjects design. Within-subjects designs have the advantage that they are more powerful than between-subjects designs and so they need relatively fewer subjects. The disadvantage of this design is that steps must be taken to eliminate practice effects and fatigue effects. These are collectively known as *order effects* and can sometimes lead to uninterpretable results. The order of testing of conditions should be determined randomly to try to cancel these out. Alternatively, you can counterbalance, in which case exactly half of the subjects receive one order, and the other half receive the opposite order of conditions – more elaborate procedures are necessary if there are more than two. Order effects can occasionally cause very serious problems, so if you have the time and resources available to you, think about using a between-subjects design; sometimes you will not have a choice.

Error and bias

Whenever something is to be measured, there is always the potential for measuring it inaccurately. Some measurement errors can be reduced, but some can never be eliminated. As long as the size of the error is sufficiently small in relation to the size of the effect that you are trying to detect, measurement error will not be a problem. There are arguments against over-controlling an experiment in order to reduce errors to a minimum. The 'perfect experiment' would be impossible to implement, and if you can still get clear cut results despite 'noisy data' then this indicates that the results are robust.

Random errors are caused by non-systematic variations in performance in addition to those that are intended by the experimental manipulation. Hence, performance always differs from person to person, and even among individuals from trial to trial. People differ in motivation, knowledge, experience, health, attention span, etc. It is impossible to control for everything, although a within-subjects design can reduce these problems. Sometimes there may be random errors due to the actual running of the experiment, though these should not be too much of a problem unless the experimenter is very sloppy indeed. Random errors can never be completely removed, but if you run enough subjects, their effects should cancel each other out. Their consequences are to muddy results and make them less clear cut.

Systematic errors bias the results because they vary in tandem with the experimental conditions and confound them. This could be caused by, for example, testing subjects for one condition in the morning and for another in the afternoon. Unless you are careless, these errors should not be a problem.

In addition, *floor effects* and *ceiling effects* can bias the results of an experiment. A floor effect occurs when most subjects are performing so badly that their performance cannot get any worse. A ceiling effect occurs when performance is so good that it cannot get any better.

Statistical hypotheses: the null and the alternative hypothesis

Whenever a statistical procedure is used, at least one statistical hypothesis is being tested. This is distinct from a research hypothesis, which is a general statement that makes a prediction about the outcome of an experiment. A research hypothesis might be the prediction that one group will be, say, faster than another. A statistical hypothesis is a more explicit statement of the different possible outcomes that are associated with a particular research hypothesis. Instructions on how to write up a laboratory report often advise you to end the introduction section with your experimental hypotheses. You should take this to mean research hypotheses rather than statistical hypotheses. This is a common source of confusion.

Unfortunately, it is never possible to prove that anything is true. If you see 1,000 white swans, this does not prove that swans are always white. However, if you see just one black swan, this *disproves* that swans are always white. Because of this problem, statisticians think in terms of *disproving* that there is *no difference* between the means of two groups rather than proving that there is a difference between them. Disproving that there is no difference involves testing the null hypothesis.

For a two-condition experiment, the null hypothesis (H_0) would be that there is no difference between the means of the two conditions. The alternative hypothesis (H_1) would then be that there is a difference between the means of the two conditions. The purpose of a statistical test is to tell whether you should *either* reject the null hypothesis *or* fail to reject the null hypothesis. If you reject the null hypothesis, then you have disproved that the means of the groups do not differ, and you can safely accept the alternative hypothesis: that the means of the groups do differ. If the means are different, and this is an experiment, then the only possible reason for this difference is the experimental treatment, so you conclude that the different levels of the independent variable caused the behaviour of the groups to differ. If you fail to reject the null hypothesis, then you have failed to disprove that the means of the two groups do not differ, and you therefore cannot accept the alternative hypothesis. This does not prove that there is no difference between the means of the two groups. Instead this shows that there is not sufficient evidence to reject the null hypothesis. A new, better designed experiment might supply this evidence.

Statistical errors

Statistical testing is based upon confidence and not certainty. You could be extremely confident that the means of two groups differ, or you could lack confidence that the means of two groups differ. Without certainty, however, there is always the possibility that there might be a statistical error. A *Type I Error* occurs when the null hypothesis is rejected by mistake. You conclude that there is a difference between the means of two groups when in fact the null hypothesis is true for the population from which the sample was taken. In other words, you have concluded that the independent variable influences performance, when really it is not related to performance in the general population. A *Type II Error* occurs when there is a failure to reject the null hypothesis by mistake. You conclude that there is no evidence for a difference between the means of the two groups when, in fact, the null hypothesis is false for the population from which the sample was taken. In other words, you have concluded that there is no evidence that the independent variable influences performance, when really it does influence performance in the general population.

Significance levels

It is possible to calculate the probability that the difference between a pair of means arose due to chance. If the probability is unlikely enough, the null hypothesis is rejected and therefore the independent variable must have been responsible for the difference. Psychologists use an arbitrary cut-off point in order to decide whether to reject or fail to reject the null hypothesis. They thus decide upon a significance level. If the probability that the results arose due to chance is 0.05 (or 1/20, or 5%) or less, then you can say that $p < 0.05$ and the null hypothesis can be rejected. Thus, the difference in means between the two groups is said to be significant, as opposed to non-significant, *never* insignificant. Hence, statisticians are accepting that 1 time in 20, a Type I Error will be made. There is nothing you can do about this except replicate findings, although if you are really unlucky the replication may also be a Type I Error. Sometimes, a more stringent cut-off is used ($p < 0.01$). However, this increases the risk of making a Type II Error. Statistical testing involves compromise.

It is easier to interpret a significant difference than a non-significant difference. A significant difference arises due to the independent variable. There are many factors that could lead to finding a non-significant difference; for example, a poorly implemented experiment, too few subjects, inappropriate materials, etc., quite apart from the fact that there could be no effect due to the independent variable. For this reason, avoid experiments where you predict as your main research hypothesis that there will not be a difference between the means. If you fail to find a difference this either shows that the theory is correct, or that the experiment was an inappropriate test of the theory. There is no way of telling these two apart.

One important point to beware of: in statistical terms, a significant difference indicates that you can generalise the finding to the populations from which the samples were drawn and that you are likely to get similar findings with other samples. Think of this as a *reliable* difference. In statistics, *significant* does not necessarily mean that the results are *exciting*. A highly significant difference simply shows that the null hypothesis is very unlikely to be true, and that the means are very likely also to be different in the populations under the same conditions. Also, you should never confuse the size of an effect with its significance; a tiny difference between a pair of means can be significant while in other circumstances a huge difference could be non-significant. For these reasons, avoid using the phrase 'significant result'. Not only is it technically incorrect, it is also ambiguous. Always talk about significant differences or significant effects instead.

Parametric statistical tests

Introductory courses in statistics usually make the distinction between *parametric* and *non-parametric* (or *distribution-free*) statistical tests. Although these can be used in similar situations, they work in different ways.

Parametric statistical tests include the t-test and Pearson's r correlation. Analysis of Variance also comes under this heading. These statistical tests are more powerful than their non-parametric equivalents. This means that if there is an effect to find, they will be more likely to find it. These types of statistical test are all based upon the use of means, standard deviations and variances, and make the assumption that only certain types of data with certain properties will be analysed (see Chapter 5). If data that do not have these properties are analysed, the tests will be more prone to error. However, it has been found that most of the time, these tests will be effective even with minor violations of the assumptions. Hence, they are *robust*.

Non-parametric statistical tests are generally less powerful than parametric tests, but fewer assumptions about data are necessary in order to use them. This means that the tests are much less likely to be affected by data which are, for example, highly varied from group to group or perhaps very skewed (see Chapter 2). Most parametric tests have a non-parametric equivalent. For example, there is the Wilcoxon test for comparing pairs of scores in a within-subjects design; the Mann–Whitney test for comparing pairs of groups in a between-subjects design; and the Spearman correlation. There are many other useful tests that may be used (see, for example, Neave and Worthington, 1988). Unfortunately, complicated experimental designs which require intricate analyses are less suited to non-parametric tests, and so more care has to be taken to ensure that the data are suitable for analysis by a parametric statistical test.

Chapter 2

Averages, measures of dispersal and the *t*-test

This chapter is intended for people who have recently completed a course in introductory statistical techniques. These courses usually cover a very wide variety of topics: measures of central tendency and dispersion; parametric and non-parametric tests; tests for differences; and tests for association to name but a few. This chapter gives a guided tour of the basic topics that are the most essential in order to understand Analysis of Variance and related statistical techniques.

Analysis of Variance is a statistical test used to assess whether means obtained from experimental conditions are significantly different from each other. In order to achieve this, a series of calculations must be carried out using *Sums of Squares* and *variances*. However, before describing these steps, we will review some of the most important measures of central tendency and variability, and some issues about the distribution of data, which are relevant to Analysis of Variance. Given that this test is related to the *t*-test we will provide a brief recap of this, followed by a discussion of the use of one- and two-tailed tests and the importance of statistical power.

Summarising data

When data are collected, they must be summarised so that a reader can make sense of them. Presenting raw data is unhelpful because humans simply find it impossible to make sense of a mass of numbers. Instead of this, the reader will need to know the most typical value for each experimental condition, and a measure of how well this value summarises the data or, in other words, a measure of dispersion. It is essential that *both* of these are presented in the results section of a formal report.

Measures of central tendency: averages

The most common form of average used to summarise a set of data is the *arithmetic mean*. This is calculated by adding all the obtained scores and then dividing this sum by the number of scores:

$$\text{mean: } \bar{X} = \frac{\sum X}{N}$$

where $\bar{X}$ is a shorthand way of referring to the mean of a set of numbers, $\sum X$ refers to the total of the set of numbers and N stands for the number of scores that made up the total. For example, the mean of 45, 34, 23, 12 and 36 is [45 + 34 + 23 + 12 + 36] / 5 = 30.

Other common measures of central tendency are the *mode* and the *median*. The mode is the most commonly occurring value in a distribution, while the median is the middle value (or the mean of the two middle values) of a set of numbers rearranged in rank order. For example the median of 2, 2, 2, 9, 10, 12, 14, 55 and 137 is 10 while the mode is 2. Although the arithmetic mean is the most widely used measure of central tendency, it is not always appropriate. For example, a mean can be distorted by a single very small or very large score in the way that a mode or a median cannot. In addition, means are sometimes meaningless. Although it is often claimed that the mean size of family is 2.4 children, this is unhelpful. An average is supposed to represent the most typical value that best summarises a set of data, and very few families have 2.4 children.

Distribution

Knowing the shape of the distribution of a set of data is an extremely important, and often neglected, part of the data analysis process. Awkwardly distributed data may require a rethink of the way in which they will be analysed, or worse still, no statistical analysis may be possible. *For this reason, it is essential that the shape of the data is known before any number crunching is to take place.* Plotting the data on a frequency histogram is the best way of gaining a useful first impression of their distribution, even though histograms rarely need to be displayed in formal reports.

The top of Figure 2.1 shows data whose 'shape' resembles a normal distribution. There is a clear central point and the distribution is reasonably symmetrical either side of it. Normally distributed data have characteristic mathematical properties which enable the computation of *parametric statistical tests*, such as *t*-tests, Pearson correlations and Analysis of Variance. Many psychological and biological variables are normally distributed in the general population.

Unfortunately, many psychological and biological variables are not normally distributed in the general population. Usually, the data are not symmetrical and instead are negatively or positively skewed. Negatively skewed distributions have a prominent tail to the left, and an example is depicted in Figure 2.1 (middle left). Positively skewed distributions have a prominent tail to the right, and an example is also shown in Figure 2.1 (middle right). Response times, a very common measure of performance in psychology, are usually positively skewed and care may be required when analysing any skewed data. This is because parametric statistical tests such as the *t*-test are intended to compare means. For skewed data, the mean is distorted by the tail of the distribution and the mean is hence a less suitable measure of the most typical value of the data. Approaches to deal with skewed distributions are suggested in Chapter 5.

Bimodally distributed data (see Figure 2.1, bottom) should be treated with caution. At an extreme, the data will be unanalysable *by any method*. With a bimodal distribution, the data have two clear separate 'central' points as can be seen in the rather extreme example. Suppose we are comparing two group means by using a *t*-test and the data of one of the groups are distributed as in Figure 2.1. We could calculate the mean of these data, and this would be about 50, but there would be little point. The mean, like any average, is supposed to represent the most typical value of a set of data, but in this example, the mean represents one of the *least typical values*. Hardly anyone scored 50, so this value is a poor benchmark of group performance for the purpose of comparing the overall group performance with others.

Whatever the statistical test used, whether parametric or non-parametric, bimodally distributed data are particularly difficult to interpret. Ultimately, any group with data distributed in this way

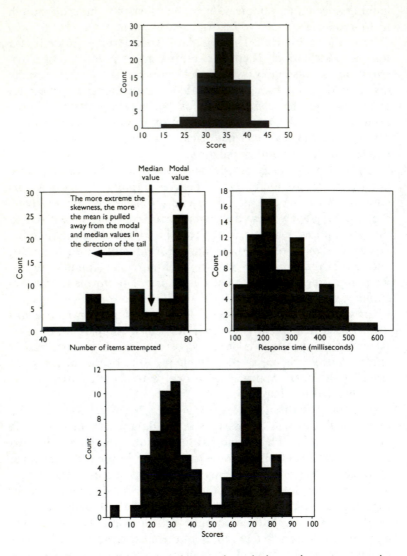

Figure 2.1 Frequency histograms showing data which are close to a normal distribution (top), a negatively skewed distribution (middle left), a positively skewed distribution (middle right) and a bimodal distribution (bottom)

appears to contain two types of subject. Faced with this pattern of data, you should consider dividing a bimodal group into sub-groups and see whether there is a clear reason why these should exist.

Variability

Two normal, or approximately normal, distributions with the same mean may still be very different due to the different dispersions, or variabilities, of the values around the means (see Figure 2.2). Some measure of the *variability* of the data is therefore also essential to summarise them. This will show the diversity of the performance and, indirectly, how effectively the measure of central tendency describes the data.

Variance and standard deviation

There are several ways of describing the variability of data numerically, but the most important measures for parametric statistical tests, including Analysis of Variance, are the *variance* and the *standard deviation*. Both represent the variability of data in relation to a mean, so that the larger the variance or standard deviation, the more varied the scores. The first step for calculating a variance for a set of numbers is to calculate the distance between every single data point and the overall mean. These distances are known

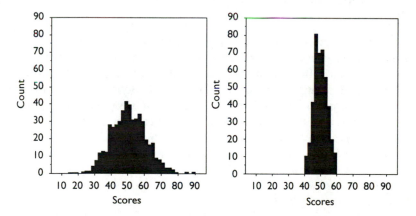

Figure 2.2 Frequency histograms showing highly varied data (left) and more uniform data (right)

as *deviation scores*. If data are highly varied with many data points some distance from the mean, then these deviation scores will mainly be large. The next step is to square these deviation scores and find their total. The total of the squared deviations, usually known as the *Sum of Squares*, is a useful measure of variability, but only when comparing groups of equal size. The Sum of Squares is therefore not always a meaningful figure by itself; a group with a larger number of scores will usually have a higher total than a smaller group, even if the data are equally diverse. The next step is therefore to find the *mean* of the total of the squared deviations. It is here that the equations can go down two separate routes.

If you have collected an entire population of scores, such as an entire school, then an exact value for the variance can be calculated as follows:

$$\text{variance: } \sigma^2 = \frac{\Sigma(X - \mu)^2}{N}$$

where σ^2 stands for the variance, but only if the exact value can be calculated, and μ (pronounced 'mew') is the symbol that stands for the mean of the population that has been tested.

The standard deviation for the population is the square root of the variance:

$$\text{standard deviation: } \sigma = \sqrt{\frac{\Sigma(X - \mu)^2}{N}}$$

If the scores represent a *sample* drawn from the *population* of interest, it is necessary to estimate the variance and standard deviations of this population from the values of the sample. Instead of taking the mean of the Sum of Squares, the Sum of Squares must be divided by the *degrees of freedom*. Hence, the denominator of the equation is $N - 1$ rather than N. *When reporting a standard deviation in a formal report, the population estimation value should always be used unless you have tested an entire population. This value is always the slightly larger when both equations are applied to the same data.*

$$\text{Variance estimated for a population from a sample: } S^2 = \frac{\Sigma(X - \bar{X})^2}{N - 1}$$

Standard deviation estimated for a population from a sample: $S = \sqrt{\dfrac{\sum (X - \bar{X})^2}{N - 1}}$

where $\bar{X}$ is the mean of the set of scores. Subtracting the mean from every score, squaring each deviation, etc. is a time-consuming exercise, so the above equation is usually written as follows:

Standard deviation estimated for a population from a sample: $S = \sqrt{\dfrac{\sum X^2 - \dfrac{(\sum X)^2}{N}}{N - 1}}$

The part of the equation:

$$\sum X^2 - \frac{(\sum X)^2}{N}$$

is exactly equal to $\sum (X - \bar{X})^2$ and this component is *always* called the Sum of Squares however it is written. Because its basis is the sum of a set of squared numbers, and because squared numbers cannot be negative, the Sum of Squares can never take a negative value (in the same way that a person can never have a negative height). Hence a standard deviation can never be a negative value.

To experienced statisticians, in conjunction with a mean, a standard deviation is a highly informative value, which is why this should *always* be reported along with a mean. For example, if a standard deviation is zero, then there is no variability and every single data point is the same. As a standard deviation increases, the greater the variability and the fatter and flatter a distribution of data becomes. More subtle information can also be conveyed. Given that a standard deviation is a measure of the variability of a set of data, and given that the more varied data are, the less well a mean summarises them, then a standard deviation can also form an initial warning that something may be amiss with data. *As a rule of thumb, if a standard deviation is greater than its mean, then the mean may not be an informative summary of the data. If data are highly varied, then some caution should be exercised in analysing them.*

Standard error

When research is carried out it is unlikely that an entire population will be tested – there are simply too many people. Even opinion polls rarely sample more than 1,500 people. The intention is that the behaviour of the sample will exactly mirror the behaviour of the population from which it was drawn, assuming that the population has been appropriately sampled. Hence, it is possible to predict how 30,000,000 people will vote by interviewing only 1,500 of them (0.005%). Despite the care taken in their compilation, opinion polls still make incorrect predictions; hence whenever the behaviour of a population is predicted from a sample, it is possible that an error will be made. If errors can be made from a sample of 1,500, particular care is required in interpreting the results of a psychology study, where as few as 16 people may have taken part. In general it is true that *the more people in a sample, the more likely the sample mean will be an accurate reflection of the population mean, and hence the less likely that the estimate is wrong by a large degree.* Just how likely can be estimated by calculating *standard errors.*

Imagine that you take a very large number of equally sized samples from a population of scores and that you calculate the mean of each sample. The means of these samples can be plotted on a frequency histogram in the same way as the distribution of individual scores. If many samples are taken, according to the central limit theorem (see Chapter 5), the distribution of their means will be more and more likely to be normal as the size of each sample increases. The mean of this distribution will be identical to the population mean from which the samples were drawn, while the *standard error*, rather than the standard deviation, is a measure of the dispersion of the distribution of the sample means in relation to the population mean.

The standard error of the mean is calculated as follows:

$$\text{standard error: } SE = \frac{\sigma}{\sqrt{N}}$$

where σ is the standard deviation of the population and N is the number of scores in the sample drawn from the population, although if σ is not known, this value can be estimated from a single sample of scores (i.e. S above). Therefore, when data are collected from a sample it is possible to estimate the standard error of the mean using the following formula:

standard error of the mean estimated from sample data: $SE = \dfrac{S}{\sqrt{N}}$

The working of this equation reflects the principles discussed above. The larger the number of scores in a sample, the smaller the standard error and the more likely that the mean of the population has been accurately estimated. Similarly, the smaller the variability of scores in a sample, the smaller the standard deviation and the smaller the standard error. In other words, the more uniform a set of scores in the population, the more likely that a set of scores in a sample will accurately reflect the population. Hence, standard error is a measure of how accurately you can pinpoint the population mean using your sample data. The smaller the value, the greater the accuracy.

Testing for differences with the t-test

Whenever research is performed, researchers work with sample data and virtually never know the standard deviations of the population(s) from which samples are drawn. Given that one of the aims of research is to extend the results obtained from sample data to the population, it is then necessary to make some inferences about the population parameters by using sample data.

Consider the case where there is a single sample of subjects who, because of the treatment that they received, are expected to differ in some way from the expected mean of an appropriate population. For example, if a large sample of children, let us say 144, are drawn randomly from a population and are given IQ boosting nutrients, it would be possible to compare their scores with the standardised average for their age-group, which is 100 IQ points. If the mean IQ obtained in the treated sample is, for example, 105 we have to decide whether the administered treatment improved IQ, or whether the mean obtained is only *apparently* larger than the mean IQ of the population, and sampling error was responsible for the inflated mean IQ in the sample. In order to conclude that the treatment was effective, it is necessary to show that it is highly unlikely that the obtained sample mean of 105 could have been obtained simply by drawing a random sample from the general population of children. The standard error of the mean provides a suitable measure of the dispersion of sample means drawn from a population, and can be used to estimate how unlikely it is that drawing children at random from a population with a mean of 100 will give a sample with a mean of 105.

Assuming that the sample standard deviation is 16, it is possible to calculate the standard error of the mean, which would then be equal to:

$$SE = \frac{S}{\sqrt{N}} = \frac{16}{\sqrt{144}} = 1.33$$

With this information it is then necessary to apply the *t*-test. This is used to determine whether the sample was likely to have been drawn from a population of normal IQ children with a mean of 100. If this is highly unlikely, we can conclude that the sample must have been drawn from a notional population of children with a higher mean IQ than the normal population. The basic form of the *t*-test is the same irrespective of the experimental design and it is as follows:

$$t = \frac{\text{the difference between two means}}{\text{the relevant standard error of the difference}}$$

In the above case the difference between the two means (i.e. 105 minus 100) is 5, and the standard error is 1.33, therefore the obtained *t* value is about 3.76. The *t* value then has to be compared with statistical tables in order to see whether the *obtained value* exceeds the *critical value* so that the null hypothesis, i.e. that the sample mean does not differ from the population mean, can be rejected. If the null hypothesis can be rejected then the alternative hypothesis is accepted. In the above case this would mean that the treatment affected children's IQ scores. The usual critical value is one which shows that the difference between two means could only occur by chance less than 5% of the time.

The example described above refers to the application of the *one-sample t*-test. This is used when there is a single sample of subjects who, because of the treatment that they received, are expected to differ in some way from the expected mean of an appropriate population. The equation for the one-sample t-test is as follows:

$$t = \frac{\bar{A} - \mu}{\sqrt{\dfrac{\sum A^2 - \dfrac{(\sum A)^2}{N}}{N - 1} \left[\dfrac{1}{N}\right]}}$$

where $\bar{A}$ is the mean of the scores in the sample, $\sum A$ is the total of the scores in the sample, $\sum A^2$ is the total of each score squared from the sample, μ is the population mean and N is the number of scores in the sample. Notice how this equation works by dividing the size of the effect – the difference between the mean of the sample and the mean of the population – by the error entailed in measuring the size of the effect. Of course, this test can only be used if the expected population value is genuinely known. There are two other types of t-test which are described below.

The within-subjects t-test

This is also called the *related-means*, *paired-means*, or *related-samples* t-test.

With a two-condition within-subjects design, there are two scores for every contributor to the data: one score for each condition. Every person has contributed a pair of scores and the analysis is performed on a single set of difference scores – i.e. the difference between each pair of scores for each subject:

$$t = \frac{\bar{D}}{\sqrt{\dfrac{\sum D^2 - \dfrac{(\sum D)^2}{N_D}}{N_D - 1} \left[\dfrac{1}{N_D}\right]}}$$

where $\bar{D}$ is the mean of the set of differences between pairs of scores. Consistency in the direction of subtraction is essential here, so that some differences may be negative while others may be positive. $\sum D$ is the total of the differences, $\sum D^2$ is the total of each of the squared differences, and N_D is the number of differences.

The between-subjects t-test

This is also called the *unrelated-means, unpaired-means,* or *independent-samples t*-test.

For a between-subjects design, there are two entirely separate sets of scores that are to be compared. If people are being tested, then each person contributes one score only to one group only. An equation for the between-subjects *t*-test for comparing two sets of scores, A_1 and A_2, is given below:

$$t = \frac{\bar{A}_1 - \bar{A}_2}{\sqrt{\frac{\left(\sum A_1{}^2 - \frac{(\sum A_1)^2}{N_{A_1}}\right) + \left(\sum A_2{}^2 - \frac{(\sum A_2)^2}{N_{A_2}}\right)}{(N_{A_1} - 1) + (N_{A_2} - 1)} \left[\frac{1}{N_{A_1}} + \frac{1}{N_{A_2}}\right]}}$$

where $\bar{A}_1$ is the mean of the scores in group A_1, $\sum A_1$ is the total of the scores in group A_1, $\sum A_1{}^2$ is the total of each of the squared scores in group A_1, N_{A_1} is the number of scores in group A_1, and so on.

Overall, the *t*-test takes account of three aspects of data in order to determine whether or not a difference is large enough to be significant: the difference between the means, the number of subjects, and the variance, the latter two making up the error of measuring the difference. These are shown in Figure 2.3 in relation to the between-subjects *t*-test.

To summarise, *t* is a measure of confidence: the bigger the difference between the means and the smaller the error of measuring the difference, the greater the value of *t*. Hence a large value of *t* shows that we can be confident that the independent variable, and not error, led to a difference between a pair of means. A small value of *t* indicates that the samples were likely to have been drawn from the same population, hence the difference between the means of the groups is an error. However, remember that *t* is simply a measure of confidence, and that people can still be wrong even when they are highly confident. Occasionally, *t* will be large due to chance rather than due to the independent variable; 1 time in 20 at the 5% level of significance. Concluding that the independent variable was the cause of the effect in this case would be a Type I Error. Occasionally, *t* will be small despite the independent variable genuinely influencing performance and so, here, concluding

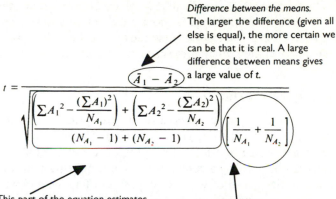

Difference between the means. The larger the difference (given all else is equal), the more certain we can be that it is real. A large difference between means gives a large value of *t*.

$$t = \frac{\bar{A}_1 - \bar{A}_2}{\sqrt{\left[\dfrac{\left(\sum A_1{}^2 - \dfrac{(\sum A_1)^2}{N_{A_1}}\right) + \left(\sum A_2{}^2 - \dfrac{(\sum A_2)^2}{N_{A_2}}\right)}{(N_{A_1} - 1) + (N_{A_2} - 1)}\right]\left[\dfrac{1}{N_{A_1}} + \dfrac{1}{N_{A_2}}\right]}}$$

Variability. This part of the equation estimates the variance in the population by averaging the individual variances estimated from each sample. The less varied the data (given all else is equal), the more certain we can be that we have measured accurately. Low variability gives a large value of *t*

Number of scores. The more subjects that have been run (given all else is equal), the more certain we can be that we have sampled accurately. A large number of scores gives a large value of *t*.

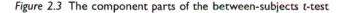

Together, the variability and the number of scores give a measurement of the degree of error in measuring the difference between the means. The smaller the error, the more confident we can be that the difference is real. Low error gives a large value of *t*.

Figure 2.3 The component parts of the between-subjects *t*-test

that the independent variable had no effect would be a Type II Error.

Determining whether or not a t value is significant

Tables of *t* values (see Appendix B) are used to see whether a value of *t* is big enough for rejection of the null hypothesis. These take the form of critical values which can be thought of as hurdles that must be cleared by the value obtained from the calculations. The hurdle for a given value of *t* depends upon the *degrees of freedom* of its calculation. The way in which degrees of freedom are calculated depends upon the *t*-test: $N_{A_1} + N_{A_2} - 2$ for the between-subjects test; $N_D - 1$ for the within-subjects test; $N - 1$ for the one-sample test. Each degree of freedom has several hurdle values associated with it. These include one for the $p < 0.05$ significance level and one for the $p < 0.01$ level (both two-tailed). The critical t values for the 0.01 significance level are always larger than for the 0.05 level. The 0.01 level is more stringent and so the hurdles are harder to clear. If a calculated value of t is big enough to clear either hurdle, then the null hypothesis is rejected at that significance level.

Intuitive statistics

Irrespective of the actual equations, with practice it is possible to get an intuitive feel for statistical tests. The information used by the t tests – size of effect, variability of scores, number of scores – can also be used by a researcher when inspecting tables of means. An intuitive grasp of when to expect a difference and when not is an extremely useful skill to possess. This will enable erroneous calculations to be spotted before they do damage. It is therefore a useful exercise to look at summary statistics and predict the outcome of statistical tests before they are performed.

The first details to look out for are the group means. If standard deviations and numbers of scores are equal for each of two experiments, then a larger difference between means is always more likely to be significant than a smaller difference. In Table 2.1, there is more likely to be a significant difference for experiment 2, as this has the larger difference between the means. If you ever find the reverse of this to be true, then something has gone wrong with the calculation.

The next detail to look out for is the number of scores. If everything else is equal, then for any given pair of means, a larger number of scores is more likely to lead to a significant difference. In Table 2.2, there is more likely to be a significant difference for experiment 1, as this has the larger number of scores.

Table 2.1 Two experiments which are identical apart from the differences between means

	Experiment 1			Experiment 2	
	Group A_1	Group A_2		Group A_1	Group A_2
N	24	24	N	24	24
$\bar{X}$	4.2	4.7	$\bar{X}$	5.8	10.8
S	3.5	3.5	S	3.5	3.5

Table 2.2 Two experiments which are identical apart from the numbers of subjects

	Experiment I			Experiment 2	
	Group A_1	Group A_2		Group A_1	Group A_2
N	24	24	N	12	12
$\bar{X}$	5.8	10.8	$\bar{X}$	5.8	10.8
S	3.5	3.5	S	3.5	3.5

Table 2.3 Two experiments which are identical apart from the standard deviations

	Experiment I			Experiment 2	
	Group A_1	Group A_2		Group A_1	Group A_2
N	24	24	N	24	24
$\bar{X}$	4.2	5.7	$\bar{X}$	4.2	5.7
S	0.7	0.5	S	3.5	3.3

Finally, look at the standard deviations. If everything else is equal, then for any given pair of means, smaller standard deviations are more likely to lead to a significant difference than larger standard deviations. In Table 2.3, there is more likely to be a significant difference for experiment 1, as this has the smaller standard deviations.

Using one- and two-tailed tests

There is often disagreement among psychologists about when and when not to use a one-tailed statistical test. For much of this book, the distinction is not important because one-tailed statistical hypotheses cannot be tested for most of the designs that are discussed. However, psychologists do use simple two-condition experiments, but rarely report the use of a one-tailed statistical test. As a reminder, here is an example of a *two-tailed* alternative hypothesis followed by its null hypothesis:

There will be a difference between the means of groups A_1 and A_2.
There will be no difference between the means of groups A_1 and A_2.

The direction of the difference has not been stated, so a significant difference in either direction is acceptable to the researcher. By comparison, here is an example of a *one-tailed* alternative hypothesis followed by its null hypothesis:

The mean of group A_1 will be greater than the mean of group A_2.
The mean of group A_1 will not be greater than the mean of group A_2.

For the one-tailed hypotheses, the direction of the difference has been stated clearly. By implication, a significant difference in the other direction will not be acceptable to the researcher *no matter how large*. One-tailed statistical hypotheses are tested by *one-tailed tests*. In order to understand their logic, it is necessary to look at normal distribution curves showing the distribution of differences between pairs of means. The key point is that, in adopting the 0.05 significance level, psychologists are agreeing that they will not be interested in differences between means for which there is a 95% chance that the differences could have occurred due to sampling errors. Whether or not a hypothesis is one- or two-tailed affects the location on the distribution where the other 5% of differences will be searched for. This is shown in Figure 2.4.

Suppose a researcher has made a clear prediction about the expected direction of a difference in an experiment, for instance by expecting that a new drug will be better or the same as a placebo, but will not make people worse. Thus it is possible to argue that any difference in the wrong direction makes no sense and must be due to error no matter how big. Therefore, only differences in the expected direction will be of interest to the researcher. The benefit of this is that because one of the tails of the distribution is of no interest, a larger portion of the other tail can be allocated to the potential rejection of the null hypothesis. *For a difference in a specified direction, a one-tailed statistical test is less stringent than a two-tailed test.* Thus, if a difference between means of, say, 2 units is just significant for a two-tailed test, then this converts into a difference between means of about 1.7 units that will be just about significant for the one-tailed test.

Despite this advantage, the use of one-tailed tests is controversial and they are rarely found in journals. To begin with, one-tailed tests do not really make sense when investigating more than one independent variable or more than two conditions in the same

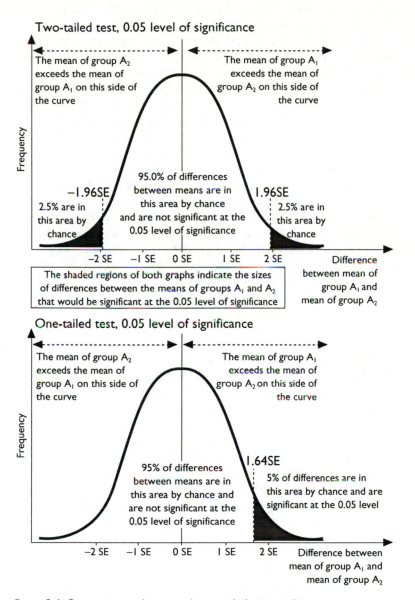

Figure 2.4 Comparisons of one- and two-tailed statistical tests

Note: SE is the standard error of the difference between the means. For example, for a two-tailed test, if the SE is 1.5, then a difference between the means of 2.94 will be just large enough to be significant (1.5 × 1.96 = 2.94).

experiment. Thus the option is simply not available for the majority of studies in psychology.

A further problem is that, because the one-tailed statistical hypotheses are directional, an unexpected difference in the opposite direction is uninterpretable no matter how large. In this case the null hypothesis should not be rejected. This can be illustrated by taking the drug example above to an extreme. Suppose that a one-tailed test was to be used because the drug might be better or the same as the placebo but definitely no worse, and clinical trials commenced. If the trials went horribly wrong, and every single volunteer died immediately on receiving the drug, the logic of the one-tailed test would mean that the null hypothesis still could not be rejected. The experimenter would be forced to conclude that chance could still have played a role in their deaths and that there was insufficient evidence to conclude that the drug was responsible. In such a situation, a replication of the study would be required, although common-sense would almost certainly prevail here! If an experimenter is prepared to respond to an unexpected difference in the opposite direction from that predicted, then a two-tailed test should be used.

The final problem is that it is not clear when one-tailed tests may be used. It is often asserted that all that is required for the use of a one-tailed test is a prior prediction by the experimenter of a difference in a particular direction. However, many pieces of research in psychology are intended to resolve contradictions between rival theories and these studies are often designed so that the competitors make opposite predictions. To use a one-tailed prediction favouring the personal preference of the researcher would guarantee that the rival theory would never be supported, as a difference between means in the opposite direction from that predicted is uninterpretable with a one-tailed test.

There are further problems due to the potential of abusing the use of one-tailed tests. This is because, for any given significance level, if the direction of an effect is ignored, the one-tailed test is less stringent than a two-tailed test. Suppose a researcher used a two-tailed test to analyse some data and found that a significant difference was just missed, perhaps $p = 0.06$. The researcher might decide retrospectively that a prediction in a specific direction was justified and therefore a one-tailed test and a significant effect could be substituted instead. Alternatively, the direction of the effect might have been predicted in advance and a one-tailed test planned, but the results might be the opposite from what were expected, which could be a particularly interesting finding. For a one-tailed test the null hypothesis cannot be rejected, but for a two-tailed test, rejection of the null hypothesis might be possible, and so this test could be substituted instead. Neither of these practices is ethical and, in such a situation, the entire experiment should be repeated. In both cases, the researchers are effectively working at the 0.075 significance level, stacking the odds in their favour, but without reporting this in the research report. Thus, the intention to use one-tailed tests coupled with the risk of finding unexpected but interesting results can lead to the need to ignore the findings, or the need to collect additional data, or the temptation to lie. None of these is a desirable outcome, and so the simplest solution except in exceptional circumstances is to stick to two-tailed statistical tests.

However, these comments should not discourage readers from predicting the outcomes of studies, or from describing these predictions in the *introduction* sections of formal reports. The key point here is to distinguish between *statistical hypotheses* – null and alternative hypotheses – and *research hypotheses*. Broadly, statistical hypotheses are concerned with the logic and mechanics of statistical tests, while research hypotheses are concerned with the overall outcome of a study: 'It is predicted that the new cold cure will speed recovery when compared with a placebo' is a research hypothesis, while 'The mean recovery time for people receiving the new cold cure will differ from the mean recovery time for people receiving the placebo' is a statistical hypothesis. Statistical hypotheses do not need to be made explicit in a report; it is safe to assume that the reader understands them. Research hypotheses are far more important. The overall rule of thumb for when and when not to make directional predictions is as follows: *make directional research hypotheses whenever possible, but use two-tailed statistical tests in order to investigate them.* Where two or more rival theories make different predictions, rather than committing yourself, *make clear exactly which pattern of results is predicted by each theory, and use two-tailed statistical tests.*

A note on statistical power

The concept of statistical power has been hinted at throughout this chapter, but a full discussion is beyond the scope of the book, and readers who wish to know more should consult a more advanced text such as Cohen (1988) or Rosenthal and Rosnow (1991). However, it is possible to give an informal idea of the various concepts without the need for an in-depth discussion.

The first point to note is that the significance of the difference between a pair of means is a poor measure of the impact of their difference. A statistically significant difference indicates that a difference between a pair of means is likely to match the general population, and so is likely to be replicated in future experiments. A highly significant difference ($p < 0.01$) is more likely to match the general population than a less significant difference ($p < 0.05$) but is not necessarily more exciting. Think about a study in which reading speed is compared between a group of subjects who have their eyes open while reading, and a group who have their eyes closed while attempting to read. It is easy to guess which group will be able to read faster, and the difference will be highly significant: $p < 0.01$ at the very least. However, it is hardly worthwhile conducting an experiment to demonstrate that people who cannot see text cannot read it! Hence, the significance level should always be taken as a measure of confidence rather than a measure of profundity. A highly significant effect indicates that we can be very confident of findings, but it tells us nothing about their theoretical importance or magnitude.

The next point to note concerns effect size. Although this can be formally defined, we will use an intuitive definition here: given that standard deviations are equal, a small difference between a pair of means indicates a small effect size, while a large difference between a pair of means indicates a large effect size. Although a large effect size might indicate that an independent variable has a large impact on performance, this might also be for trivial reasons (consider the example in the last paragraph). On the other hand, a small effect size might be of profound importance if it, say, represents the outcome of taking a life-saving drug. The advice here is that readers should consider their data and analysis in the light of the theories that they are testing. Sometimes a large effect size will be important, sometimes it will represent a trivial finding. Sometimes a small effect size will be important.

The final point to note is that whether or not a difference is likely to be significant, i.e. trustworthy, depends upon the number of subjects tested. Assuming that all else is equal, more subjects means that a difference is more likely to be significant and hence, provided that the null hypothesis is false, such a study has more *statistical power*. This is very important when planning studies, and if the expected effect size is known, it is possible to calculate backwards in order to see how many subjects must be tested in order to be reasonably confident of obtaining a significant effect. This number can be quite eye-opening when running a between-subjects design; sometimes it may turn out that hundreds of subjects may be required for a reasonable chance of a successful outcome. In this case, a simple within-subjects design may be preferable if possible. In practical terms, the consideration of effect size, sample size and statistical power leads to an important piece of advice: when attempting to replicate a piece of work performed by another researcher, *never* be tempted to attempt the replication with a smaller number of subjects than were previously tested.

Chapter 3

Using variance to test hypotheses

In the following pages you will be introduced to the theory behind the technique known as *Analysis of Variance* (*ANOVA*). In subsequent chapters, you will be shown how to compute the statistic for simple experiments. The arithmetic is straightforward but can be time consuming and so, for more complicated designs, you will be shown how to interpret analyses instead. Throughout the rest of the book, the word *factor* will be preferred to the phrase *independent variable*. The word *level* will be preferred to the word *condition*. Hence, a study with two independent variables, each with two conditions, would be described as having two *factors*, each with two *levels*. Since any experiment must have at least two conditions, it follows that a factor must always have at least two levels.

Limitations of the t-test

If you wish to look at more than two levels and/or more than one factor, the principles underlying the derivation of the *t*-test prevent it from being expanded to cope. As shown in Chapter 2, the equation gives a single value of *t* based upon comparing a pair of group means. You run into difficulties if you have three or more means to compare. You could use several *t*-tests to compare every mean with every other mean, but a typical experiment could consist of three *factors* each with two *levels* giving eight different *cells* (groups). Comparing every mean with every other mean would give a total of 28 comparisons. Not only would this be cumbersome and time consuming to calculate and interpret, even with a computer, but you might run into problems because the more comparisons that are made, the more likely it is that one or more of the comparisons will be significant by chance. A Type I

Error is a significant difference that does not really exist in the general population. Normally, this will happen about once in 20 studies, a consequence of setting the significance level to 0.05; but if each study involves over 20 *t*-tests, then at least one error is likely to happen *for nearly every study*. This is known as the *problem of multiple comparisons*.

Analysis of Variance

Analysis of Variance (ANOVA) is based upon slightly different first principles from the *t*-test. Because of this, ANOVA is more flexible and is used for the analysis of more complicated designs. Its principles are based upon the reasons why scores might vary – why it is the case that usually no two people in an experiment perform exactly alike. Also, what are the consequences of this for deciding whether or not any of the experimental manipulations have had an effect on performance?

Box 3.1 An example of a simple between-subjects design experiment

Suppose I ran an experiment with two separate groups of subjects: a one-factor between-subjects design with two levels. In this example, I looked at the effects of memory strategy on the recall of names that go with faces. I started off with a pilot study in order to make sure that I was not going to waste time looking for an effect that might not be there, so I began by looking at the performance of ten subjects. Before I instructed them, I randomly allocated them to two groups of five in order to ensure that they were not likely to differ in their general memory ability.

One group of subjects was instructed to use a mnemonic which should have helped them to recall names that go with faces, but not the other group. They were left to use their usual strategies and so constituted a control group. I showed both groups 15 slides of faces along with their surnames. Next I showed the same 15 slides but this time without the names, leaving the subjects to recall them as accurately as they could. Hopefully, the mnemonic had been successful, and those people taught to use it were better at recalling names than those who were not.

The memory performance is given below (the dependent variable is the number of correctly recalled names out of 15):

Mnemonic group	No-mnemonic group
11	11
12	8
15	10
12	10
10	11

LEVEL MEANS:	12	10
GRAND MEAN*:	11	

There does seem to be something happening here. The mnemonic group remembered 2 more names on average than the no-mnemonic group. The mnemonic did appear to help so I am probably justified in going on to run a full-scale experiment. However, taking a closer look at the scores, there is some overlap in performance between the two groups, and the scores within each group vary. Thus, the five scores in the mnemonic group differ from each other despite the fact that the five subjects in that level were treated exactly alike. The same also applies to the no-mnemonic group.

*Mean of all scores irrespective of group

Sources of variability in raw data

In order to understand Analysis of Variance, we need to understand the causes of variability in data. Why is it that within a group of people, the scores of any pair of subjects are likely to differ although they are all treated alike? In other words, what are the causes of *within-group variability?* Why does it persist despite all precautions taken to ensure that all people within the same group are treated in exactly the same way? Why is it that between two groups of people, the scores of any pair of subjects are also likely to differ? In other words, what are the causes of *between-group variability?* Three reasons (sources of variability) can be identified.

1   Treatment effects (the effects of the independent variable)

These are the effects that I am looking for, since as a result, the subjects should be behaving differently. I hope to find that the scores of a group of people who are treated in one way are different from those of a group of people who are treated in another way, resulting in an overall difference between experimental conditions. Ideally, there would be no overlap between levels, so that in Box 3.1 the people who are taught to use the mnemonic strategy are always better at remembering names than people who are not taught it. This is not the case here, and it is highly unlikely to be the case for any study that you may encounter, and differences in performance within each level are leading to some overlap between them.

2   Individual differences

A group of subjects will perform differently even when all individuals have been treated in exactly the same way. In the mnemonic group performance ranged from 10 names recalled to all 15 of them. These differences could have been due to some subjects being naturally more proficient at using the mnemonic than other subjects; or perhaps some had used it before and had had more practice at using it. Some of the subjects may have decided that they did not want to use the mnemonic and used a different strategy instead. Hence people can differ in quantitative ways, performing the same processes at different levels of skill. They can also differ in qualitative ways, performing completely different processes. Individual differences are also certain to be present in the no-mnemonic group: without any instructions, each subject was free to choose his or her own personal preferred method for remembering names and faces. This will lead to different strategies, which are guaranteed to lead to individual differences in performance. In any situation, individuals will differ in skill, ability, knowledge and strategies used, so that even if a group of people are treated identically, individuals will differ in performance simply because they *are* different.

3   Random (residual) errors
It could be argued that, in theory, each subject should have a true skill level for any given task, and that under ideal conditions it should be possible to measure this accurately. Even if this were true, in practice perfect measurement would be impossible, and errors of measurement can arise from a variety of sources of which just a few are suggested below:

i   varying external conditions such as time of day, temperature, etc.
ii   the state of the subject (current focus of attention, etc.)
iii the experimenter's or the computer's ability to measure and score accurately.

These can all lead to random errors of measurement of performance. Within reason, they should be minimised, but the law of diminishing returns will apply here. Random errors will always creep in however careful experimenters are.

Collectively, individual differences and random errors are known as *experimental errors*. The aim of every experiment is to minimise experimental errors so that they do not obscure the *treatment effects*. Experimental errors manifest themselves by spreading data away from the group means, i.e. increasing the variability in the scores, and hence the standard deviations. The greater the standard deviations, the greater the experimental error, and the less confident we can be that a difference between a pair of means has been accurately measured. In addition, experimental error can manifest itself by distorting the values of group means away from the means of the populations from which they were drawn. For example, a randomly drawn sample may, by chance, consist of abnormally proficient people in relation to the population.

In any experiment, it is also possible to make a distinction between two types of variability. *Within-group variability* is the extent to which the individuals within a single group of subjects differ, despite all the members of a given group having been treated exactly alike. *Between-group variability* is the extent to which over-all groups as a whole differ from each other, hopefully because they have been treated differently. Ideally, for any experiment, the within-group variability should be low in relation to the between-group variability (see Figure 3.1).

The easiest way to conceptualise between-group variability is by considering the overall means of the groups: for two groups with identical means, the between-group variability is zero; if the difference between means were to be increased, the between-group variability would increase. Variability is the same as diversity: the more diverse a set of group means, the larger the between-group variability. The within-group variability for a group depends upon the diversity of data within it. If everyone in the group attained an identical score, there would be no diversity and the within-group variability would be zero. The more diverse the data within a group, the greater the within-group variability.

Between-group variability arises not only because of treatment effects, but can also arise because of experimental error, despite all your precautions of randomisation etc. Hence, even when samples are drawn from an identical population, their means

In the diagrams below, the means of four samples, A, B, C and D, are shown by the circles. The means for groups A and C are greater than the means for groups B and D by the same magnitude for both sets of samples. The tails are error bars (which are calculated from standard errors) and show that for each individual sample, we can be confident that 95% of the time, the true mean of the population from which it was drawn will be somewhere between the tails.

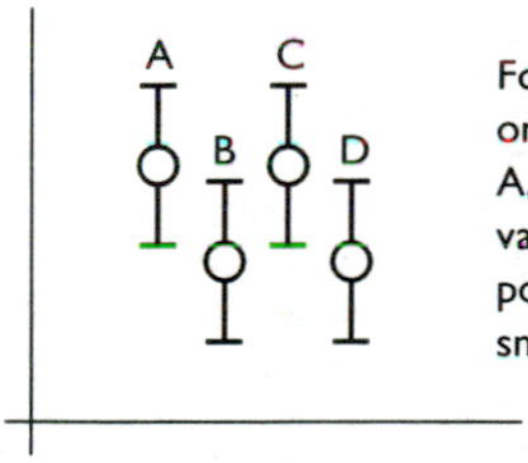

For these data, the between-group variability (calculated on the basis of the difference in means between groups A, B, C and D) is small in relation to the within-group variability. It could easily be the case that in the general population, the mean of either A or C could actually be smaller than the mean of either B or D.

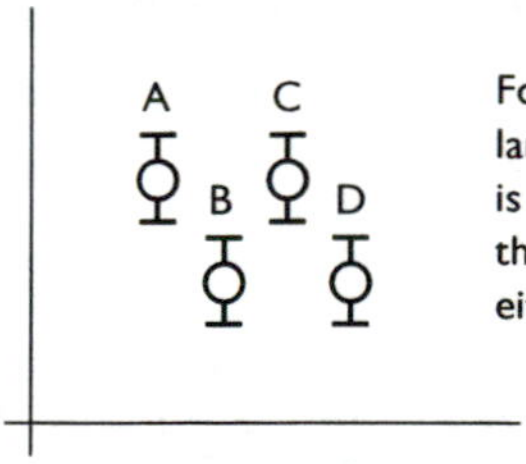

For these data, the between-group variability is large in relation to the within-group variability. It is highly unlikely that in the general population, the mean of either A or C could be smaller than either the mean of B or D.

Figure 3.1 Low within-group variability, and hence low standard error, is important when comparing group means

are likely to differ from the population mean, and also from each other, entirely due to chance. Furthermore, in unfortunate circumstances, this could give the illusion that an experimental manipulation caused the difference. Thus, differences between groups can occur not only due to treatment effects, but also due to the fact that individuals differ and that true performance, even if it exists, could never be accurately measured. Hence, if you are unlucky, with perhaps too many skilled performers in one group, too few in another, experimental error might lead you to find a spurious difference. This could give the impression that the treatment effects were responsible for differences between groups when in fact they were not.

Within-group variability will arise due only to experimental error, since all subjects in a single group are receiving the same treatment. Treatment effects cannot possibly be the cause of differences in scores within that group. In a perfect world, there would be no within-group variability in any study. This is because all subjects in a group, who have been treated in the same way, should behave in the same way. In reality this is never the case due to the effects of experimental error. Table 3.1 shows another way of comparing between- and within-group variability, this time numerically. S refers to the standard deviation for each sample of five scores.

Table 3.1 Examples of between- and within-group variability

High between-group variability, no within-group variability			No between-group variability, high within-group variability			Moderate between-group variability, moderate within-group variability		
Group A	Group B	Group C	Group A	Group B	Group C	Group A	Group B	Group C
10	20	30	10	15	5	10	10	20
10	20	30	25	20	25	10	20	20
10	20	30	30	30	25	10	20	30
10	20	30	35	40	45	20	20	30
10	20	30	50	45	50	20	30	30
Mean 10	20	30	30	30	30	14	20	26
S 0	0	0	14.6	12.8	18.0	5.5	7.1	5.5

The F ratio for a between-subjects design

The t-test is a useful statistical test because it is possible to calculate the probability of getting a particular value of t, by chance alone, for a given degrees of freedom value, which is related to the number of subjects that were run. If the value of t, calculated for an experiment, exceeds the critical value for a chosen significance level, you can conclude that the difference between the pair of means was unlikely to have arisen due to chance. This would happen less than 1 time in 20 at the 5% significance level. If chance can be ruled out, then all that is left to account for the difference in performance is the way in which the treatment of the two levels differed (the independent variable). Performing Analysis of Variance gives one or more statistical values called *F ratios*. Like t, obtained F ratio values should be compared against a critical value from tables. A significant value means that you can rule out experimental error as the reason for a set of means differing. At this point, it is necessary to distinguish between variability and *variance*. Variability is an informal term for conceptualising diversity, while variance is a precisely defined mathematical measure of variability, diversity or dispersion of data (see Chapter 2).

The general equation for the F ratio is defined as follows:

$$F = \frac{\text{between-group variance}}{\text{experimental error}}$$

The numerator, i.e. the top of the F ratio equation, is always the between-group variance whatever the design of an experiment. Although this value can be influenced by individual differences and random errors of measurement, it is the only way of measuring the size of the treatment effects for a study. The denominator of the equation, i.e. the underneath, is known as the *error term. It is extremely important that you commit this phrase and its meaning to memory*. It is a measure of the extent to which experimental error, and not the treatment effects, caused the scores to differ. For a between-subjects design, both individual differences and random errors of measurement can cause scores to vary within a group, despite everyone in the group being treated identically, and it is not possible to distinguish between the two. Each person contributes only a single score to the data, and this score may deviate from the 'true' score for either reason or both. Collectively, individual differences and random errors cause within-group variance, and so this value is used as the error term for a between-subjects design:

$$F = \frac{\text{between-group variance}}{\text{within-group variance}}$$

Alternatively, we can rewrite the F ratio to show the various sources of variability:

$$F = \frac{\text{treatment effects} + \text{experimental error}}{\text{experimental error}}$$

and, given that experimental error has two sources of variability for a between-subjects design, the equation can also be expressed thus:

$$F = \frac{\text{treatment effects} + \text{individual differences} + \text{random errors}}{\text{individual differences} + \text{random errors}}$$

Thus, in order to conclude that an experiment has 'worked', the variance due to the treatment effects, i.e. the effects due to the independent variable, must be sufficiently large to stand out mathematically from the 'noise' that constitutes the variance due to experimental error.

Notice that the equation is expressed in terms of overall variances rather than differences between means. This gets us away from the problem of how to analyse more than two levels – for now at least. Since variances can be calculated relatively easily, F can be calculated by using straightforward arithmetic.

It is helpful to think about the extreme values that F can take. If a treatment has no effect on performance, then the amount of variability between groups caused by the treatment effects is zero. Hence, any variability in subject scores and overall means is due only to experimental error. If this is the case, the equation becomes:

$$F = \frac{0 + \text{experimental error}}{\text{experimental error}}$$

If the calculated value of F is 1 or near to 1, you can be certain that your treatment had no effect. However, it is not enough simply to find a value of F that is greater than 1 to conclude that the treatment has had a significant effect on performance. With small numbers of subjects, it is possible to get F values larger than 1 by chance more often than 1 time in 20. Instead, it is possible to calculate the probability of finding a particular value of F for a given number of degrees of freedom (see the section on the *central limit theorem* in Chapter 5 for an explanation as to why this is the case). For ANOVA, the degrees of freedom take account of both the number of subjects that you run and the number of levels (conditions) that each factor has. Like the t-test, you are more likely to find a significant effect if you run, say, groups of 30 subjects rather than groups of 15 subjects. F tables must therefore be used in order to determine whether or not an effect is significant. The tables give critical values – hurdles – for given degrees of freedom that must be equalled or exceeded in order to conclude that there is some sort of significant effect.

If the within-group variance is very low in relation to the size of the treatment effects, so that the overall level means are different but the subjects within each level yield virtually identical scores, then the value of F will be large. At an extreme, consider a situation in which there is no experimental error at all within groups, so that everyone within a group has exactly the same score. If the treatment still has an effect, so that the groups differ, then F will be infinite:[1]

$$F = \frac{\text{treatment effects} + 0}{0} = \infty \text{ (infinity)}$$

Most observed F values will be somewhere between the extremes above, normally towards the smaller end. F values above 20 are rare in psychological studies. Overall, you are looking for your F values to be as large as possible. *The larger the value of F, the more the treatment effects are standing out from the experimental error, and the less likely that differences in level performance were caused by chance.*

Final comments

If you can keep sight of the underlying principles discussed above, then you will find that most of the rest of the book will be straightforward. Mathematically, ANOVA is simple but time consuming to perform and the most difficult part will be getting used to the notations that are used. There is little point in calculating F ratios for complicated designs. Hence, later you will be shown how to use Analysis of Variance appropriately and interpret its outcomes, rather than how to compute statistical values by hand.

Hopefully, you will gain some insight into how the techniques work and hence be able to spot mistakes and any odd output given by a computer. This can be caused by incorrect data entry or file formatting, but sometimes by an incorrectly written program. You should also be able to get to grips with the limitations of ANOVA, and avoid designing studies that make you particularly vulnerable to them. ANOVA can be an extremely powerful tool, and like any other powerful tool it can be dangerous in untrained or careless hands.

Chapter 4

Calculating *F* ratios for one-factor between-subjects designs

This chapter aims to show you how to compute the Analysis of Variance *F* ratio for the simplest possible design: one-factor, between-subjects with two levels. The basic equations can also be extended so that designs with three or more levels can also be analysed. As a reminder, the word *factor* is equivalent to *independent variable* while *level* refers to the different conditions of the factor. By convention, in a single-factor two-level experiment, the factor is designated by the letter *A*, while its two levels are designated A_1 and A_2. NB These labels are just statisticians' shorthand, and should never be used as labels in a formal report. Meaningful names should be used instead. If a second independent variable is added, that factor is designated *B* by statisticians, and then the third factor is designated as *C*, and so on. Before beginning, here are some reminders of the notation which will be used. At the end of the chapter, some of the notation will be simplified, so bear this in mind while working through the examples:

X will only be used in order to give examples of equations; it stands for either a single arbitrary number or an entire set of numbers, depending on the example.

Y stands for the set of all scores in a study ignoring the condition that they are in. Thus, $\sum Y$ means *add up all of the scores, irrespective of which level a score is in.* $(\sum Y)^2$ means *add up all the scores, and square this total.* However, $\sum Y^2$ means *take each score, square it and add these squares together. Be careful not to confuse* $\sum Y^2$ *and* $(\sum Y)^2$.

In addition, $\bar{Y}$ denotes the grand mean: the mean of all scores irrespective of their level.

Y	1	2	3	$\sum Y$ 6	$(\sum Y)^2$ 36

| Y^2 | 1 | 4 | 9 | $\sum Y^2$ 14 | |

A_X in order to calculate the F ratio, we will need to know various details about the scores in individual levels. A_1 stands for the set of scores in a particular level, A_2 stands for the scores in the next level, and so on. For example, $\sum A_1$ means *add up all of the scores in level A_1*, $(\sum A_2)^2$ means *add up all of the scores in level A_2 and square this total*, and so on. In addition, $\bar{A}_1$ denotes the mean of the scores in level A_1, and $\bar{A}_2$ denotes the mean of the scores in level A_2 and so on.

N stands for the total number of *scores* in a study. *This will not always be the same as the number of subjects. In a one-factor two-level within-subjects design, with 10 subjects, there will be 20 scores.*

N_X will be used when we refer to the number of scores in one of the levels. If every level has the same number of scores, we can simply refer to N_A, the number of scores in any one of the levels of factor A. If there are different numbers of scores in each level, then further suffixes are necessary. N_{A_1} stands for the number of scores in level A_1, N_{A_2} stands for the number of scores in level A_2 and so on. Box 4.1 applies this notation to the mnemonic example from Chapter 3.

The one-factor between-subjects design

This is the most straightforward design to analyse both conceptually and mathematically. The outcome will be an F ratio whose statistical significance can be determined from tables (see Appendix B). When a factor has two levels, a significant value for F means that the treatment has caused the means of the two levels to differ, as for a t-test. When the factor has three or more levels, a significant value for F means that the treatment has caused the three level means to differ in some unspecified way, and further follow-up tests may be required (see Chapter 6). Like all statistical

Box 4.1 **The performance of mnemonic and control groups**

Below are the raw data. The dependent variable is the number of correctly recalled names out of 15:

Mnemonic group	No-mnemonic group
11	11
12	8
15	10
12	10
10	11

LEVEL MEANS: 12   10
GRAND MEAN: 11

For the factor being investigated, A_1 will represent the scores of the mnemonic group and A_2 will represent the scores of the no-mnemonic (control) group. N, the total number of scores, is 10.

	A_1		A_2
$\sum A_1$	60	$\sum A_2$	50
$(\sum A_1)^2$	3600	$(\sum A_2)^2$	2500
$\sum A_1^2$	734	$\sum A_2^2$	506
N_{A_1}	5	N_{A_2}	5

tests, computation and interpretation are far more straightforward if there are an equal number of subjects in each of the levels. If this is possible then there is the added bonus that if the data violate any of the underlying assumptions of ANOVA, which are the same as for any parametric test, these violations are far less likely to be important (see Chapter 5). In the following explanations, the term *variability* will be used to refer to how varied the data are, i.e. the extent to which scores differ from each other. *Variance* has a more specific meaning (see Chapter 2 for a reminder of this).

Whenever variance is being calculated, the general equation is always the same. Estimating the variance of a population from a sample of scores always involves the following:

$$\text{variance} = \frac{\text{Sum of Squares}}{\text{degrees of freedom}}$$

Either of the following equations may be used when calculating the variance of a set of scores:

$$\text{variance} = \frac{\sum(X - \bar{X})^2}{N - 1} \quad \text{or variance} = \frac{\sum X^2 - \frac{(\sum X)^2}{N}}{N - 1}$$

$\sum(X - \bar{X})^2$ is exactly equal to $\sum X^2 - \frac{(\sum X)^2}{N}$

Whichever way you choose of writing the variance equation and calculating the value, the numerator, i.e. the top of the variance equation, is always known as the *Sum of Squares*, and the two versions always give the same answer. As a reminder, the more numbers that are a long way from the mean, the greater the variance. If these numbers represent the scores of a single sample of subjects who have all been treated identically, then the higher the variance, the greater the experimental error. If the square root of a variance is calculated, this gives the standard deviation. Although standard deviations are usually given in formal reports, ANOVA uses variances because it is far easier to add and subtract values without square root signs getting in the way. Recall from Chapter 3 that the F ratio for a between-subjects design is the between-group variance divided by the within-group variance, which is also known as the *error term*. In order to perform Analysis of Variance, both of these must be calculated.

Calculating within-group variance

Figure 4.1 shows where we need to look in order to find a value for the within-group variance. For a between-subjects design, calculating the within-group variance gives the error term. For now, we will ignore the degrees of freedom and concentrate on calculating the Sum of Squares, which indicate the total variability present in the data.

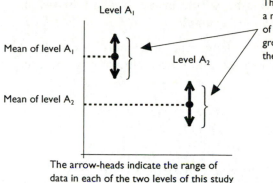

The within-group variance is a measure of the variability of the data within each of the groups, averaged over all of the groups

The arrow-heads indicate the range of data in each of the two levels of this study

Figure 4.1 The location of the within-group variance in a two-group study

The total Sum of Squares within groups can be calculated by taking the Sum of Squares for each of the levels, whether there are two, three, four or more. These are then added together to give the total Sum of Squares within groups. To calculate the variance, this is then divided by the total within-group degrees of freedom. Hence, in words (SS is short for Sum of Squares):

$$\text{total within-group variance} = \frac{SS \text{ level } A_1 + SS \text{ level } A_2 \text{ (and so on)}}{\text{total within-group degrees of freedom}}$$

Or, numerically:

$$\text{total within-group variance} = \frac{\sum(A_1 - \bar{A}_1)^2 + \sum(A_2 - \bar{A}_2)^2 \text{ (and so on)}}{\text{total within-group degrees of freedom}}$$

The equation can be extended no matter how many levels the factor has. The SS_{WITHIN} (Sum of Squares within groups) part of the equation is $\sum(A_1 - \bar{A}_1)^2 + \sum(A_2 - \bar{A}_2)^2$ and so on, for as many levels as you have. Box 4.2 shows the calculation for SS_{WITHIN} using this equation with the mnemonic experiment data.

Box 4.2 Calculating the within-group Sum of Squares for the mnemonic example

These are the data from the mnemonic experiment example. In order to calculate the within-group variance proceed as follows:

						LEVEL MEANS
Mnemonic group	11	12	15	12	10	12
No-mnemonic group	11	8	10	10	11	10
GRAND MEAN (mean of all scores):						11

1   For the mnemonic group (A_1) the Sum of Squares within this group is given by the following equation: $\sum(A_1 - \bar{A}_1)^2$. The level mean for this group, $\bar{A}_1$, is **12**; we need to calculate the total of every score's deviation from this mean:

$11 - 12 = -1; 12 - 12 = 0; 15 - 12 = 3; 12 - 12 = 0;$
$10 - 12 = -2$

$(-1)^2 + (0)^2 + (3)^2 + (0)^2 + (-2)^2 = 1 + 0 + 9 + 0 + 4 = 14$

2   For the no-mnemonic group (A_2) the Sum of Squares within this group is given by the following equation: $\sum(A_2 - \bar{A}_2)^2$. The level mean for this group, $\bar{A}_2$, is **10**; we need to calculate the total of every score's deviation from this mean:

$11 - 10 = 1; 8 - 10 = -2; 10 - 10 = 0; 10 - 10 = 0;$
$11 - 10 = 1$

$(-1)^2 + (-2)^2 + (0)^2 + (0)^2 + (1)^2 = 1 + 4 + 0 + 0 + 1 = 6$

3   $\text{total within-group variance} = \dfrac{\text{total within-group Sum of Squares}}{\text{total within-group degrees of freedom}}$

$$= \frac{\sum(A_1 - \bar{A}_1)^2 + \sum(A_2 - \bar{A}_2)^2}{\text{total within-group degrees of freedom}}$$

$$= \frac{14 + 6}{\text{total within-group degrees of freedom}} = \frac{20}{df}$$

Calculating all of the differences between every score and its respective mean is a very time-consuming exercise, and so it is better to use the alternative Sum of Squares equation given earlier. Using this enables the formula for the within-group Sum of Squares to be simplified considerably:

$$\text{total within-group variance} = \frac{\sum A_1{}^2 - \dfrac{(\sum A_1)^2}{N_{A_1}} + \sum A_2{}^2 - \dfrac{(\sum A_2)^2}{N_{A_2}}}{\text{total within-group degrees of freedom}}$$

Thus

$$SS_{WITHIN} \text{ (Sum of Squares within groups)} = \sum A_1{}^2 - \frac{(\sum A_1)^2}{N_{A_1}} + \sum A_2{}^2 - \frac{(\sum A_2)^2}{N_{A_2}}$$

But $\sum A_1{}^2$ and $\sum A_2{}^2$ together mean: *find the sum of every square of every score* and is identical to writing $\sum Y^2$. Also, a well-planned study should always have equally sized groups if possible, with the result that we do not have to worry about any difference between N_{A_1} and N_{A_2}. They will be identical and both can be written as N_A. Hence, the equation can be greatly simplified. From this point onwards in this chapter, equations will apply only to designs with equal numbers of subjects in each group; calculations for unbalanced designs can be very time-consuming, and interested readers should consult an advanced text such as Kirk (1982) for details. The simplified equation for the within-group Sum of Squares is as follows:

$$SS_{WITHIN} = \sum Y^2 - \frac{(\sum A_1)^2 + (\sum A_2)^2}{N_A}$$

Box 4.3 demonstrates the use of this equation on the mnemonic example.

Box 4.3 The preferred method for calculating the within-group Sum of Squares

For the mnemonic example, in order to calculate the SS_{WITHIN} proceed as follows:

A_1 mnemonic group   11   12   15   12   10 $\sum A_1 = 60$ $(\sum A_1)^2 = 3600$

A_1^2 121   144   225   144   100 $\sum A_1^2 = 734$

A_2 no-mnemonic group   11   8   10   10   11 $\sum A_2 = 50$ $(\sum A_2)^2 = 2500$

A_2^2 121   64   100   100   121 $\sum A_2^2 = 506$

$$SS_{WITHIN} = \sum Y^2 - \frac{(\sum A_1)^2 + (\sum A_2)^2}{N_A} \; ;$$

but $\sum Y^2 = \sum A_1^2 + \sum A_2^2 = 734 + 506 = 1240$

and N_A = the number of scores in any level of the experiment = 5

therefore, $SS_{WITHIN} = 1240 - \dfrac{3600 + 2500}{5} = 1240 - \dfrac{6100}{5} = 1240 - 1220 = 20$

Calculating between-group variance

Figure 4.2 shows where we need to look in order to find a value for the between-group variance. For all designs, calculating the between-group variance gives a measure of how different the overall groups are from each other. Again, we will ignore the degrees of freedom and concentrate on calculating the Sum of Squares for now. For the between-group variance, we are not interested in the individual variability of subjects, and so this is ignored when looking at the overall mean level of performance of several groups. For a two-level experiment, we *could* base a calculation of the between-group variance on the difference between the pair of means (cf. the *t*-test).

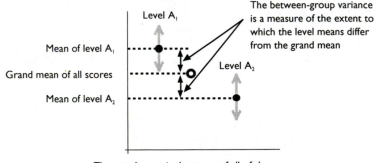

Figure 4.2 The location of the between-group variance in a two-group study

However, basing the measure of between-group variance on this would prevent the equations from being extendable to studies where there are more than two levels. Instead, the equation for the between-group variance is based upon the size of the difference between each group mean in comparison to the *grand mean*, the overall mean of all scores. The greater the deviations of the level means from the grand mean, and hence the bigger the differences between groups, the greater the size of the between-group variance, and hence the more different the groups are from each other. The more different the groups are from each other overall, the more likely that the treatment has genuinely changed the performance of them.

The way in which all equations for calculating between-group variance effectively work is as follows. First the variability of the scores within the groups must be ignored and so *we set the value of each score within a level to its level mean*. In order to find the variability between groups, *we take each adjusted score and find the square of the difference between every score and the grand mean*. The formula for the between-group variance can therefore be written as follows, and is demonstrated in Box 4.4:

$$\text{between-group variance} = \frac{N_{A_1}(\bar{A}_1 - \bar{Y})^2 + N_{A_2}(\bar{A}_2 - \bar{Y})^2 \text{ (and so on)}}{\text{between-group degrees of freedom}}$$

Box 4.4 **Calculating the between-group Sum of Squares for the mnemonic example**

For the mnemonic example, in order to calculate the between-group variance, we need to know the number of scores in each level: N_{A_1} and N_{A_2}; the mean score for each level: $\bar{A}_1$ and $\bar{A}_2$; and the grand mean: $\bar{Y}$;

$\bar{A}_1$: mnemonic group mean   12
$\bar{A}_2$: no-mnemonic group mean   10
$\bar{Y}$: grand mean (mean of all scores)   11

$$\text{between-group variance} = \frac{N_{A_1}(\bar{A}_1 - \bar{Y})^2 + N_{A_2}(\bar{A}_2 - \bar{Y})^2}{\text{between-group degrees of freedom}}$$

$$= \frac{5(12 - 11)^2 + 5(10 - 11)^2}{\text{between-group degrees of freedom}}$$

$$= \frac{5(1)^2 + 5(-1)^2}{\text{between-group degrees of freedom}} = \frac{10}{df}$$

Again, the above formula for the between-group variance is somewhat cumbersome, but if the groups are equally sized, it can be rearranged to make the formula below. The intermediate steps in converting the formula are not shown, but the brave are welcome to try to convert one into the other. This formula is demonstrated in Box 4.5.

$$\text{between-group variance} = \frac{\dfrac{(\sum A_1)^2 + (\sum A_2)^2}{N_A} - \dfrac{(\sum Y)^2}{N}}{\text{between-group degrees of freedom}}$$

Thus

$$SS_{BETWEEN} \text{ (Sum of Squares between groups)} = \frac{(\sum A_1)^2 + (\sum A_2)^2}{N_A} - \frac{(\sum Y)^2}{N}$$

Box 4.5 The preferred method for calculating the between-group Sum of Squares

For the mnemonic example, in order to calculate the $SS_{BETWEEN}$ proceed as follows:

A_1 mnemonic group	11	12	15	12	10	$\sum A_1 = 60$	$(\sum A_1)^2 = 3600$
A_2 no-mnemonic group	11	8	10	10	11	$\sum A_2 = 50$	$(\sum A_2)^2 = 2500$

$$SS_{BETWEEN} = \frac{(\sum A_1)^2 + (\sum A_2)^2}{N_A} - \frac{(\sum Y)^2}{N}$$

But $\sum Y = \sum A_1 + \sum A_2 = 60 + 50 = 110;$

therefore $(\sum Y)^2 = (110)^2 = 12100$

N_A = the number of scores in a level = 5,

N = the total number of scores = 10

therefore, $SS_{BETWEEN} = \dfrac{3600 + 2500}{5} - \dfrac{12100}{10} = \dfrac{6100}{5} - \dfrac{12100}{10} = 1220 - 1210 = 10$

In addition to the Sums of Squares for the two types of variance above, it is also possible to calculate the variance of all data while ignoring the levels that the scores are in. This simply uses the standard equation for variance:

$$\text{total variance} = \frac{\sum Y^2 - \dfrac{(\sum Y)^2}{N}}{N - 1}$$

For the total Sum of Squares (SS_{TOTAL} – the total variability of all of the data), this is effectively the total of the squared differences between every single score and the grand mean. For the mnemonic experiment example, SS_{TOTAL} comes to 30. This is a useful value to know because it enables calculations to be double-checked.

So far, three Sums of Squares have been discussed:

$$SS_{WITHIN} = \sum Y^2 - \frac{(\sum A_1)^2 + (\sum A_2)^2}{N_A}$$

$$SS_{BETWEEN} = \frac{(\sum A_1)^2 + (\sum A_2)^2}{N_A} - \frac{(\sum Y)^2}{N}$$

$$SS_{TOTAL} = \sum Y^2 - \frac{(\sum Y)^2}{N}$$

Although there are three equations, each with two components, there are only three different values to calculate:

$\sum Y^2$ for SS_{WITHIN} and SS_{TOTAL}; $\dfrac{(\sum Y)^2}{N}$ for $SS_{BETWEEN}$ and SS_{TOTAL}

and $\dfrac{(\sum A_1)^2 + (\sum A_2)^2}{N_A}$ for SS_{WITHIN} and $SS_{BETWEEN}$

In fact, $SS_{TOTAL} = SS_{BETWEEN} + SS_{WITHIN}$. This is always true however many levels there are and is a fundamental, and extremely useful, property of Sums of Squares which enables working to be checked and notation to be simplified later. Effectively, the variability of a set of data can be completely split into two different, independent sources – between and within groups. An explanation as to why this is the case is beyond the scope of the discussion here, but if you are curious, think of Pythagoras (or see Wickens, 1995 for a further discussion).

What do the degrees of freedom come to?

So far, the degrees of freedom, i.e. the denominators, of the variance equations have not been calculated. The Sums of Squares give the total variability between groups or within groups, but it is necessary to know average variabilities in order to compute variances. Degrees of freedom are used in order to enable estimates of the variances for the general population to be computed. Although it is relatively straightforward to explain what a degree of freedom is, explaining why these values give the required answers is far more difficult.

Put simply, the degrees of freedom are *the number of scores that are free to vary once you know what is the mean of the set of scores.* Hence, in theory, if a mean is calculated from a set of values, all but one of these scores could be any value – they are free to vary – but whatever values these scores take, this fixes the value of the remaining score in order to keep the mean at the same value.

Between-group degrees of freedom

The degrees of freedom for between-group variance are the *total number of levels minus 1.* When using the level means to calculate the grand mean, if there are two levels, only one level mean can vary freely once the grand mean is known. For any value that one level mean takes, the fact that the grand mean is known fixes the value of the other level mean.

For example, if there are two levels, A_1 and A_2, given that the grand mean $\bar{Y}$ is 10;

if $\bar{A}_1$ takes the value of 12 then $\bar{A}_2$ *must* take the value of 8
if $\bar{A}_1$ takes the value of 13 then $\bar{A}_2$ *must* take the value of 7

and so on. Only one of the two means is free to take any value and so, given that there are two levels, then the between-group degrees of freedom is 1.

If there are three levels and the value of the grand mean is known, two level means can vary freely, but once the values of these are known, the value of the third level mean is fixed. For example, if there are three levels, A_1, A_2 and A_3, given that the grand mean is

10, if $\bar{A}_1$ takes the value of 12 and $\bar{A}_2$ takes the value of 13, then $\bar{A}_3$ *must* take the value of 5. If $\bar{A}_1$ takes the value of 6 and $\bar{A}_2$ takes the value of 22, then $\bar{A}_3$ *must* take the value of 2 and so on. Only two of the three means can take any value, and so if there are three levels, then the between-group degrees of freedom are 2.

The general formula for the between-group degrees of freedom is $(a - 1)$ where a is the number of levels in factor A.

Within-group degrees of freedom

For within-group variance, the total within-group degrees of freedom are calculated in a similar way to the total within-group Sum of Squares. The degrees of freedom for each of the individual levels are calculated, and then these degrees of freedom are added together to give the total within-group degrees of freedom. Within each level, the Sum of Squares is calculated from the variability of the level scores in relation to their level mean, and the degrees of freedom are the number of level scores that are free to vary given that the level mean is fixed. Hence, the degrees of freedom for each of the individual levels are given by the total number of scores in that level minus 1: once the level mean is determined, $N_A - 1$ individual scores are free to vary. The total within-group degrees of freedom are the total of the degrees of freedom for each of the individual levels:

$$\text{total within-group variance} = \frac{SS \text{ level } A_1 + SS \text{ level } A_2 \text{ (and so on)}}{df \text{ level } A_1 + df \text{ level } A_2 \text{ (and so on)}}$$

Thus, if there are three levels of a between-subjects factor, each with 10 subjects and hence 9 degrees of freedom per level, the *total* within-group degrees of freedom are $9 + 9 + 9 = 27$. The general formula for the within-group degrees of freedom is therefore $a(N_A - 1)$ where a is again the number of levels in the factor and N_A is the number of scores in each of the levels of factor A.

Like Sums of Squares, degrees of freedom can also be added and subtracted. Thus, not only does

$$SS_{TOTAL} = SS_{BETWEEN} + SS_{WITHIN}$$

but

$$df_{TOTAL} = df_{BETWEEN} + df_{WITHIN}$$

The df_{TOTAL} is the total degrees of freedom of all of the scores, irrespective of their groups, in relation to the grand mean. SS_{TOTAL}, the total Sum of Squares, was the variability of all scores in relation to the grand mean; thus df_{TOTAL} is the number of individual scores that are free to vary given that grand mean is known, and is always one less than the total number of scores. Hence, the formula for the total degrees of freedom is either $(aN_A - 1)$ or $(N - 1)$, where N is the total number of scores. The degrees of freedom for the mnemonic example along with the final calculation of the variances are given in Box 4.6.

Box 4.6 Calculating the degrees of freedom for the mnemonic example

In the mnemonic example there are two levels, each with five scores:

$a = 2$	$N_A = 5$	$N = 10$	
$df_{BETWEEN}$	$= (a - 1)$	$= 2 - 1$	$= 1$
df_{WITHIN}	$= a(N_A - 1)$	$= 2(5 - 1)$	$= 8$
df_{TOTAL}	$= (N - 1)$	$= 10 - 1$	$= 9$

From previous calculations:

$$SS_{BETWEEN} = 10$$
$$SS_{WITHIN} = 20$$
$$SS_{TOTAL} = 30$$

and so, to calculate the variances:

between-group variance $= \dfrac{SS_{BETWEEN}}{df_{BETWEEN}} = \dfrac{10}{1} = 10$

within-group variance $= \dfrac{SS_{WITHIN}}{df_{WITHIN}} = \dfrac{20}{8} = 2.5$

$F = \dfrac{\text{between-group variance}}{\text{within-group variance}} = \dfrac{10}{2.5} = 4$

Extending the equations if there are three or more levels

The general equations for calculating variances are easy to extend if an experiment has three or more levels in a factor; it is just a matter of adding the extra components on to the equations as and when necessary. For example, Table 4.1 shows a comparison of the equations for two- and three-level designs. $(\sum A_3)^2$ means take the scores in the third level, add all of these scores together and square the total. In theory, these formulae can be extended to accommodate as many levels as required, so that if a fourth level is added, $(\sum A_4)^2$ must be computed, and so on.

The ANOVA table

The outcome of performing an Analysis of Variance is usually a table such as that shown in Table 4.2. This displays the various Sums of Squares and the degrees of freedom, along with the variances, which are also known as *Mean Squares*. Even if the analysis is performed by hand, fully filling in an ANOVA table is a useful way of ensuring that all of the necessary components have been completed. If the analysis is performed by computer, a table will almost certainly be the result, but the exact format will vary. It is therefore important that the various components discussed above and how they are related to each other are understood.

Table 4.1 ANOVA equations for two- and three-factor between-subjects designs

	Two levels in the factor	Three levels in the factor
$SS_{BETWEEN}$	$\dfrac{(\sum A_1)^2 + (\sum A_2)^2}{N_A} - \dfrac{(\sum Y)^2}{N}$	$\dfrac{(\sum A_1)^2 + (\sum A_2)^2 + (\sum A_3)^2}{N_A} - \dfrac{(\sum Y)^2}{N}$
SS_{WITHIN}	$\sum Y^2 - \dfrac{(\sum A_1)^2 + (\sum A_2)^2}{N_A}$	$\sum Y^2 - \dfrac{(\sum A_1)^2 + (\sum A_2)^2 + (\sum A_3)^2}{N_A}$
SS_{TOTAL}	$\sum Y^2 - \dfrac{(\sum Y)^2}{N}$	$\sum Y^2 - \dfrac{(\sum Y)^2}{N}$ (same equation)
$df_{BETWEEN}$	$(a-1) = 2-1 = 1$	$(a-1) = 3-1 = 2$
df_{WITHIN}	$a(N_A - 1) = 2(N_A - 1)$	$a(N_A - 1) = 3(N_A - 1)$
df_{TOTAL}	$(N-1)$	$(N-1)$

Table 4.2 ANOVA table based on the mnemonic experiment example

SOURCE	Sum of Squares	Degrees of freedom	Mean Square	F	p
A	10	1	10	4	> 0.05
S/A	20	8	2.5		
TOTAL	30	9			

A computer will print out an ANOVA table, but it will not explain what it means. Table 4.2 shows the details filled in with the numbers from the mnemonic example. Even if a computer printout uses unfamiliar column headings, it is usually still possible to work out which component is which.

Often, the highly descriptive terms, $SS_{BETWEEN}$, SS_{WITHIN} and so on, are felt to be too cumbersome for daily usage, and so these are shortened:

> $SS_{BETWEEN}$ is usually written as SS_A;
> $df_{BETWEEN}$ is usually written as df_A
> SS_{WITHIN} is usually written as $SS_{S/A}$;
> df_{WITHIN} is usually written as $df_{S/A}$.

Looking at the individual columns of Table 4.2:

- The *SOURCE* heading refers to the source of the variability. *A* is between groups, *S/A* is within groups. Some computer packages may not print a TOTAL row.
- The *Sums of Squares*, sometimes abbreviated to *SS*, are taken directly from the calculations in Box 4.6, as are the degrees of freedom, usually abbreviated to *df*.
- *Mean Square* is the mean of each of the Sums of Squares or, in other words, the variances. Looking across each row, each Mean Square corresponds to the Sum of Squares divided by its degrees of freedom. Hence, the between-group variance, the *A* row, is 10. The within-group variance, the *S/A* row, is 2.5. Mean Square may be abbreviated to *MS*.
- The *F* ratio is obtained by dividing the between-group Mean Square by the within-group Mean Square. There is just one *F* ratio for this design, but it is essential that you learn to navigate ANOVA tables because later designs in this book

will have up to seven F ratios on a single table. The TOTAL row is not used for calculating the F ratio, but can help you check your values. Of particular importance on the ANOVA table is the *error term*. This is the measure of the experimental error, the denominator of the F ratio equation, and is the within-group variance for a between-subjects design. Other values may be used for other designs. It is important that you learn to recognise this phrase and learn where to look on ANOVA tables for error terms. It is also essential to know which is the error term when reporting F ratios. The error term may be required if any follow-up tests are to be performed after the main ANOVA.

● Finally, a p value in the form of a significance level has been included on the table. Computer programs usually calculate an exact probability: the exact chance of getting a treatment effect of a given size coupled with an error of a given size and a given number of degrees of freedom. This exact probability has to be converted into a significance level. If the exact probability is greater than 0.05, for example, 0.9, 0.1, or 0.06, this is more probable than the 5% cut-off, and the effect is non-significant at $p > 0.05$. If the exact probability is less than 0.05, for example 0.044, 0.02, or 0.001, this is less probable than the cut-off and $p < 0.05$. If there is no probability given, or the calculation is being performed by hand, the significance of the obtained F value must be determined by using tables of critical values in order to see whether the obtained F is large enough for a significant effect.

An F value is always reported with its degrees of freedom, given for the between-group variance first, then for the error term. Thus, from Table 4.2, $F(1,8) = 4$, and the F ratio has both 1 *and* 8 degrees of freedom. F tables are two dimensional. Both values of the degrees of freedom need to be taken into account when determining whether or not an effect is significant. On most tables you go across and then down by the number of degrees of freedom (see Appendix B for a table of critical F values). To complete the mnemonic experiment example, the critical value of F for df (1,8) is 5.32 for the 5% level of significance; our observed value of 4 was not high enough to reject the null hypothesis, so we conclude, for now – as this was just a pilot study – that the instruction to use a mnemonic apparently had no effect on memory for names.

Simplifying the notation

Although the notation used above is practical for simple ANOVA designs, it becomes cumbersome and unwieldy when complexity increases. Rather than use unsatisfactory notation, some changes will be introduced in this section which will enable us to tackle within-subjects designs and two-factor designs in later chapters. The sigma notation ($\sum$) used so far is also somewhat redundant. Simpler symbols can be used because there are very regular patterns to the equations, and it is possible to take advantage of these. Recall that there are only three basic components to the Sums of Squares equations:

$$\sum Y^2 \text{ for } SS_{WITHIN} \text{ and } SS_{TOTAL}; \quad \frac{(\sum Y)^2}{N} \text{ for } SS_{BETWEEN} \text{ and } SS_{TOTAL}$$

$$\text{and } \frac{(\sum A_1)^2 + (\sum A_2)^2}{N_A} \text{ for } SS_{WITHIN} \text{ and } SS_{BETWEEN}$$

For every single component, there is a repeating pattern, with the result that the equations can be shortened. In words, all formulae have the format:

$$\frac{(\text{component 1})^2 + (\text{component 2})^2 + (\text{component 3})^2 \text{ (and so on)}}{\text{the number of scores that make up each component}}$$

Taking each component in term:

$\dfrac{(\sum Y)^2}{N}$ is $\dfrac{(\text{grand total})^2}{\text{the number of scores that make up the grand total}}$

$\dfrac{(\sum A_1)^2 + (\sum A_2)^2}{N_A}$ is $\dfrac{(\text{level total } A_1)^2 + (\text{level total of } A_2)^2}{\text{the number of scores that make up each level}}$

$\sum Y^2$ is $\dfrac{(\text{score}_1)^2 + (\text{score}_2)^2 + (\text{score}_3)^2 + (\text{score}_4)^2 \text{ (and so on)}}{1 \text{ (only one number makes up each individual score)}}$

Overall, the original formulae for the Sums of Squares can be summarised by the following general equation:

$$[X] = \text{basic ratio of } X = \frac{\text{the sum of (each and every } X)^2}{\text{the number of contributions to each } X}$$

Therefore, for the between-subjects design, instead of writing the three components in full, the following shorthand will be used, and is demonstrated in Box 4.7:

for $\dfrac{(\sum Y)^2}{N}$ $\qquad$ [T] $\quad$ *the basic ratio of the grand total*

for $\dfrac{(\sum A_1)^2 + (\sum A_2)^2}{N_A}$ $\qquad$ [A] $\quad$ *the basic ratio of the level totals*

for $\sum Y^2$ $\qquad$ [Y] $\quad$ *the basic ratio of the individual scores*

Box 4.7 Demonstrating basic ratios

Taking the mnemonic experiment example:

A_1 mnemonic group $\qquad$ 11 $\quad$ 12 $\quad$ 15 $\quad$ 12 $\quad$ 10
A_2 no-mnemonic group $\quad$ 11 $\quad$ 8 $\quad$ 10 $\quad$ 10 $\quad$ 11

[T] is the basic ratio of the total of the scores. There is only one total, 110, so if you square this you get 12,100. Divide this by the number of contributions to the total, these were the 10 scores. Thus:

$$[T] = \frac{(\text{grand total})^2}{\text{the number of scores that make up the grand total}}$$

$$[T] = \frac{(110)^2}{10} = \frac{12100}{10} = 1210$$

[A] is the basic ratio of the level totals, or *treatment sums*. There are two levels and therefore two totals in this study: 60 and 50. Square each score and add the squares together. Divide the total by the number of contributions to each *individual* total, i.e. the number of scores in each level – there are 5 scores in each. Thus:

$$[A] = \frac{(\text{level total of } A_1)^2 + (\text{level total of } A_2)^2}{\text{the number of scores that make up each level}}$$

$$[A] = \frac{(60)^2 + (50)^2}{5} = \frac{3600 + 2500}{5} = \frac{6100}{5} = 1220$$

$[Y]$ is the basic ratio of the individual scores. Square each individual score and add the squares together. Only one score contributed to each square, and so there is no need for division in this case. Thus:

$$[Y] = \frac{(\text{score}_1)^2 + (\text{score}_2)^2 + (\text{score}_3)^2 + (\text{score}_4)^2 \text{ (and so on)}}{1 \text{ (only one number makes up each individual score)}}$$

$$[Y] = \frac{(11)^2 + (12)^2 + (15)^2 + (12)^2 + (10)^2 + (11)^2 + (8)^2 + (10)^2 + (10)^2 + (11)^2}{1}$$

$$[Y] = \frac{121 + 144 + 225 + 144 + 100 + 121 + 64 + 100 + 100 + 121}{1} = 1240$$

Using basic ratios

Basic ratios are a shorthand way of writing out the equations for the between-subjects F ratio. By simplifying the equations this saves on space and reduces the chance of making an error. The point to remember is that the new symbols stand for familiar formulae and processes. Using these three basic ratios, it is possible to calculate the various Sums of Squares and variances in exactly the same way as before, but without having to write out long equations every time. Thus:

$$SS_{WITHIN} \ (SS_{S/A}) \ = \ \sum Y^2 - \frac{(\sum A_1)^2 + (\sum A_2)^2}{N_A} \ = [Y] - [A]$$

$$SS_{BETWEEN} \ (SS_A) \ = \ \frac{(\sum A_1)^2 + (\sum A_2)^2}{N_A} - \frac{(\sum Y)^2}{N} \ = [A] - [T]$$

$$SS_{TOTAL} \qquad = \ \sum Y^2 - \frac{(\sum Y)^2}{N} \qquad = [Y] - [T]$$

Box 4.8 completes the mnemonic example using basic ratios.

A final advantage of using basic ratios, with their compact formulae, is that instructions for performing an ANOVA can be displayed on an ANOVA table, so that it is easy to see which cells need to be filled and how they should be filled. This is shown in Table 4.3.

Box 4.8 Basic ratios for the mnemonic example

SS_{TOTAL} $\quad = [Y] - [T] \quad = 1240 - 1210 = 30$
SS_A $\quad\quad = [A] - [T] \quad = 1220 - 1210 = 10$
$SS_{S/A}$ $\quad\quad = [Y] - [A] \quad = 1240 - 1220 = 20$

If you look back over the chapter, you will find that whatever formulae are used, these answers are always the same.

Table 4.3 ANOVA table summarising the component parts for a between-subjects design

SOURCE	Sum of Squares	Degrees of freedom	Mean Square	F	p
A	$[A] - [T]$	$(a - 1)$	$\dfrac{[A] - [T]}{(a - 1)}$	$\dfrac{\text{Mean Square}_A}{\text{Mean Square}_{S/A}}$	See tables
S/A	$[Y] - [A]$	$a(N_A - 1)$	$\dfrac{[Y] - [A]}{a(N_A - 1)}$		
TOTAL	$[Y] - [T]$	$(N - 1)$			

Finally, here are some helpful points to bear in mind if you are performing ANOVA by hand:

(a) $[Y]$ is always the largest basic ratio.
(b) $[T]$ is always the smallest basic ratio.
(c) Sums of Squares can NEVER take a negative value.
(d) If one basic ratio is more than twice the others, check your working.
(e) $[Y]$ is the basic ratio that people usually make computational mistakes on.
(f) If you do suspect an error, check the basic ratios.

Chapter 5

One-factor between-subjects ANOVA

Advanced topics

Chapter 4 discussed the essentials of Analysis of Variance, and these details will be sufficient for the vast majority of undergraduate students for most of their project work. However, for those who are curious, or who are conducting or planning more advanced research, the topics covered in this chapter are well worth studying. First, we will discuss why the Analysis of Variance test 'works' (the *central limit theorem*). We will then discuss the key assumptions underlying these designs, how to determine whether they have been violated, and some suggestions for action to take if this is the case. Some of the points raised will apply equally to future chapters as to previous chapters, and you will find it worthwhile to bear them in mind as you progress through the book.

ANOVA and the central limit theorem

As we have seen, Analysis of Variance is a statistical test used to compare two or more means. The *F* ratio is calculated by comparing two different estimates of variance for the population(s) from which the samples are drawn. It might seem odd to compare means by comparing variances, but read on. One estimate of variance, called the *within-group variance*, is not affected by treatment effects because everyone within each group should have been treated identically. In other words, this variance estimate should be unaffected by whether or not the null hypothesis is true or false. The second variance estimate is the between-group variance, and the size of this *will* be related to the size of the treatment effects. In other words, this variance estimate *is* affected by whether or not the null hypothesis is true or false. If the null hypothesis is true in the general population, the size of the between-group variance should tend towards the size of the within-group variance. This is because, given that the treatment is not affecting the group means, then the only sources that can cause them to differ are individual differences and random errors of measurement. These are also the *only* sources that affect the within-group variance. If the null hypothesis is false, the between-group variance should exceed the within-group variance. This happens because the treatments are acting upon the group means *in addition* to individual differences and random errors of measurement. The *F* ratio, used in ANOVA to test the null hypothesis, is obtained by dividing the between-group variance by the within-group variance. Therefore a decision about the presence or absence of differences between a set of means is taken from the ratio of the two variance estimates. In order to understand why this should be the case, it is necessary to introduce the *central limit theorem*.

Let us designate the true mean of a normally distributed population by μ, with its variance designated as σ^2. If numerous different random samples are drawn from this population, and the size of each sample is N in every case, where N is an arbitrary number, then the central limit theorem states that the distribution of sample means will be more likely to resemble a normal distribution as N increases. In addition, the theorem states that the mean of the sample means will be identical to μ, and that the variance in the means of the samples (designated $\sigma_{\bar{x}}^2$) will be equal to the variance of the individual scores in the population(s) divided by the number of scores in each sample:

$$\text{variance of sample means, } \sigma_{\bar{x}}^2 = \frac{\sigma^2}{N}$$

The major assumptions which allow us to compute the *F* ratio for Analysis of Variance are discussed later in this chapter, but two of these will be mentioned here: (i) the scores in the population(s) from which samples are selected are normally distributed, and (ii) the scores in the populations from which the samples are drawn have equal variances: $\sigma_1^2 = \sigma_2^2 = \ldots = \sigma_n^2$. This is the *homogeneity of variance assumption*. When the central limit theorem is combined with these assumptions, it is possible to show why the *F* ratio works as a statistical test, and this will be demonstrated for a single-factor between-subjects design.

First of all, consider a situation where the null hypothesis is true, i.e. where scores have been drawn from two different populations whose means are identical (so that $\mu_1 = \mu_2$). Where this is the case, it is additionally assumed that the samples have been drawn from populations which also are normally distributed and have the same variance. Effectively, therefore, the samples have been drawn from the same population. Ideally, the means of the samples should also be identical, but if they are not, this is due to sampling error.

We need to calculate the F ratio in order to test whether the means obtained from the two samples are different, in other words to test whether they have been selected from populations that have different means. It is necessary first to calculate the total within-group variance for the samples, also called the Mean Square$_{WITHIN}$, or Mean Square$_{ERROR}$. This will enable the variance of the individual scores in the population(s), from which the samples have been taken, to be estimated. Whether or not the null hypothesis is true or false, i.e. whether or not the experimental treatment affects performance, should be irrelevant to the size of this variance because this is based upon an aggregate of the variability within each group. Within each group, everyone should have received the same treatment. The variances of the populations from which the samples are drawn are assumed to be the same under the homogeneity of variance assumption, even if the samples are selected from populations with different means. Hence, an estimate of the variance of the scores in the population (i.e. S^2) can be calculated from each sample using the standard formula:

variance estimation for the population, $S^2 = \dfrac{\sum(X - \bar{X})^2}{N - 1}$, where N is the sample size.

Since each variance for each sample is an estimate of the (assumed to be) same population variance, any differences between these are assumed to be due to error. An average *across samples* of these obtained estimates will therefore provide the best overall estimate of the population variance because the random errors will cancel each other out. The obtained average is the Mean Square$_{WITHIN}$ and an example calculation is given in Box 5.1.

According to the central limit theorem, it is possible to obtain another estimate of the variance of the individual scores in the population on the basis of the sample data. This can be obtained using the means of the samples, and is called Mean Square$_{BETWEEN}$. This estimation of the population variance is expected to coincide with the estimation given by the Mean Square$_{WITHIN}$ but only if the null hypothesis is true (i.e. $\mu_1 = \mu_2$ if there are two levels). If the null hypothesis is true, then each sample mean is calculated from a set of data samples drawn from the same population. Therefore, these means are members of the sample distribution of the means, obtained by drawing samples from a single population. Consequently, it is possible first to estimate the variance of the distribution of these sample means, and then, from these, to estimate the variance of the individual scores in the population.

The estimate of the variance in the distribution of the sample means can be found by calculating the squared difference between each sample mean and the mean of these means, and adding these squares together. In other words:

$$\text{variance in the distribution of the sample means, } S_{\bar{x}}^2 = \frac{\sum(\bar{X} - \mu)^2}{N_{\bar{x}} - 1}$$

Here $\bar{X}$ corresponds to each sample mean, and μ to the population mean, estimated by calculating the mean of the sample means. $N_{\bar{x}}$ is the number of sample means taken, and *not* the number of scores in each sample. From the estimated variance in the distribution of the sample means, it is possible to estimate the variance of the individual scores in the population. According to the central limit theorem, the variance in the distribution of the sample means is equal to the variance in the individual scores of the population divided by the number of scores in each sample:

$$\sigma_{\bar{x}}^2 = \frac{\sigma^2}{N}$$

Therefore, given $\sigma_{\bar{x}}^2$ and N it is possible to obtain σ^2. As shown above, we can obtain an estimate of $\sigma_{\bar{x}}^2$ (i.e. $S_{\bar{x}}^2$). We know N since this is the number of scores in each selected sample. Therefore an estimate of σ^2 (i.e. S^2) can be calculated by multiplying $S_{\bar{x}}^2$ by N. An example of this calculation is also given in Box 5.1. In this example, the estimate of the population variance S^2 obtained by the Mean Square$_{WITHIN}$ is 3.5 while the estimate of the population variance S^2 obtained by the Mean Square$_{BETWEEN}$ is 2.5. As expected, given that the null hypothesis is true ($\mu_1 = \mu_2$), these two estimates are similarly sized, as is shown on the ANOVA table.

Box 5.1 **Estimating the population variance when the null hypothesis is true**

	Sample 1		Sample 2
$Score_1$	4	$Score_6$	3
$Score_2$	7	$Score_7$	6
$Score_3$	7	$Score_8$	7
$Score_4$	8	$Score_9$	6
$Score_5$	4	$Score_{10}$	3

Mean	6.0	5.0
Variance	3.5	3.5
Grand mean:	5.5	

$$\text{Mean Square}_{WITHIN} = S^2 = \frac{3.5 + 3.5}{2} = 3.5$$

$$\text{Mean Square}_{BETWEEN} = S_{\bar{x}}^2 N = \left(\frac{(6.0 - 5.5)^2 + (5.0 - 5.5)^2}{1}\right) 5 = \left(\frac{0.5}{1}\right) 5 = 2.5$$

$$F = \frac{\text{Mean Square}_{BETWEEN}}{\text{Mean Square}_{WITHIN}} = \frac{S_{\bar{x}}^2 N}{S^2} = \frac{2.5}{3.5} = 0.714$$

ANOVA table:

SOURCE	Sum of Squares	Degrees of freedom	Mean Square	F	p
A (between)	2.5	1	2.5	0.714	>0.05
S/A (within)	28.0	8	3.5		
TOTAL	30.5	9			

Next, consider the case in which the null hypothesis is false. This time the samples whose means are to be calculated have not been selected from the same population. However, we will continue to assume that the different populations all have normally distributed scores, and the variances of the individual scores in all of the populations are equal. Therefore, it follows from this assumption that Mean Square$_{WITHIN}$ will still provide a sound estimate of the variance in individual scores of every population. Box 5.2 provides an example where the null hypothesis is false. The scores of sample 2 are identical for both Boxes 5.1 and 5.2, but the scores of sample 1 in Box 5.2 have been created by adding 5 to each of the scores in sample 1 of Box 5.1. The means of sample 1 and 2 in Box 5.2 are now considerably apart, but their respective variances are unchanged compared with Box 5.1. This shows us that the Mean Square$_{WITHIN}$ obtained from the example in Box 5.2 is identical to the one obtained in Box 5.1, and this highlights the fact that Mean Square$_{WITHIN}$ should be unaffected by whether or not the null hypothesis is true or false, i.e. it is unaffected by whether or not an experimental manipulation is effective.

If the null hypothesis is false, then the Mean Square$_{BETWEEN}$ *cannot* be used to give an accurate estimate of the variance of individual scores in the population. Where this is the case, Mean Square$_{BETWEEN}$ will usually be greater than Mean Square$_{WITHIN}$. Why should this be the case? If the null hypothesis is false, then the samples have not all been drawn from the same population, although these different populations only differ in their means. If we were to draw numerous samples from a single population (population A_1), we could plot a frequency distribution and calculate how often we would expect each sample mean to be observed. However, if we were to draw further samples from another population (population A_2) with, say, a greater mean than population A_1, we would find that these samples would have larger sample means more often than expected were we using distribution of sample means of population A_1 to predict their frequency. If we were to plot the sample means of population A_2 on the same frequency histogram as population A_1, we would obtain a broader distribution than if we were to take the individual population distributions separately, hence artificially inflating the estimated variance in the distribution of sample means for either population A_1 or population A_2. If the estimate of the variance in sample means, $\sigma_{\bar{x}}^2$ is inflated when the null hypothesis is not true, it follows that using this to estimate the variance of individual scores in the population, σ^2, will also result in an inflated value. Therefore, estimating σ^2 from $\sigma_{\bar{x}}^2$ (Mean Square$_{BETWEEN}$) will produce a larger value than if σ^2 is calculated directly (Mean Square$_{WITHIN}$). Thus, dividing Mean Square$_{BETWEEN}$ by the Mean Square$_{WITHIN}$ will, on average, give a value larger than 1 (see the example in Box 5.2). Hence, if the Mean Square$_{BETWEEN}$ is substantially larger than the Mean Square$_{WITHIN}$, then the estimate of the population variance obtained by the Mean Square$_{BETWEEN}$ must have been inflated due to the fact that the null hypothesis was not true. Thus the means reflect samples that have been drawn from populations whose means differ; and only their means. This allows the researcher to conclude that the means obtained in a study differed due to the experimental treatment.

Box 5.2 **Estimating the population variance when the null hypothesis is false**

	Sample 1		Sample 2
Score$_1$	9	Score$_6$	3
Score$_2$	12	Score$_7$	6
Score$_3$	12	Score$_8$	7
Score$_4$	13	Score$_9$	6
Score$_5$	9	Score$_{10}$	3

Mean	11.0		5.0
Variance	3.5		3.5
Grand mean:		8	

Mean Square$_{WITHIN}$ $= S^2 = \dfrac{3.5 + 3.5}{2} = 3.5$

Mean Square$_{BETWEEN}$ $= S_{\bar{X}}^2 N = \left(\dfrac{(11.0 - 8)^2 + (5.0 - 8)^2}{1}\right) 5 = \left(\dfrac{18}{1}\right) 5 = 90$

$F = \dfrac{\text{Mean Square}_{BETWEEN}}{\text{Mean Square}_{WITHIN}} = \dfrac{S_{\bar{X}}^2 N}{S^2} = \dfrac{90}{3.5} = 25.7$

ANOVA table:

SOURCE	Sum of Squares	Degrees of freedom	Mean Square	F	p
A (between)	90.0	1	90.0	25.7	<0.05
S/A (within)	28.0	8	3.5		
TOTAL	118.0	9			

Assumptions underlying ANOVA

Analysis of Variance is a parametric test. Like all other parametric tests, certain assumptions are made about data so that they can be analysed in this way. Today these assumptions are often ignored by researchers and journals. This is because ANOVA is a robust test under most circumstances. Even major deviations from the assumptions are unlikely to reduce the power of the test, resulting in Type II Errors, or lead to Type I Errors. However, this robustness is only true as long as a design with equal numbers of subjects per level is analysed (or equal cell sizes – see Chapter 8). If this is not the case, then considerably more care is required.

Various ways of getting round the difficulties are discussed below, although usually these actions make no difference to the outcomes of the significance tests anyway. As a rule of thumb, small violations of any of the assumptions are unlikely to have a great effect on significances. If a p value is less than 0.01 or greater than 0.1, it is therefore highly unlikely that an incorrect statistical inference will be drawn. On the other hand, care is always required for borderline cases. If there is a shortage of subjects, and if p is between, say, 0.03 and 0.07 then it is quite possible for violations of the assumptions to lead to incorrect statistical inferences.

Ideally, all data should be on an interval scale when performing an Analysis of Variance, although it is usually possible to analyse ordinal data in this way, e.g. response data from questionnaires. Ask yourself whether means are an appropriate way of summarising your data. If not, then Analysis of Variance may not be an appropriate statistical test.

There are three major assumptions underlying Analysis of Variance.

I Individual differences and errors of measurement are independent from group to group

This assumption means that all subjects should be randomly allocated to groups for between-subjects factors, or that the order of testing of conditions for within-subjects factors should be randomised or counterbalanced. Hence, if all subjects receive all conditions in the same order, or subjects are not randomly allocated to conditions, for example you have divided them by gender or expertise – *classification variables* – then this assumption has been violated.

Consequences of violating this assumption

The consequence of violating this assumption is that the study becomes difficult to interpret. If subjects have not been randomly allocated to groups, then any differences between groups may be because of the way in which people were allocated to them, rather than the experimental treatment. In addition, the effects of classification variables are always difficult to interpret because their values cannot be manipulated randomly. Overall, for any instance where subjects cannot be randomly allocated to condition (between-subjects designs) or cannot be randomly allocated to task order (within-subjects designs) then problems with interpreting the ANOVA outcome are inevitable.

Action to avoid this violation

Always take action to minimise order effects for within-subjects factors. Always randomly allocate subjects to between-subjects factors where possible. For designs involving classification variables this will not be possible; take care to ensure that there are equal numbers of subjects in each and every group and even if you achieve all of these, be aware of the resulting restriction in any conclusions that you can draw concerning causality.

2 Individual differences and errors of measurement are normally distributed within each group

In a perfect world, every individual in a sample would be treated exactly alike and so every score should be identical. Unfortunately this will never be the case for real research because experimental error causes scores to differ from each other. Most of these scores will also differ from the sample mean and also the mean of the notional population from which the sample was drawn. This assumption asserts that these errors of measurement will be normally distributed, both in the population and, therefore, in the sample drawn from the population, *and hence the data in each and every group will be normally distributed*. Skewed and bimodal data are the usual deviations from a normal distribution. The easiest way to understand why this assumption is important is to consider the ways in which non-normal distributions make the mean a less accurate measure of group performance (see Chapter 2). Given that, ultimately, the purpose of ANOVA is to enable groups to be compared by comparing their means, if the means of the data are not an accurate measure of group performance, then means, and hence ANOVA, should not be used to compare the groups.

Consequences of violating this assumption

This will depend upon the nature of the distortion. Some possibilities are shown in Figure 5.1. For the left-hand experiment, scores in all three levels are clearly normally distributed and all is well. If the data are skewed, but all by roughly the same degree in the same direction, then overall there is also no problem. This is shown by the middle experiment. Here, the scores are skewed negatively in all three cells. Although the means have been distorted by this, the distortion is identical for all groups, and so it is still meaningful to see which means differ. If some cells are skewed positively and other cells are skewed negatively then there will be serious problems in interpreting differences between means, or the lack of them. This may lead to Type I or Type II Errors. For the right-hand experiment, there are different distributions in every level. It is no longer meaningful to compare means since any outcome may just as much be due to artefacts of distribution as to the treatments. Bimodal data (not shown, but see Chapter 2) are difficult to analyse in any meaningful way.

Action to avoid this violation

It is not easy to determine by eye whether or not this assumption has been violated. Unfortunately, two of the most usual measures of

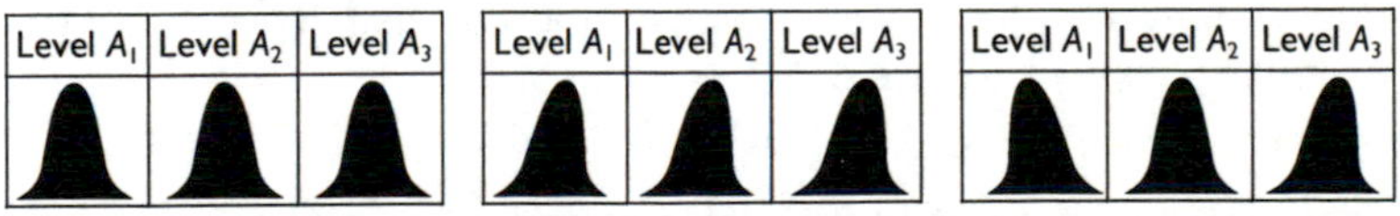

Figure 5.1 Distributions of data in three experiments showing normal data which conform to the assumptions of ANOVA (left), skewed data that are still analysable by ANOVA (centre) and mixed data that cannot be analysed by ANOVA (right)

performance – reaction times and error rates – are usually skewed (see Chapter 2). Fortunately, the skew for reaction times will almost always be positive. The skew for error rates will depend on whether or not there are floor or ceiling effects. If a wide range of performance is being sampled, it is easily possible to experience both, in which case the only satisfactory remedy is to redesign the measures.

If this might be a problem, the Kolmogorov–Smirnov test can be used to see whether distributions differ significantly from normal. See Siegel and Castellan (1988, pp. 51–8) for a description of this, and another test that can be used to see whether or not data are significantly skewed.

Alternatives include (i) calculating medians from the scores of each subject and analysing the medians rather than the means, (ii) performing a data transform, changing the overall score of every subject in a systematic way, or (iii) using a non-parametric Analysis of Variance. Unfortunately, transforming data is unlikely to help where different cells are skewed in different directions.

3 The size of variance in the distribution of individual differences and random errors is identical within each cell

This is the homogeneity of variance assumption. As discussed earlier, one of the fundamental assumptions of ANOVA is that samples are drawn from populations whose variances are identical, and therefore the variances in the samples should not differ significantly from each other. Hence, experimental treatments should affect the population means and the sample means, but not the population variances and the sample variances. Thus, if the variances of the groups differ markedly, this implies that the treatment not only affected the level of performance, but also the variety of performance within each group. If there are big differences in the standard deviation from group to group, there is a likelihood that this assumption has been violated, though usually not to the extreme shown in Figure 5.2.

Consequences of violating this assumption

Violating this assumption tends to increase the likelihood of making Type I or Type II Errors, depending on how the assumption has been violated.

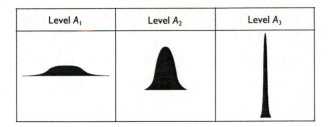

Figure 5.2 Distributions of data which clearly violate the homogeneity of variance assumption

Action to avoid this violation

As a general rule of thumb, if the largest group variance in a study is no more than four times the size of the smallest group variance, then it is safe to analyse the data. The test below can be used if more certainty is required. Analysis of Variance can be used to test for significant differences between means *and also variances*. To test pairs of variances, it is necessary to calculate the variance of the data within each group, and then calculate an F ratio by dividing the largest variance by the smallest variance:

$$F = \frac{\text{largest group variance}}{\text{smallest group variance}}$$

The degrees of freedom of the F ratio are found in the same way as for a conventional ANOVA: df = (degrees of freedom of the numerator, degrees of freedom of the denominator). Degrees of freedom are found by subtracting one from the number of scores in a group. A worked example is shown in Box 5.3.

Ensuring that scores are equally varied across groups is not an easy matter. If some tasks are harder than others, it is almost inevitable that the harder tasks will also be subject to the more varied performance. Ensuring that subjects are as similar as possible to each other is one possible action. The more similar subjects are, the smaller the extent to which a more difficult task will spread out their performance. If this assumption has been violated, data can either be transformed or a non-parametric Analysis of Variance may be used. If you are unlucky enough to

Box 5.3 An example showing a comparison of variance between groups

I have conducted a small study and these are the scores:

Level A_1	Level A_2	Level A_3
1	1	1
1	1	1
1	3	2
2	3	6
2	4	7

The equation for the variance of a set of scores is as follows:

$$\text{variance} = \frac{\sum X^2 - \frac{(\sum X)^2}{N}}{N - 1}$$

For level A_1, variance = $\dfrac{11 - \dfrac{49}{5}}{4}$ = 0.3

For level A_2, variance = $\dfrac{36 - \dfrac{144}{5}}{4}$ = 1.8

For level A_3, variance = $\dfrac{91 - \dfrac{289}{5}}{4}$ = 8.3

$$F = \frac{\text{largest group variance}}{\text{smallest group variance}} = \frac{8.3}{0.3} = 27.7 \text{ with } df\,(4,4)$$

$F(4,4) = 27.7$, $F_{CRIT} = 6.39$, $p < 0.01$.

The significant F tells us that we have violated the homogeneity of variance assumption; there is a significant difference in variance between two of the groups.

have violated the homogeneity of variance assumption *and* have unequal numbers of subjects in the groups, then you should refer to an advanced text such as Kirk (1982).

Dealing with rogue data

This section discusses the different methods that may be employed in order to solve the various problems that are encountered if data violate any of the assumptions of ANOVA discussed above. Although these solutions may improve matters, they are not universal panaceas, and on rare occasions it may be necessary to admit defeat and redesign a study. A useful alternative is to consider a non-parametric equivalent of Analysis of Variance. For between-subjects designs, the *Kruskal–Wallace One-Way Analysis of Variance by Ranks* may be used as an alternative to a standard ANOVA. A significant test result indicates that scores between groups differ, and then the Mann–Whitney test may be used to follow this up by determining exactly which groups. This is similar to the follow-up tests to be described in Chapter 6. Unfortunately, these tests are restricted to single-factor designs and so are limited in their usefulness. If it is necessary to perform a non-parametric test by hand, a text such as Neave and Worthington (1988) or Siegel and Castellan (1988) should be consulted.

Transforming data

Dependent variables are usually convenient but imperfect measures of the effects of independent variables on performance. Not only may they be subject to errors of measurement, but also they may not be related in simple, linear ways to the skill levels etc. that are ultimately being measured. Floor and ceiling effects are an obvious example. The alternative to using non-parametric tests, which cannot easily be used if there are two or more factors, is to *transform the data*. This involves taking every overall score of every subject and applying a mathematical function to each. The rationale for this is that the measurement scale may not have a linear relationship to the true scale of performance.

For example, suppose I give subjects a set of problems such as anagrams to solve in a set time. I decide to measure skill at problem solving by seeing how many are solved correctly in this time. Most people will be able to solve quite a few, say 20.

However, the time limit, combined with constraints on human performance, means that it will be extremely difficult to get a very large score, and so very few people will solve many more than 20. Those who do are clearly very skilled problem solvers indeed. The consequence of this is that the difference in skill level between someone who has solved 10 problems and someone who has solved 15 problems may be far smaller than the difference between someone who solved 20 problems and someone who solved 25 problems. Hence, the number of problems solved is not linearly related to problem solving skill and this is shown in Figure 5.3. In other words, the dependent variable, *number of problems solved,* is measured on an ordinal scale, not an interval scale. Perhaps, in this example, taking the number of problems solved by each subject and squaring this score would be a more appropriate indication of problem solving skill.

To get around these types of problem, and other violations of the assumptions underlying Analysis of Variance, the following data transforms may be used in the following circumstances. These are the most frequently used, but there are others that you may come across (see, for example, Howell, 1997).

Standard deviation is proportional to the mean

If the homogeneity of variance assumption is violated, it is often the case that the cells with the higher means are also the cells that have the higher standard deviations. If a set of means are unequal and if

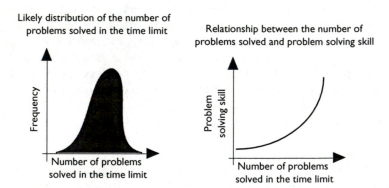

Figure 5.3 A plausible relationship between the number of problems solved and problem solving skill

$$\frac{\text{group mean}}{\text{group standard deviation}}$$

gives roughly the same answer for each of the groups, then try a *logarithmic transform*; take each overall subject score and calculate the logarithm of that value:

new score = $\log_{10}$ (old score)

and perform the statistical test on the new set of transformed scores. If any of the scores are zero or negative, a constant must be added to each before it can be transformed. For example, if some scores are zero, then the transform should be:

new score = $\log_{10}$ (old score + 1)

Variance is proportional to the mean

At other times, if the homogeneity of variance assumption is violated, groups with higher means may also be the groups that have the higher variances. If a set of means are not equal and if

$$\frac{\text{group mean}}{\text{group variance}}$$

gives roughly the same answer for all of the groups, then a *square root transformation* may improve homogeneity;

new score = $\sqrt{\text{old score}}$

If the scores are small, i.e. less than 1, then:

new score = $\sqrt{\text{old score} + 0.5}$

or

new score = $\sqrt{\text{old score}} + \sqrt{\text{old score} + 1}$

may be better transforms. If any of your scores are negative, then it is necessary to add a constant to all of the scores in order to remove the negatives. For example, if the smallest score is -2, then the following should be applied:

$$\text{new score} = \sqrt{\text{old score} + 3}$$

Positively skewed distribution

The two transforms outlined above will reduce both any positive skew in a set of data because they have a tendency to reduce large scores by a large amount and small scores by a small amount. If the data are only slightly positively skewed, the transform will not necessarily be helpful, and is probably not necessary for the purposes of removing skewness.

Several extreme values

For response time data, or solution time data for reasoning and problem solving tasks, there will often be occasional extreme values which add a long tail to one side of the distribution. For example, either a problem solving task is solved relatively quickly, say in 30 seconds, or the subject gets hopelessly lost and is no nearer a solution after 5 minutes. Alternatively, mis-pressing a button or losing attention can also prolong reaction times considerably without being informative about cognition. Rather than removing these values, the solution times could be converted to solution speeds by performing a *reciprocal transformation,* which will reduce the effect of the outliers and reduce the standard deviations, hence improving the homogeneity of variance.

$$\text{new score} = \frac{1}{\text{old score}}$$

If any score is equal to zero, then the following should be used, though it should not be possible to obtain a score of zero when response times are being investigated:

$$\text{new score} = \frac{1}{\text{old score} + 1}$$

When should data be transformed?

Usually, a transform will not be necessary as ANOVA is a very robust test. Only if data markedly deviate from the assumptions outlined above should a data transform be considered. Unfortunately, this topic, perhaps more than any other in this book, is one in which decisions are more or less always taken on the basis of a personal opinion.

How skewed is skewed? How heterogeneous must the variance be before warning bells start to ring? There are various statistical tests that were mentioned above that can answer these questions. One possible strategy, if the data fail these, is to try a data transform and compare the ANOVA output with the output for the untransformed data. Usually, transforming the data has no effect on whether or not differences between means are significant. If this is the case, then there is no need to be concerned and the analysis of the untransformed data should be reported. A sentence in the report that states that transforming the data had no effect might be useful in this situation. If there are differences in significances between transformed and untransformed data, then more care is needed, and if any of the transforms above do improve distribution or homogeneity of variance, then the analysis of the transformed data should be reported. Remember that the intention is to make data as suited as possible for Analysis of Variance, not to obtain the most favourable ANOVA results which are most in line with predictions. Ideally, the ANOVA should not be performed until the best transform has been determined.

Reporting data transforms

Data transforms are often potentially confusing to report, especially for a reciprocal transformation, which will reverse the directions of differences between groups and reverse the sign of correlations. It is therefore essential to describe the transformation process as carefully as possible in the results section of a report. Graphs and tables must be clearly labelled so that the reader knows what is on display. It is usual to show means in their original units in tables and figures, as these are easier for readers to understand. However, rather than giving means for the untransformed data, it is usual to take the means of the transformed values, e.g. take the mean of the set of logarithms that were calculated, and then convert this value back to the original units. This will give values that are not the same as the original means, but will bear a closer relationship to the actual values which have been analysed. An example of an analysis and the reporting of transformed data is given in Appendix A.

Deleting outliers

An alternative approach to the problem in which a few data points are very different from the rest is to delete the offending data. This is particularly the case where a set of scores have been collected from an individual, and although most are similar, one or two are exceptionally large or small. This will often happen when an individual is having to make several rapid responses, e.g. to words presented on a computer. Most response times will be fast, but lapses in attention may mean that a few uncharacteristic times are much longer than the rest. These exceptional responses may well distort the overall mean for that individual. Therefore, there may be some justification in deleting them, since the reason for the exceptions may be irrelevant to the theory under test. If any responses are to be deleted, it is essential that standardised and accepted criteria are applied consistently. If data deletion is to take place, the scores of every subject must be investigated, and the usual accepted criterion is as follows:

> For a set of scores for an individual, calculate the mean and standard deviation. Any scores which are greater than the mean plus two standard deviations or the mean minus two standard deviations may be deleted.

In practice, deleting some scores from a set of data will change both the mean of the data and the standard deviation. If these are recalculated, then it may be found that more data should be deleted from the same subject: deleting exceptions may create more exceptions, and so if the criterion is to be applied recursively in this way, and it should be, there is the risk of rapidly running out of data for an individual. In practice, the two-standard deviation cut-off is somewhat draconian and a three-standard deviation cut-off is also sometimes reported in the research literature. The best solution is to collect plenty of scores for each subject. The more scores collected, the less effect any extreme score can have on the data. However, unless quantities of data are small, deleting occasional exceptional scores usually makes little difference to the data, and this action is rarely taken by researchers. Transforming data or redesigning a study are usually preferable actions.

Chapter 6

Following up a one-factor between-subjects ANOVA

In the previous chapter, you were shown how to compute the F ratio for the simplest possible ANOVA: one-factor between-subjects. However, unlike simpler statistical tests, the meaning of the F ratio, whether significant or non-significant, is not always straightforward. This chapter discusses the further steps necessary in order to understand fully the outcome of a study in relation to the hypotheses under test.

The meanings of ANOVA outcomes

What does a significant F mean?

A significant value of F shows that the treatment has had a *significant effect* on the means of that factor. In other words, the different levels of the factor are related to different levels of performance in some way. In the simplest possible terms, this indicates that the difference between at least one of the pairs of the level means is significant. When there is one factor with only two levels, the meaning of a significant value of F is therefore unambiguous. There are only two level means, so it must be those two that are different. When there are three or more levels in a factor, matters become less clear. For three levels, there are at least three different combinations of pairs of means (see Figure 6.1). Every pair of means could be significantly different, or just one pair. In order to determine the exact pattern of differences, extra tests are required. The first follow-up tests to be described in this chapter are *pairwise comparisons* in which differences between pairs of means are tested for significance. These may be conducted either as *planned comparisons* or as *post-hoc* tests. Later, tests of more specific hypotheses, *linear contrast analysis*, will be discussed, but for now we will stick to simple pairwise comparisons.

What does a non-significant F mean?

If there is a non-significant value of F, there is insufficient evidence in support of any differences amongst the means and the null hypothesis cannot be rejected. Any differences which are apparent are not sufficiently large and consistent to stand out from differences in performance due to experimental error and are therefore unlikely to be due to treatment effects (see Figure 6.1). Sometimes you may be justified in performing certain follow-up tests, if you had planned to make them *before* running the experiment, but if you made no such plans, this is the end of the analysis.

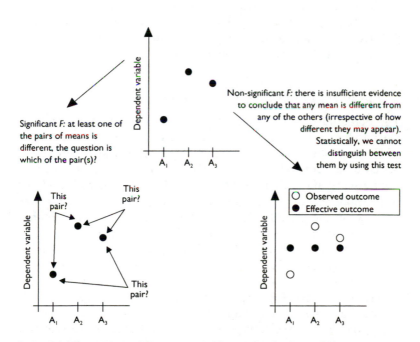

Figure 6.1 The two possible outcomes when using Analysis of Variance to analyse a single-factor design

Pairwise comparisons for single-factor designs: planned comparisons and *post-hoc* testing

There are two strategies for following up an Analysis of Variance after the initial *F* test. One of the essential parts of the research process is planning ahead; you should have decided which you are going to use before any analysis is performed on the data.

1   You may wish to know exactly which of the means differ significantly from which of the others, and thus you need to make every possible comparison. This would require you to look at every single combination of pairs of means, to see which of these are significantly different, in which case you will need to embark upon *post-hoc comparisons*. Usually, this situation will occur either because you did not, or could not, plan which means to compare, or because a particularly intricate hypothesis was under test.

2   You may have decided *in advance* that you will only be comparing particular pairs of means, and thus you do not need to compare all the possible pairs. In which case you will be making *planned comparisons*.

The problem of multiple comparisons

The potential difficulty with all of these follow-up tests, and the reason why you do not simply use *t*-tests to compare every mean with every other mean, is that multiple statistical comparisons increase the probability of making a Type I Error. A Type I Error occurs when the null hypothesis is mistakenly rejected, and the conclusion that there is a significant effect is in error, and there was no effect in the general population to detect. The 5% significance level means that this will happen about 1 time in 20 for any instance of using a statistical test. This Type I Error is also known as *per comparison Type I Error*. The 5% level is chosen as a compromise; a more stringent significance level would reduce the occurrence of Type I Errors but increase the occurrence of Type II Errors. The consensus amongst psychologists is generally, though implicitly, that 1 per comparison Type I Error in 20 will not damage the field too badly. However, we can also talk about *familywise Type I Error*. This occurs if a Type I Error has occurred at least once when performing a set of statistical tests on data from a single study. For a study with multiple factors/levels, if every mean is compared with every other mean using the *t*-test at the 5% significance level, this greatly increases the chance that the outcome of one of the comparisons will be a Type I Error, hence the familywise Type I Error rate could become as high as 100% in every experiment. This would occur if 20 comparisons were made, all at the 5% level of significance: 5% times 20 is equal to 100%. The greater the number of statistical tests performed, the greater the chance that one of the results will be a Type I Error. This needs to be taken into account with both *post-hoc* tests and planned comparisons.

Unfortunately, there is little agreement amongst statisticians on the best way in which to control familywise Type I Error, so that different textbooks often disagree on the best follow-up tests to use. If you plan to make a career of using statistical tests, you will put yourself at an advantage if you at least try to understand what is taking place when you make pairwise comparisons. Sooner or later you might have to justify using a particular analysis, and saying that your textbook told you to use a particular technique may not be enough *because the person you are justifying yourself to might have read a different textbook*. The approach taken by this book is to present all of the commonly used approaches; explaining their pros and cons, not only so that readers who feel confident can make their own decisions, but also to give advice on reasonable courses of action in particular situations. Thus less confident readers will not be forced to make a decision they do not feel able to take.

Using the t-test to make planned comparisons

Box 6.1 shows some example data which will be used for illustrating pairwise planned comparisons. The effect of three teaching techniques on examination performance is to be investigated: (i) Lectures supported by Computer Assisted Learning; (ii) Lectures supported by Tutorials; and (iii) Lectures without support. Suppose I am only interested in whether or not Computer Assisted Learning (CAL) is an improvement over, or at least as good as, traditional teaching techniques. In this case, before I ran the experiment, I would plan to compare the LCAL-group with the Lecture/Tutorial group (the LT-group) and the LCAL-group with the Lecture only group (the

L-group). These comparisons are all I need to make to decide whether or not to equip a large, expensive computer room. I am not interested in whether or not there is a difference between the L-group and the LT-group. Although this might be an interesting comparison, it is irrelevant for the purposes of this study. *Thus, certain hypotheses may be tested without comparing every mean with every other mean.*

Box 6.1 An example study involving planned comparisons

Suppose I have decided to investigate whether Computer Assisted Learning techniques (CAL) might be a worthwhile way of teaching. Three groups of students are chosen at random. One group is given lectures only (the L-group), another is given lectures and tutorials (the LT-group) and another is given lectures and a set of CAL programs to work through (the LCAL-group). The success of the teaching method will be measured by the final year exam mark. Although this study is a bit rough and ready, it should give some sort of indication of whether or not CAL is worth pursuing.

Data for the study are given in the first table in this box, and the second table shows the outcome of an Analysis of Variance that has been performed. Note that this is a one-factor three-level between-subjects design. Each subject is given only one of the teaching techniques. *NB These data are fictitious.* Unfortunately, the ANOVA table shows that the value of *F* just fails to exceed the critical value, which for degrees of freedom of (2,27) is 3.35, suggesting that there is no difference between the three means. Perhaps we should have run more subjects as the data are quite varied. However, all is not lost, but only if I *planned in advance* to compare certain pairs of means and not every pair, i.e. if I intended to make some *planned comparisons*.

Raw data:

Group	LCAL	LT	L
	58	63	52
	62	57	54
	65	58	56
	62	64	58
	60	63	63
	64	67	61
	56	67	58
	67	72	58
	65	65	63
	75	64	67
Means	63.4	64.0	59.0

ANOVA summary table:

Source	Sum of Squares	Degrees of freedom	Mean Square	F	p
A	149.1	2	74.5	3.31	>0.05 non-sig.
S/A	608.4	27	22.5		
TOTAL	757.5	29			

Before the study was run, I explicitly decided to make the two pairwise planned comparisons outlined above.[1] Deciding upon this regime *before* I ran the experiment *is an extremely important detail*. Also important is that I keep the numbers of planned comparisons as low as possible in order to reduce the likelihood of multiple comparisons leading to a high familywise Type I Error rate. One rule of thumb is that there should be one less comparison than the number of levels, i.e. $(a - 1)$ comparisons where a is the number of levels in the factor. This is suggested by, for example, Keppel, Saufley and Tokunaga (1992). Two comparisons are planned in this example, each at the uncorrected 5% level of significance. This gives a family-wise Type I Error rate of 10%, but the restrictions above make this is a permissible risk, and no further corrections to the significance level are required. For rare occasions where a design might have six or more levels, even this rule of thumb will make the chance of a familywise Type I Error somewhat too likely, and under such circumstances, the Bonferroni adjustment is recommended even if the comparisons were planned in advance. Here, the preferred significance level for a single comparison is divided by the total number of comparisons to be made in order to obtain a new significance level. Hence, with five comparisons at the 5% level of significance, 5% divided by five comparisons gives the 1% significance level, and only pairwise comparisons significant at this level will be accepted.

However many explicit planned comparisons are intended, they can be made despite the lack of a significant F value. This is, therefore, an *unprotected test* because the non-significant F ratio is not a barrier to using the follow-up tests. There is no real need to perform or report the ANOVA at all, except that one of the values from the table is needed in order to compute the planned comparisons by hand. Overall, these reasons show that deciding to make planned comparisons before running an experiment is a very good strategy.

The formula for using the t-test for making planned comparisons is given below, and has the same basic structure that all t-test equations have (see Chapter 2). The t-test must only be used to make the specified planned comparisons: two in the example. If your curiosity gets the better of you and you wish to make extra unplanned comparisons after you have made the planned comparisons – and hence have seen the means – you have to use a different test.

$$ t = \frac{\bar{A}_1 - \bar{A}_2}{\sqrt{(\text{Mean Square}_{ERROR}) \left(\dfrac{2}{N_A} \right)}} $$

Where $\bar{A}_1 - \bar{A}_2$ is the difference between the pair of means to be compared, and Mean Square$_{ERROR}$ is the error term used to test the F ratio. This is taken straight from the ANOVA table. This is why the ANOVA needed to be performed despite this test being unprotected. N_A is the number of scores in each of the levels of the factor whose means are being compared; this assumes an equal number of subjects per level. Given the assumption that the group variances are equal, and that any differences in variances are due to random error, the best estimate of the experimental error is based upon the *aggregate* of *all* of the group variances. Hence, the error term, Mean Square$_{ERROR}$ from the ANOVA table is used rather than just the variances of the pair of groups being compared. The obtained value of t has the same degrees of freedom as the Mean Square$_{ERROR}$ from the ANOVA table, and these degrees of freedom are used to determine the critical value of t if needed. Box 6.2 demonstrates the equation for the example data.

Box 6.2 **Making planned comparisons on the example data**

Comparing the mean of the LCAL-group with the mean of the L-group:

$$t = \frac{63.4 - 59}{\sqrt{(22.5)\left(\frac{2}{10}\right)}} = \frac{4.4}{\sqrt{4.5}} = \frac{4.4}{2.12} = 2.08$$

and comparing the mean of the LT-group with the mean of the LCAL-group:

$$t = \frac{64 - 63.4}{\sqrt{(22.5)\left(\frac{2}{10}\right)}} = \frac{0.6}{\sqrt{4.5}} = \frac{0.6}{2.12} = 0.28$$

From the ANOVA table (Box 6.1), the t value has 27 degrees of freedom, the same as for the ANOVA error term. Looking at the tables, the critical value t with 27 degrees of freedom at the 5% level of significance is 2.052, so the mean exam performance of the group who were given lectures with Computer Assisted Learning was significantly greater than the mean of the group that received lectures alone. However, there was no significant difference between the means of the group given lectures with Computer Assisted Learning and the group given lectures with tutorial support.

I will now have to decide whether tutorials are cheaper or more expensive to provide than computers . . .

Using post-hoc tests in addition to making planned comparisons

Suppose in a discussion with another member of staff, we get on to the topic of the effectiveness or otherwise of tutorials. My colleague suggests that they are of little educational value because few students try to take part in them fully. I remember that the data from my CAL study included exam results from students who received lectures only and students who received lectures supported by tutorials. If I have already analysed the data using my planned comparisons, especially if a small number was used and the significance level was not adjusted for them, and if I wish to further analyse the data, this is one situation in which I need to use a *post-hoc* test.[2]

In order to take account of the problem of multiple comparisons leading to high familywise Type I Error rates, *post-hoc* tests make the criteria for a significant difference more stringent than would normally be the case if you simply used a *t*-test to compare a pair of means, even if the Bonferroni adjustment has been applied. This is because *post-hoc* tests correct the significance level for every single possible comparison, including ones that you might have no intention of ever making. *Post-hoc* tests are thus less powerful than planned comparisons, as you are less likely to find a significant difference between a pair of means for a given set of data. Thus, where possible, you should always make planned comparisons.

In the example here, where a number of planned comparisons have been specified and made, and it is desired to make an additional comparison not previously intended, then the *Scheffé* test should be used. With the Scheffé test, *t* is calculated using the same equation given above, but this time, rather than looking up the critical value on tables, a new critical value is calculated using the equation below:

$$t_{\text{SCHEFFÉ}} = \sqrt{(a - 1)(F_{\text{CRIT}})}$$

where a is the number of levels in the factor whose means are being compared, and F_{CRIT} is the original critical value of F for that factor from the ANOVA that was performed. If the value of t, found by comparing a pair of means, is greater than $t_{\text{SCHEFFÉ}}$, you can then conclude that these means significantly differ. The result of this equation is to give a higher critical value of t, and hence a more difficult hurdle to cross, than would otherwise have been the case. This is the reason why the Scheffé test is more stringent than the ordinary t-test. Box 6.3 shows a demonstration of the Scheffé test for the example data.

The result in Box 6.3 may at first seem odd. The difference between the means of the L-group and the LT-group is not significant, yet the difference was even bigger than the difference between the means of the LCAL-group and the L-group, which was previously found to be significant. At first sight this may appear counterintuitive.

Box 6.3 Performing a Scheffé test on the example data

When comparing the mean of the LT-group with that of the L-group from the example in Box 6.1, the first step is to find the critical value of F for the original ANOVA. For degrees of freedom of (2,27) this is 3.35, hence:

$$t = \frac{64 - 59}{\sqrt{(22.5)\left(\frac{2}{10}\right)}} = \frac{5}{\sqrt{4.5}} = \frac{5}{2.12} = 2.36$$

$$t_{\text{SCHEFFÉ}} = \sqrt{(a - 1)(F_{\text{CRIT}})}$$

$$t_{\text{SCHEFFÉ}} = \sqrt{(3 - 1)(3.35)} = \sqrt{2(3.35)} = \sqrt{6.70} = 2.59$$

The original critical value of t for the planned comparisons was 2.052. Note how it has been increased for this test and thus a stiffer hurdle has been presented. The observed value of t is not greater than the new critical value which was calculated, so I do not have evidence that tutorial support of lectures leads to better mean exam performance than lectures alone.

The first point to note is that the Scheffé test is very conservative. The correction to guard against the problem of multiple comparisons takes into account not just every possible pairwise comparison of means that could be made, but also the different *contrast comparisons* that could be made as well (see later). Hence, the contradiction in the example makes sense mathematically because this *post-hoc* test makes a stringent correction to the significance level.

The second point to note is how hypothesis testing works. The aim is to disprove the null hypothesis, this being that the means are equal in the general population. In the example, I have failed to do so. This does not mean that I have *proved* that the null hypothesis is true; instead, the non-significant difference tells me that I do not yet have sufficient evidence to reject the null hypothesis. Instead, I need to collect some more evidence. The stringent correction may seem unfair, but do not forget that earlier I made several lenient planned comparisons without making any correction to the significance level. The payoff for this is that if I wish to make further unplanned comparisons, I need to be much more stringent in order to avoid the problem of making a Type I Error.

Making comparisons between every possible pair of means

Sometimes, for example in an exploratory study or a pilot study, you may not have any ideas about exactly which means you need to compare. In this case, you can use a test intended to compare every possible pair of means, but without the stringent correction used by the Scheffé test. There are a very large number of tests that can be used for comparing sets of means in this way, and it can be very difficult to choose between them (see Howell, 1997, for a fuller discussion of the various available tests). Two possible tests will be mentioned here – along with the computation of one – but all such tests function in similar ways and share two common features:

1   They take account of the magnitude of the difference between a pair of means; the larger the difference, the more likely that it is significant.

2   They make a correction for the numbers of pairs of means that
     are being compared, so that the probability of making a
     familywise Type I Error is reduced, but not to the extent
     that the criterion for significance is made so stringent that it
     is impossible to find any significant differences at all.

The major differences between the various pairwise tests
concern the exact way in which the correction for multiple
comparisons is made. *Post-hoc* tests assume that every single
possible comparison will be made and correct the significance level
accordingly. For a complicated design with many levels and many
possible comparisons, this correction can yield unacceptably low
levels of statistical power unless many subjects are run. There is a
very fine balancing point between making too many Type I Errors
and making too many Type II Errors, and the difficulties associated
with this are unlikely to be resolved. The consequence of this is that
if several of the possible pairwise comparisons do not make sense or
are genuinely unimportant, then making selected comparisons with
t-tests and applying the Bonferroni adjustment to the significance
level will almost always give a more powerful, less stringent statistical test than using a *post-hoc* procedure. This means that *post-hoc*
tests should only be used if every single possible comparison is
genuinely important; prior selectiveness will almost always yield a
more sensitive analysis.

One problem with the use of *post-hoc* tests occasionally arises
when the overall F ratio for an effect is of borderline significance
(e.g. $p = 0.049$). Since *post-hoc* tests apply corrections to the
significance level to take account of multiple comparisons, it is
occasionally possible to find a significant F, but then to find that
none of the pairwise comparisons is significant. This situation,
where encountered, is very difficult to interpret, and changing to
a less stringent *post-hoc* test (e.g. from Tukey to Newman–Keuls
see below) is not really recommended. The best solution, short of
rerunning the entire study, is probably to run additional subjects,
or alternatively to plan comparisons for a future replication.
Ideally, this situation would not have arisen had plenty of subjects
been tested to begin with.

Two common *post-hoc* tests are *Newman–Keuls* and *Tukey HSD*
(HSD stands for *Honestly Significant Difference*[3]). The second of
the two is the more stringent, and so this test should be used if
more caution is necessary. Many researchers object to any use of

the Newman–Keuls test because of this. However, when comparing up to and including three group means, the test is completely safe to use. Only for four or five means does the test become problematic, and the Tukey HSD should always be used if there are five or more groups to compare. Both tests work best with roughly equally sized groups, with similar variances and with normally distributed data. If the data appear to depart from these criteria (see Chapter 5), the *Games–Howell* correction to the Tukey test should be used (this test is not described here; see Howell, 1997, for formulae). Well-written computer software should make performing any *post-hoc* test very straightforward, and since the tests all work in similar ways to the *t*-test, there is no real need to go into their workings in great detail. The Newman–Keuls test is somewhat more involved to perform than the Tukey test and so only the latter will be demonstrated here, but this should not be taken as an implicit statement against the use of the Newman–Keuls test; in the right circumstances it is completely safe to use. One final point to note before describing the Tukey test: in psychology, if all means are to be compared with no firm prior predictions, the *post-hoc* tests to be described are usually not applied unless the *F* ratio for a factor is significant, indicating that there are differences among the means to be searched for.

Post-hoc analysis with the Tukey HSD test

Box 6.4 shows the working for the Tukey test should you ever be without a computer. Note that the equation requires an equal number of subjects in each level. The basic equation is set out below. It calculates a minimum critical difference for a pair of means to be significant, given the number of means that are to be compared. If the difference between the means is greater than the critical difference, then it is significant. Note that the statistic makes use of the error term from the ANOVA table.

$$W = q_{(r, df_{ERROR})} \sqrt{\frac{\text{Mean Square}_{ERROR}}{N_A}}$$

W	is the critical difference between the means. A difference between a pair of means is only large enough to be significant if it is greater than this value.
$q_{(r, df_{\text{ERROR}})}$	is the appropriate value of the *studentized range statistic* for the chosen significance level (see Appendix B). This is a single value taken from tables. Its exact value depends upon the number of means under comparison and the degrees of freedom of the error term from the ANOVA table.
r	is the number of means to be compared. The Tukey test automatically assumes that every possible comparison will be made.
df_{ERROR}	is the degrees of freedom for the error term from the original ANOVA table used to test the significance of the factor to which the means belong.
N_A	is the number of scores in each of the levels of the factor that is under test.

Box 6.4 **Performing the Tukey test (equal numbers of subjects per group)**

Cough mixtures often contain drugs known to make people drowsy and less responsive. Suppose the effects of various cough mixtures on performance are being determined. The scores represent people's mean performance on a lexical decision task, in which each person is presented with a number of words and non-words one at a time, and for each letter string has to decide whether or not it is a word. The mean response times in milliseconds are given in the first table: the greater the time, the more the mixture has degraded performance. This is a one-factor between-subjects design with four levels and the second table shows the outcome of the analysis. There are 10 subjects per level.

Table of means:

Group	Placebo	Drug 1	Drug 2	Drug 3
Means	550	562	653	601

ANOVA summary table:

Source	Sum of Squares	Degrees of freedom	Mean Square	F	p
A (drug type)	9600.0	3	3200.0	10.2	<0.05
S/A (error)	11282.4	36	313.4		
TOTAL	20882.4	39			

$$W = q_{(r, df_{\mathrm{ERROR}})} \sqrt{\frac{\text{Mean Square}_{ERROR}}{N_A}}$$

There are four means to be compared, and therefore the value of q corresponds to an r value of 4. There are 36 degrees of freedom for df_{ERROR}, also from the ANOVA table, and the error term is 313.4. Thus, for each pair of means, the equation for calculating the critical difference for significance, at the 0.05 significance level, W, is:

$$W = 3.82 \sqrt{\frac{313.4}{10}} = 3.82 \ \sqrt{31.34} = 21.4$$

Hence, only means which are different by 21.4 milliseconds or more are far enough apart for the difference to be significant.

Computer printouts often show the results of a *post-hoc* test in the form of a grid. This is illustrated below; asterisks indicate pairs of mean that are different from each other, at least at the 0.05 level of significance.

	Placebo	Drug 1	Drug 3	Drug 2
Placebo	—	NS	*	*
Drug 1		—	*	*
Drug 3			—	*
Drug 2				—

Hence, all differences are significant apart from the one between the placebo and drug 1. This cough mixture does not appear to degrade performance when compared with the placebo; all others significantly degrade performance. The patterns of significance can also be written as shown below. The means are in order of size and the underlining links together those means that are not different from each other. Thus, the placebo and drug 1 appear to be equally good, drug 3 significantly degrades performance in comparison with both, and drug 2 is the worst of all:

Placebo   Drug 1   Drug 3   Drug 2

However, this notation should only be used in a clear-cut case such as this. More often the significance of every single comparison between means should be reported. When reporting findings of *post-hoc* tests, only the significance of the difference need be reported ($p < 0.05$, $p < 0.01$, $p > 0.05$); neither the degrees of freedom nor an actual statistical value are required.

Post-hoc analysis with the Newman–Keuls test

The basic principles of the Newman–Keuls test are very similar to the Tukey test, and the equation for calculating critical differences is the same. The outcome of the test is information on whether or not the difference between a pair of means is large enough to be significant, possibly with the exact significance level. The format of presentation of the analysis, when performed by computer, is usually identical. However, for various reasons the Newman–Keuls test uses different critical differences for different pairs of means and the result of this is a test that is slightly more lenient than the Tukey test. Hence, if the outcome of a Tukey HSD test and a Newman–Keuls test are compared, a difference that is non-significant with the Newman–Keuls test will never, under any circumstances, be significant with the Tukey test. However, a difference that is non-significant with the Tukey test may, occasionally, be significant with the Newman–Keuls test. *Choose the post-hoc test before you perform the analysis for sound statistical reasons. NEVER compare the outcome of several different post-hoc tests, choosing the one that you prefer.* However, more often there are no differences in outcome between the two tests for a given data set, and if a Newman–Keuls analysis of the example data were to be attempted, this would be found to be the case here.

Linear contrast analysis for single-factor designs

Earlier, we saw how pairwise planned comparisons are used in order to focus on specific tests of interest, while *post-hoc* tests are used to trawl for differences by comparing every mean with every other mean. The advantage of using planned comparisons is that, in exchange for resisting the temptation to perform endless statistical tests, the sensitivity of each specified comparison is relatively high. In fact, pairwise comparisons using the *t*-test are a specific type of *linear contrast analysis*, and we will finish this chapter by looking at the other types of hypothesis that this type of analysis may be used to test. In general, any Analysis of Variance in which the $df_{BETWEEN}$ for a factor is greater than one, i.e. there are more than two levels in the factor, is said to be unfocused.[4] As stated earlier, a significant F ratio indicates that there are some significant effects somewhere among the means, but without follow-up tests it is hard to be sure exactly where. In general, linear contrast analysis enables a researcher to make focused inferences within a large unfocused analysis.

Linear contrast analysis enables a researcher to compare any combination of means from an ANOVA design. For example, in a single-factor between-subjects ANOVA with three levels, a researcher may wish to compare the mean of the control group with the *combined* mean performance of the two experimental groups. In other words, is the following comparison significant?

$$\bar{A}_1 \text{ versus } \frac{\bar{A}_2 + \bar{A}_3}{2}$$

If it is known in advance that an exact comparison, such as this, is sufficient in order to test a hypothesis, then there is little point in performing the entire unfocused Analysis of Variance with its associated loss in sensitivity. This runs the risk of finding a non-significant overall F ratio when the specific null hypothesis for the comparison of interest was false. In other words, a Type II Error has been made. Similarly to pairwise planned comparisons, a significant overall F ratio is not required in order to test these hypotheses for significance, as long as the specific contrasts were *planned* before performing any statistical analysis on the data, and as long as not too many contrasts are intended (i.e. $a - 1$ comparisons, where a is the number of levels and the number of comparisons does not exceed four).

The reason why a contrast analysis is always more sensitive than an unfocused analysis is because of the way in which between-group variance – Mean Square$_{BETWEEN}$ – is calculated: between-group variability (i.e. the Sum of Squares) is divided by the between-group degrees of freedom. Hence the overall F ratio for a between-subjects design is as follows:

$$F = \frac{\text{Mean Square}_{BETWEEN}}{\text{Mean Square}_{WITHIN}} \text{ and Mean Square}_{BETWEEN} = \frac{SS_{BETWEEN}}{df_{BETWEEN}}$$

If the F ratio of a three-factor between-subjects design is calculated, then $df_{BETWEEN}$ is 2 and so the $SS_{BETWEEN}$ is halved to give the between-group variance. However, if a contrast analysis is performed, the $df_{BETWEEN}$ is always 1, and so if most of the between-group variability is in line with the hypothesis that is being tested by a linear contrast, then $SS_{CONTRAST}$ will be almost as high as the original value of $SS_{BETWEEN}$, and so Mean Square$_{CONTRAST}$ could be almost double Mean Square$_{BETWEEN}$. The error term, Mean Square$_{WITHIN}$, is always the same whatever the effect being tested for significance, and so a focused comparison is able to give a larger F ratio than the unfocused comparison is able to same data.

As a more concrete example, consider the following fictitious study. The intention of this was to investigate the effects of different levels of stress on a manual dexterity task. There were three groups of subjects and the stress level was manipulated by administering a pre-task. Subjects spent either 5 minutes, 10 minutes or 15 minutes attempting to solve insoluble puzzles. According to the Yerkes–Dodson law, moderate levels of stress should facilitate performance at a dexterity task when compared with low or high levels. Given that this pattern of data has been predicted in advance, then it makes considerable sense to focus the analysis on seeing whether or not the data match this prediction. Suppose that the total between-group variability, $SS_{BETWEEN}$, is 100. Since there are three levels, $df_{BETWEEN}$ is two and Mean Square$_{BETWEEN}$ is therefore 50. Additionally, suppose that our prediction accounts for 90% of the between-group variability while the remaining 10% is variability that is not in line with our hypothesis. If we split $SS_{BETWEEN}$ accordingly, then $SS_{CONTRAST}$ is 90. There is only one degree of freedom and so Mean Square$_{CONTRAST}$ is also 90. Either Mean Square would have been tested by the same error term, and so specifying the contrast would increase the size of the F ratio. Hence this will have considerably increased the chance of finding a significant effect.

Linear contrasts enable any combination of means from an ANOVA design to be compared. Thus, for example, if you have four groups you can compare:

$$\frac{\bar{A}_1 + \bar{A}_2}{2} \text{ versus } \frac{\bar{A}_3 + \bar{A}_4}{2} \quad \text{or} \quad \bar{A}_1 \text{ versus } \frac{\bar{A}_2 + \bar{A}_3 + \bar{A}_4}{3}$$

Another important type of contrast analysis is where trends are searched for in data, hence *trend analysis*. If the values of the independent variable under investigation can be ordered along a numerical interval scale, it is possible to search for a trend in the effect of this variable on the dependent variable. If we consider the example of the effect of stress level on a dexterity task, assuming that it is plausible to think of the three levels of the independent variable – 5 minutes, 10 minutes and 15 minutes – as three equal increments in the level of stress, it is possible to test to see whether a particular trend is present in the data. Specifically, given three means, it is possible to test for the presence of either a significant *linear* or a significant *quadratic* trend, or both.

A linear trend in data indicates that the values of the dependent variable either increase or decrease steadily as a function of the increase in the value of the independent variable. In other words a straight line would be a reasonable fit to the obtained means. Improvement in cognitive task performance, from childhood to adolescence, might be an example of a linear trend in psychological research. A typical linear trend is shown in Figure 6.2 (left). A quadratic trend indicates that mean performance increases *and then decreases*, or vice versa, as the independent variable increases. Hence, a U-shaped, or inverted U-shaped, curve on the graph will connect the means reasonably well. A typical quadratic trend is also shown in Figure 6.2 (right). Somewhat confusingly, even if we are looking for a quadratic relationship, this is still called a linear contrast analysis.

With more than three levels in a factor, more esoteric curves are possible in theory. However, there are virtually no psychological independent and dependent variables which can be plausibly linked by more complicated curves. Therefore, only examples of linear and quadratic functions will be discussed.

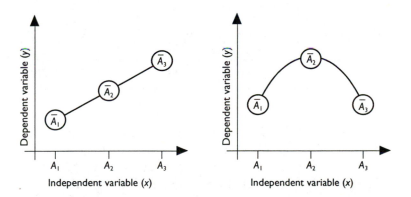

Figure 6.2 A linear trend in an experiment with three levels (left) and a quadratic trend in an experiment with three levels (right)

Calculating and testing the significance of contrasts

In this section, you will be shown how to perform various contrast analyses, illustrated by the stressed-performance example from above. A reasonable prediction would be that a moderate level of stress would be related to better performance at a dexterity task, compared with low and high levels of stress. This prediction corresponds to a quadratic trend in the means, in this case an *inverted* U-shaped curve. Some fictitious data are shown in Box 6.5. The working assumes an equal number of subjects per group. Where this is not possible and the calculations must be performed by hand, the reader should consult an advanced text such as Kirk (1982).

In order to calculate the values for linear contrasts, we first need to *weight* our means according to the hypothesis under test. These

---

Box 6.5 Data for an investigation of the relationship between stress level and performance

NB This is a between-subjects design. The raw data are as follows:

Stress level	Low	Medium	High
	42	57	39
	54	46	45
	45	54	49
	40	41	39
	36	56	44
$\bar{A}_x$	43.4	50.8	43.2
$\sum A_x$	217	254	216

The means clearly appear to have a quadratic trend: the mean dexterity performance of people with a moderate stress level is certainly higher than the mean of people with low or high stress levels. But, as is shown on the ANOVA table below, there is no significant overall effect of stress level.

ANOVA summary table:

Source	Sum of Squares	Degrees of freedom	Mean Square	F	p
A	187.6	2	93.8	2.5	> 0.05
S/A	450.8	12	37.6		
TOTAL	638.4	14			

weights, W_X, should reflect our predictions under test, but are expressed numerically, *and must add up to zero.* Table 6.1 shows some examples of weights that can be applied to a three-level design.

Once the weights have been determined, these should then be applied to the linear contrast formula in order to calculate L. The formula should be extended if more than three levels have been investigated.

$$L = W_1 \sum A_1 + W_2 \sum A_2 + W_3 \sum A_3 \text{ (given that } W_1 + W_2 + W_3 = 0)$$

Box 6.6 shows calculations of L for various possible predictions from the example data.

Having calculated L, it is necessary to use this value in order to calculate a Sum of Squares for the effect, indicating the degree of variability which can be accounted for by the particular prediction:

$$SS_{CONTRAST} = \frac{L^2}{N_A \sum (W^2)}$$

where N_A is the number of scores in each level.

Table 6.1 Some examples of weights for testing specific hypotheses

Contrast	Description	W_1	W_2	W_3
Linear trend	$\bar{A}_1 < \bar{A}_2 < \bar{A}_3$	−1	0	1
Quadratic trend	$\bar{A}_2 > \bar{A}_1, \bar{A}_2 > \bar{A}_3$ and $\bar{A}_1 = \bar{A}_3$	−1	2	−1
Pairwise comparison	$\bar{A}_1 < \bar{A}_2$ ($\bar{A}_3$ irrelevant)	−1	1	0

Box 6.6 Calculations of L for various possible predictions from the example data

Stress level:	Low	Medium	High
$\bar{A}_x$	43.4	50.8	43.2
$\sum A_x$	217	254	216

Linear trend: If we expect low stress to give us the worst performance, medium stress to result in medium performance, and high stress to result in the best performance, then the chosen weights should be (-1), (0) and $(+1)$:

$$L = (-1)217 + (0)254 + (1)216 = -217 + 216 = -1$$

Quadratic trend: If we expect both high and low stress to give us the worst performance, and medium stress to result in the best performance, then the chosen weights should be (-1), $(+2)$ and (-1):

$$L = (-1)217 + (2)254 + (-1)216 = -217 + 508 - 216 = 75$$

Pairwise comparison (I): If we expect low stress to give us worse performance than medium stress, and we are not bothered about high stress, then the chosen weights should be (-1), $(+1)$ and (0). This is equivalent to using the t-test to make a pairwise comparison, as shown earlier:

$$L = (-1)217 + (1)254 + (0)216 = -217 + 254 = 37$$

Pairwise comparison (II): If we expect medium stress to give us better performance than high stress, and are not bothered about low stress, then the chosen weights should be (0), $(+1)$ and (-1). This is also equivalent to using the t-test:

$$L = (0)217 + (1)254 + (-1)216 = 254 - 216 = 38$$

Note that the two pairwise comparisons together are the equivalent prediction to the quadratic trend prediction, and that their two values of L total to the same value of L for the quadratic trend.

Like all F ratios, contrast analysis follows the standard F ratio formula:

$$F = \frac{\text{Mean Square}_{EFFECT}}{\text{Mean Square}_{ERROR}}$$

We already have Mean Square$_{ERROR}$; this is taken from the original ANOVA table. Having calculated $SS_{CONTRAST}$, no further action is required because:

$$\text{Mean Square}_{CONTRAST} = \frac{SS_{CONTRAST}}{df_{CONTRAST}}$$

But $df_{CONTRAST}$ is always equal to one and therefore:

$$F = \frac{SS_{CONTRAST}}{\text{Mean Square}_{ERROR}}$$

Having calculated the observed F value, it should be compared with the critical value for $(1, df_{ERROR})$ degrees of freedom, in order to see whether the differences or trends under investigation are significant. Box 6.7 shows the significance tests for the contrasts identified in Box 6.6.

Box 6.7 F tests for the contrasts outlined in Box 6.6

There are five subjects per group, $N_A = 5$. The error term, Mean Square$_{ERROR}$, is taken from the ANOVA table in Box 6.5. It is 37.6 with 12 degrees of freedom. All of the F ratios below will therefore have $(1,12)$ degrees of freedom, giving a critical value of F of 4.75 at the $p < 0.05$ significance level.

$$SS_{CONTRAST} = \frac{L^2}{N_A \Sigma (W^2)} \qquad F = \frac{SS_{CONTRAST}}{\text{Mean Square}_{ERROR}}$$

Linear trend: $L = -1$, $\Sigma (W^2) = (-1)^2 + (0)^2 + (1)^2 = 2$

$$SS_{CONTRAST} = \frac{(-1)^2}{5(2)} = 0.1 \qquad F = \frac{0.1}{37.6} = 0.0027 \qquad p > 0.05, \text{ non-significant}$$

Quadratic trend: $L = 75$, $\Sigma (W^2) = (-1)^2 + (2)^2 + (-1)^2 = 6$

$$SS_{CONTRAST} = \frac{(75)^2}{5(6)} = 187.5 \qquad F = \frac{187.5}{37.6} = 4.99 \qquad p < 0.05, \text{ significant}$$

Pairwise comparison (I): $L = 37$, $\Sigma (W^2) = (-1)^2 + (1)^2 + (0)^2 = 2$

$$SS_{CONTRAST} = \frac{(37)^2}{5(2)} = 136.9 \qquad F = \frac{136.9}{37.6} = 3.64 \qquad p > 0.05, \text{ non-significant}$$

Pairwise comparison (II): $L = 38$, $\Sigma (W^2) = (0)^2 + (1)^2 + (-1)^2 = 2$

$$SS_{CONTRAST} = \frac{(38)^2}{5(2)} = 144.4 \qquad F = \frac{144.4}{37.6} = 3.84 \qquad p > 0.05, \text{ non-significant}$$

Taking the results of the example, although the overall F ratio in Box 6.5 was non-significant, with an appropriately targeted prediction, it was possible to find a significant effect for a quadratic trend in the data. Also, note that the two separate planned comparisons which were equivalent to a quadratic trend were both non-significant. This was despite not correcting for significance, giving a probability of making a familywise Type I Error of 1 in 10. However, combining these separate predictions into a single test for a quadratic trend produced a statistical result that *was* significant. The more focused and specific you can make a prediction, and the fewer significance tests that you need to make in order to assess it, the more powerful the test, and the more likely a significant effect will be found. Overall, the example shows that in order to test the hypothesis – that a moderate level of stress is uniquely beneficial for performing a dexterity task – then a straightforward Analysis of Variance looking for differences among all three levels is not the most sensitive technique. Given that a quadratic trend was explicitly predicted before the data were analysed, this trend should be directly tested.

In the example above, we also tried to fit the data to a linear trend, but a non-significant effect was obtained. This suggests that the means are not increasing as the stress level increases. However, two points should be noted. First, data *should not* be analysed endlessly in different ways until a significant effect is found. As for planned comparisons, contrasts should be specified before commencing the data analysis, and should be limited in number. The number of contrasts performed should not exceed the $df_{BETWEEN}$, had a conventional ANOVA been performed. Overall, the same strategy as given earlier is suggested here. If $(a - 1)$ linear contrasts were explicitly planned from the beginning, where a is the number of levels in the factor, then these analyses may be applied without the need for a significant F ratio for the factor. If four or fewer contrasts are intended, then the significance level need not be corrected, but if five or more comparisons are planned, then the Bonferroni adjustment should be applied.

The second point is to sound a note of caution when interpreting contrasts. Recall that the weights in order to test for a linear contrast when a factor has three levels are (-1), (0) and $(+1)$. In practical terms, what happens is that the mean of A_2 is ignored when performing a linear trend contrast analysis, as this mean makes no contribution to the $SS_{CONTRAST}$. In other words, provided that $\bar{A}_1$ is reliably greater than or less than $\bar{A}_3$, a linear trend can be found in a set of data whatever the value of $\bar{A}_2$. Figure 6.3 shows two sets of means, both of which would fit a linear trend equally well. In reality, the right graph shows a quadratic *and* a linear trend together. Overall, the suggestion here is always to be wary of any contrast analysis where one or more of the weights turns out to be zero. Only if the value of the zero-weighted mean(s) is genuinely irrelevant to the hypothesis under test can there be no problems.

Finally, the examples in this section have all been for a three-level experiment. It is possible to search for linear and quadratic trends in designs with more than three levels, and weights for these contrasts are given in Appendix B.

Directionality of contrasts

Contrasts are evaluated by comparing an obtained F value with a critical value on F tables. All values of the F ratio and the F

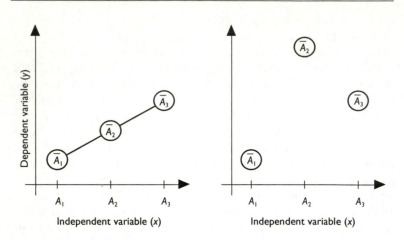

Figure 6.3 Two sets of data which fit a linear trend equally well

distribution range from 0 to $+ \infty$ (infinity) and, because of this, it is not possible to test a one-tailed statistical hypothesis. However, bearing in mind the warnings in Chapter 2, when performing a contrast analysis it may sometimes be appropriate to test a directional statistical hypothesis in order to benefit from the increase in statistical power that this entails. Consider an experiment where it is expected that a particular skill will improve with age. However, bear in mind that a one-tailed test may not be advisable here given that numerous abilities are known to decline with age during adulthood. If a standard contrast analysis for a linear trend is performed, this will not only test for an increase in skill with age, but also for a linear decline in skill with age. If it is genuinely reasonable to use a one-tailed significance test, then this is possible provided that the F ratio for the Mean Square$_{EFFECT}$ has one degree of freedom, as is the case for any contrast analysis. An F ratio with $df_{BETWEEN}$ equal to one is identical to t^2 had a t-test been performed on the data instead. By taking the square root of an obtained F ratio, it is possible to obtain the corresponding t value. With a t value, it is possible to obtain both one-tailed and two-tailed critical values of t, and hence the F ratio from any contrast analysis can be subjected to a one-tailed statistical test if appropriate.

Trends with unequally spaced intervals

Trend analysis can be applied to any situation where the independent variable can be measured on an interval scale. In the example above, we have only looked at situations where there have been equally sized intervals between the values. In this situation, the standard weights for linear and quadratic trend contrasts can be applied automatically without any modification. However, if the values of the independent variable are not evenly spaced, for example the independent variable taking values of 5, 20 and 60 minutes, new weights for linear and quadratic trends must be calculated in order to take account of this. Assignment of weights is relatively straightforward but beyond the scope of this book, and the reader is referred to an advanced source (e.g. Gaito, 1965).

Chapter 7

Calculating *F* ratios for one-factor within-subjects designs

In this chapter, the basic ANOVA calculations introduced in Chapters 3 and 4 for the between-subjects design will be modified for within-subjects designs. For a within-subjects design, every subject takes part in all of the levels of a factor, and knowing more than one piece of information about every subject enables the size of the error term to be reduced for the *F* ratio.[1] This results in a larger value of *F* and hence the effect is more likely to be significant. Overall, for a given effect size and a given number of scores, any within-subjects design study should be more powerful than an equivalent between-subjects design.

However, with the increase in statistical power comes several potential problems, and the apparent simplicity of the within-subjects design is deceptive. In practical terms, a researcher should always be on the lookout for *order effects*: the ways in which performing one task changes performance on subsequent tasks. If a person is performing three or more tasks, one after the other, it is highly likely that one of the tasks will influence the performance of the rest, usually due to learning. When using within-subjects factors, the only practical way to minimise this is to vary the order of the tasks for each person so that no consistent pattern can be allowed to develop. This would either be by counterbalancing or by randomly allocating subjects to different orders of conditions. However, even with these actions, there are problems with analysing within-subjects data which will be discussed later.

Single within-subjects factor, two or more levels

As shown in Chapter 3, the general equation for the F ratio is:

$$F = \frac{\text{between-group variance}}{\text{experimental error}}$$

For the between-subjects design, the F ratio used the within-group variance for the error term:

$$F = \frac{\text{between-group variance}}{\text{within-group variance}}$$

Because between-group variance has two sources of variability – treatment effects and experimental error – the general formula can also be written as:

$$F = \frac{\text{treatment effects} + \text{experimental error}}{\text{experimental error}}$$

However, recall from Chapter 3 that experimental error also has two sources of variability. Scores may vary because some people are naturally faster (or slower, or more accurate, etc.) than others. Hence, individual differences can be responsible for scores varying from one another. In addition, random errors of measurement may cause differences in scores, and hence the F ratio can be rewritten as:

$$F = \frac{\text{treatment effects} + \text{individual differences} + \text{random errors}}{\text{individual differences} + \text{random errors}}$$

As we will see, for a within-subjects design, because there are at least two scores per person, it is possible to remove the variability of the scores due to individual differences from the error term. This leaves the error term consisting only of random error, also called *residual error*. The effect of removing this variability and making the error term smaller is to make the overall value of F larger, so that the treatment effects stand out more and are more likely to be significant. Hence, for a within-subjects design:

$$F = \frac{\text{between-group variance}}{\text{random errors}}$$

As an aside, for a within-subjects design, as far as the between-group variance is concerned, the variabilities in scores caused by individual differences cancel each other out so that they will have no effect on the between-group variance. Effectively, they were never present to begin with, and individual differences in overall performance are not a source of variability for the between group variance. This means that the actual sources of variability for a within-subjects design are:

$$F = \frac{\text{treatment effects + random errors}}{\text{random errors}}$$

Sources of error variability

The underlying basis of within-subjects ANOVA is that, once we have two or more scores per person, we can see two ways in which people can be different from each other. They can differ in their overall level of performance or they can differ in the trends in their scores, or both.

Tables 7.1 to 7.5 each show a pair of subjects, each with two scores. We can look at the overall mean score for each subject ignoring the fact that there may be differences from level to level, but we can also look at the *trend* in scores for each subject across conditions. Trend refers to both the *size of the difference* and the *direction of the difference* in scores for a subject. Table 7.1 shows two subjects who are identical. Their overall performance is the same, a mean of 2, and the trend in scores is the same size and direction, A_2 is always two units greater than A_1. Table 7.2 shows a pair of subjects who differ in overall performance – one obtained double the scores of the other overall – but not in the trend in performance. Both obtained a larger score for A_2, the size of the difference is 2 units in both cases. If I predicted that scores in A_2 would be larger than scores in A_1, I would be completely happy with this outcome. Table 7.3 shows the opposite to Table 7.2. Here, these subjects have identical overall performance (both obtained an overall score of 2) but they have different trends. The size of the trend is identical for both (two units) but is in the opposite directions. I could not make any

Tables 7.1–7.5 Various ways in which pairs of subjects with pairs of scores can be different

Table 7.1

	A_1	A_2	Mean
S_1	1	3	2
S_2	1	3	2

Table 7.2

	A_1	A_2	Mean
S_1	1	3	2
S_2	3	5	4

Table 7.3

	A_1	A_2	Mean
S_1	1	3	2
S_2	3	1	2

Table 7.4

	A_1	A_2	Mean
S_1	1	3	2
S_2	0	4	2

Table 7.5

	A_1	A_2	Mean
S_1	1	3	2
S_2	5	3	4

guess from this as to which was the harder task. Table 7.4 also shows two subjects who do not differ in their overall score, but who again differ for the trends in their scores. The direction of the trend is the same for both, and only the size of the trend differs. This pattern is far more interpretable than the pattern in Table 7.3. In general terms, direction of trend is more crucial to interpreting data than the size of the trend. Finally, Table 7.5 shows a pair of subjects who differ both for overall performance and for their trends.

Individual difference and random error variance

In each of Tables 7.1 to 7.5, only two subjects were compared. With a real study, there will be many more subjects, and they will never have identical trends, so a statistical test is required in order to make sense of the data.

When we talk about the variety of overall performance for a set of subjects, ignoring the actual scores for individual levels, we are concerned with *individual difference* variability. This is also called *between-subject* variability and this will be the preferred term. Hence, between-subject variance is a measure of the extent to which subjects, on average, perform differently from each other *irrespective of experimental condition*. In Table 7.6, when we look at the overall means for each subject, we can see that the overall mean value for the second subject is four times larger than for the third subject, while the value for the first subject is twice as large as for the third subject. Although the individual differences are large, *the trend in performance is identical for every subject, they all scored 2 more for condition A_2 than condition A_1*. If we were to calculate the between-subject variance for these data, we would find this to be much higher for the data in Table 7.6 than for the data in Table 7.7.

In Table 7.7, the overall mean for every subject is the same, so that the between-subject variance, if calculated, would be very low. In fact it would be zero: there is no overall difference between subjects, zero differences = zero variance. However, although every subject's overall mean is the same, their trends are very different. The third subject has a greater score for condition A_1 than for condition A_2. The first and fourth subjects have a greater score for

Table 7.6 Data with high between-subject variability

	A_1	A_2	Mean
Subject 1	3	5	4
Subject 2	7	9	8
Subject 3	1	3	2
Subject 4	5	7	6
Mean	4	6	5

Table 7.7 Data with low between-subject variability

	A_1	A_2	Mean
Subject 1	1	9	5
Subject 2	5	5	5
Subject 3	6	4	5
Subject 4	4	6	5
Mean	4	6	5

condition A_2 than for condition A_1, while the second subject has performed equally well for both conditions. This variability in the consistency of trends can also be measured, and this is given either the name *random error variance* or *residual variance*. The latter term will be used here in preference. In Table 7.7, the trends are very inconsistent, and so the residual variance will be high; in Table 7.6, the trends are identical to each other and so the residual variance will be much lower: again it will be zero.

Psychologists test hypotheses about differences. Hence, if treatment A_1 is predicted to make subjects obtain larger scores than treatment A_2, this can be investigated by administering both treatments to each subject – i.e. a within-subjects design – and seeing to what extent the trend in performance of each individual is in the predicted direction: A_1 scores greater than A_2 scores. If our prediction really is true for the general population, then most subjects should obtain larger scores for A_1 than for A_2; only a minority should have scores in the wrong direction. The more subjects in the wrong direction, i.e. with the wrong trend, the more the prediction is weakened. Variability in trends is measured by *residual variance*: the more accurate our prediction that A_1 scores will be greater than A_2 scores, the smaller the residual variance. If there is no clear trend, then the residual variance will be high. However, if the majority of trends are in the opposite direction to the prediction, the residual variance will also be low, showing that there are consistent differences in levels of performance, but in the opposite direction to that predicted.

For virtually all studies in psychology, there will be a prediction that scores in one condition will be different, i.e. larger or smaller, than scores in another condition. You will rarely, if ever, see a more exact prediction of the sizes of the scores. Hence, you might read a prediction that scores in level A_1 will be lower than level A_2, but will never read a prediction that scores in level A_1 will be around 5 seconds and scores in level A_2 will be around 9 seconds. Because the overall level of performance is usually irrelevant, the between-subject variance shown in Table 7.6 should be ignored. Everyone has a difference in the same direction, so who cares that some people have much larger scores than others overall? For a within-subjects design, this is achieved mathematically by removing the between-subject variability from the within-group variability, leaving behind only random errors in trends, and hence the residual variability.

With the residual variance as the error term, then ideally this should be low compared with the between-group variance, and if this is the case then there is likely to be a significant effect. Hence, for a within-subjects design:

$$F = \frac{\text{between-group variance}}{\text{residual variance}}$$

In Table 7.8, there are two sets of data, each with two levels: A_1 and A_2. Every single subject has attained a higher score for A_2 than for A_1 for both sets of data, and the trend in performance for every one of the matched pairs of subjects is identical. For example, the S_2 subject in the left-hand data set obtained a score for A_2 that was two units larger than their score for A_1, and so did the S_2 subject in the right-hand data set. Even though one pair of scores was more than double the other, *the trends were identical in both cases*. In the right-hand set of data, there are much larger individual differences in the overall performance of subjects compared with the left-hand data set. For a between-subjects ANOVA, high between-subject variability is reflected in the calculation of the within-group variance, and masks the treatment effects by giving a small F value. Variances and Fs have been computed as though both of these experiments were between-subjects designs. Notice that although both have exactly the same between-group variance, a reflection of the same differences between the means, the data on the right have such a high within-group variance that using this as an error term gives an F value that is vanishingly small.

Table 7.8 Using between-subjects ANOVA on a within-subjects design

	A_1	A_2		A_1	A_2
S_1	7	8	S_1	7	8
S_2	7	9	S_2	17	19
S_3	5	7	S_3	25	27
S_4	4	7	S_4	14	17
Mean	5.75	7.75	Mean	15.75	17.75
Between-group variance	8		Between-group variance	8	
Within-group variance	1.583		Within-group variance	58.25	
F		5.05	F		0.14

However, in terms of a within-subjects design, the results of both experiments are identical. Each pair of subjects, for example the S_1 subjects for both the right-hand and the left-hand data, has an identically sized trend in performance in the same direction. For the right-hand data, it is irrelevant that S_3 overall had scores over three times as big as those of S_1, *they both had trends in the same direction*. If we calculate the portion of the overall variability in the data accounted for by individual differences, i.e. between-subject variability, and we remove this from the within-group variability, we will obtain the residual variability. This is our measure of the differences in the size and direction of the trends in performance, which is independent of the between-subject variability, and is hence our measure of error for this experiment. The less consistent the trends, the larger the residual variability and hence the experimental error. Expressing this variability as a variance will give the value of the error term for a within-subjects design.

It is possible to remove between-subject variability from the error term because we have more than one score for each individual. With only one score, it is impossible to know the extent to which experimental error was caused by either individual differences or random errors. With two scores, we immediately get an impression of the overall performance level for every subject. Hence, we can find out how much of the within-group variance is due to between-subject variability, and how much is due to residual variability. Removing the between-subject variability results in the size of the error term getting smaller *but without affecting the size of the treatment effects*. This means that the treatment effects are far more likely to stand out mathematically from the experimental error, and are easier to detect.

Table 7.9 shows exactly the same data as Table 7.8, but this time with a within-subjects ANOVA performed. Notice that the size of the error term is much smaller for both, but has particularly shrunk for the right-hand set of data. Now that a within-subjects ANOVA has been performed, F is extremely large, and this would be expected given the highly consistent trend in the differences. Notice also that the between-group variance is unchanged compared with Table 7.8. Furthermore, observe the identical residual variance in the two ANOVAs. This reflects the fact that for the two data sets subjects had identically sized trends in performances, and that all of these trends were in the same direction.

Table 7.9 Using within-subjects ANOVA on a within-subjects design

	A_1	A_2		A_1	A_2
S_1	7	8	S_1	7	8
S_2	7	9	S_2	17	19
S_3	5	7	S_3	25	27
S_4	4	7	S_4	14	17
Mean	5.75	7.75	Mean	15.75	17.75
Between-group variance		8	Between-group variance		8
Residual variance		0.33	Residual variance		0.33
F		24	F		24

Calculating F for a within-subjects design

Calculating *F* for a single-factor within-subjects design is relatively straightforward. The same basic ratios as for a between-subjects design are used. The only difference is that an extra one is required for the purpose of removing between-subject variability from the error term. In the calculations to follow, the between-subject Sum of Squares will be removed from the within-group Sum of Squares to leave the *residual* Sum of Squares. Likewise, the between-subject degrees of freedom will be removed from the within-group degrees of freedom to leave the *residual* degrees of freedom.

This procedure can be understood in the following way – it is mathematically identical to all of the procedures that you will be shown later. We are only interested in the consistency and the magnitude of the *trends* in the differences between levels for each subject. In other words, we need to know the average trend – or difference – between levels across subjects, and the consistency is measured by the residual variability. If there is low consistency in trends, then the residual variability will be high; if there is high consistency in trends, then the residual variability will be low. We are not interested in the magnitude of the overall differences between individuals, which is measured by the between-subject variability. Because we have more than one score per individual, we know the overall mean level of performance. If we take the overall mean for each subject, and subtract this from each level score, we will be left with just the trend in performance, and will

Table 7.10 Removing between-subject variability

	A_1	A_2	Mean		A_1	A_2	New mean
S_1	7	8	7.5	S_1	−0.5	+0.5	0
S_2	17	19	18	S_2	−1.0	+1.0	0
S_3	25	27	26	S_3	−1.0	+1.0	0
S_4	14	17	15.5	S_4	−1.5	+1.5	0
Mean	15.75	17.75	16.75	Mean	−1.0	+1.0	0

Between-group Sum of Squares	8	Between-group Sum of Squares	8
Within-group Sum of Squares	349.5	Within-group Sum of Squares	1

have completely eliminated the overall differences between individuals. Hence, this removes between-subject variability.

In Table 7.10, a set of scores and their between-group and within-group Sums of Squares are shown on the left-hand side. Notice that the measure of diversity of data, the within-group Sum of Squares, is very high. The right-hand side shows the new scores calculated by subtracting each subject's overall mean from each subject's level score. Notice the effect of this on the new overall subject means. The measure of the diversity of data is now extremely low. However, the measure of the overall difference in scores between the groups, the between-group Sum of Squares, is unchanged by this process.

This process has removed the between-subject variability from the within-group Sum of Squares, and this is now termed the *residual Sum of Squares*, and this will be used for the error term. However, we cannot simply use this Sum of Squares in a between-group analysis of variance. We need to divide Sums of Squares by appropriate degrees of freedom in order to obtain variances, and the process of removing between-subject variability from the within-group variability has also removed some degrees of freedom. The residual degrees of freedom is therefore not the same as the within-group degrees of freedom, and so this value will also need to be calculated.

Removing between-subject variability mathematically

Box 7.1 shows an example that will be used for the calculations in this section.

Box 7.1 **A digit Stroop task and data**

For over 60 years, psychologists have known that it is very difficult to name the ink colour of a word if the word happens also to be a conflicting colour name itself: the natural tendency to read the word conflicts with the required task of naming the ink colour. This is known as the Stroop effect and can also be shown with numbers: how many xs are printed here: xxxx? How many 7s are printed here: 777777? The natural tendency to name a digit tends to interfere with counting how many digits there are. Suppose we run a small experiment where subjects are given two tasks in which they have to count the number of elements in a string. Each task consists of a list of 10 strings of either xs or digits. The control task consists of 10 letter strings, with between 2 and 8 xs in a string, while the interference task consists of 10 strings of digits, with between 2 and 8 identical digits in a string, which are incongruent with their quantity. For example, 22 or 333 would never be shown.

For example, the first three items for each list might be:

Control task	Control answer	Interference task	Correct answer
xxx	'3'	444	'3'
xxxxx	'5'	77777777	'8'
xxxxxxx	'7'	33	'2'

The dependent variable is the time taken in seconds to complete a list. The prediction is that the counting time should be longer for the interference list. Given the nature of the prediction, we are only interested in the difference in performance due to the list type. It does not matter if one subject takes 10 seconds for the control task while another takes 60 seconds, as long as every subject takes a little bit longer for the interference task than the control task.

Subject no.	Control	Interference	Subject mean	Subject total
S_1	4	6	5	10
S_2	5	7	6	12
S_3	6	8	7	14
S_4	7	5	6	12
TOTAL:	22	26	24	48
MEAN:	5.5	6.5	6	12

GRAND MEAN: 6   GRAND TOTAL: 48

We are expecting that the control list times will be faster than the interference list times for each subject. Overall this might be the case, but there is one exception (S_4). On average, the interference list took one second longer to read than the control list. Notice also that there are differences in each subject's overall counting time. Thus the best subject (S_1) on average was two seconds faster than the slowest subject (S_3) *averaging over conditions.*

In Chapter 4, you were shown that Sums of Squares are additive. The total variability is equal to the between-group Sum of Squares added to the within-group Sum of Squares:

$$SS_{TOTAL} = SS_{BETWEEN} + SS_{WITHIN}$$

When the between-subject variability, $SS_{SUBJECTS}$, is removed from the within-group Sum of Squares, we are left with residual variability due to random errors, $SS_{RESIDUAL}$.

$$SS_{WITHIN} = SS_{SUBJECTS} + SS_{RESIDUAL}$$

so that

$$SS_{TOTAL} = SS_{BETWEEN} + SS_{SUBJECTS} + SS_{RESIDUAL}$$

In order to compute the within-subjects design ANOVA, it is necessary to calculate the between-subject Sum of Squares. This is directly analogous to calculating the between-group (i.e. between-level) Sum of Squares. If we calculate the Sum of Squares between subjects, $SS_{SUBJECTS}$, and remove this from SS_{WITHIN}, we will be left with the residual random errors, $SS_{RESIDUAL}$, which will be used for the error term.

For the between-subject Sum of Squares, we are not interested in the individual variability of each subject from level to level; instead we are looking at the overall mean performance of each subject. In order to calculate $SS_{SUBJECTS}$ we look at the size of the difference of each individual overall mean in comparison to the *grand mean*. The greater the deviations of each subject mean from the grand mean, the greater the size of the between-subject variability, and hence the greater the contribution of individual differences to the within-group variance.

Calculating $SS_{SUBJECTS}$ is analogous to the way in which $SS_{BETWEEN}$ is calculated, so the difference between each subject mean and the grand mean needs to be squared, and then multiplied by the number of levels in the experiment, thus taking account of the number of individual scores that contribute to each subject's mean. As a reminder, the formula for the between-group variance can be written as follows (from Chapter 4):

$$\text{between-group variance} = \frac{N_{A_1}(\bar{A}_1 - \bar{Y})^2 + N_{A_2}(\bar{A}_2 - \bar{Y})^2 \text{ (and so on)}}{\text{between-group degrees of freedom}}$$

The formula for the between-subject variance is thus as follows:

$$\text{between-subject variance} = \frac{N_{S_1}(\bar{S}_1 - \bar{Y})^2 + N_{S_2}(\bar{S}_2 - \bar{Y})^2 \text{ (and so on)}}{\text{between-subject degrees of freedom}}$$

where N_{S_1} is the number of scores that subject 1 has, i.e. the number of levels, which we have designated a until now, and $\bar{S}_1$ is the mean score of subject 1, and $\bar{Y}$ is the grand mean. This equation is demonstrated in Box 7.2.

The formula for calculating the between-group variance can be simplified considerably (see Chapter 4) and, assuming that nothing has gone seriously wrong and every subject has an equal number of

Box 7.2 Applying the formula to calculate the between-subject Sum of Squares

Subject no.	Control	Interference	Subject mean	
S_1	4	6	5	
S_2	5	7	6	
S_3	6	8	7	
S_4	7	5	6	GRAND MEAN = 6

For the counting example, the between-subject Sum of Squares would be calculated in the following way:

1 Take the difference between each overall subject mean and the grand mean and square each difference:

S_1: $5 - 6 = -1$; $-1^2 = 1$ S_2: $6 - 6 = 0$; $0^2 = 0$
S_3: $7 - 6 = 1$; $1^2 = 1$ S_4: $6 - 6 = 0$; $0^2 = 0$

2 Multiply each square by the number of levels that each subject performed (2 for this example):

S_1: $2(1) = 2$ S_2: $2(0) = 0$
S_3: $2(1) = 2$ S_4: $2(0) = 0$

3 Add these products together: $2 + 0 + 2 + 0 = 4$

scores, the formula for the between-subject variance can be simplified in exactly the same way:

$$\text{between-subject variance} = \frac{\dfrac{(\sum S_1)^2 + (\sum S_2)^2 \text{ (and so on)}}{N_S} - \dfrac{(\sum Y)^2}{N}}{\text{between-subject degrees of freedom}}$$

where $\sum S_1$ is the total of the scores of subject 1 and so on, and $\sum Y$ is the sum of all scores irrespective of condition (or in other words, the grand total of all scores) and N_S is the number of scores for each subject.

Thus the $SS_{SUBJECTS}$ (Sum of Squares between subjects) =

$$\frac{(\sum S_1)^2 + (\sum S_2)^2 \text{ (and so on)}}{N_S} - \frac{(\sum Y)^2}{N}$$

You may recognise $\frac{(\sum Y)^2}{N}$ from Chapter 4, it is the basic ratio of the grand total and is designated by $[T]$. The following component:

$$\frac{(\sum S_1)^2 + (\sum S_2)^2 \text{ (and so on)}}{N_S}$$

also follows the basic ratio pattern. Each subject total is squared, and divided by the number of scores that make up each total. Instead of writing out the equation in full, it will be designated $[S]$. Hence:

$$[S] = \frac{(\text{subject total}_1)^2 + (\text{subject total}_2)^2 + (\text{subject total}_3)^2 \text{ (and so on)}}{\text{the number of scores making up each of the subject totals}}$$

and therefore:

$$SS_{SUBJECTS} = [S] - [T]$$

The degrees of freedom are the number of subject means that are free to vary given that you have used them to calculate the grand mean: the *total number of subjects in a level minus one*, or in other words:

$$(s - 1)$$

where s is the number of scores in a level. Box 7.3 demonstrates using basic ratios to calculate the between-subject variance.

In order to complete the ANOVA, we need to know the within-group, between-group and total Sums of Squares and degrees of freedom. To calculate the required Sums of Squares, these are the ways in which the basic ratios are used (see Chapter 4):

$$SS_{TOTAL} = [Y] - [T]$$
$$SS_A = [A] - [T] \quad (SS_{BETWEEN})$$
$$SS_{S/A} = [Y] - [A] \quad (SS_{WITHIN})$$

Box 7.3 Using basic ratios to calculate between-subject variance

Subject no.	Control	Interference	Subject mean	Subject total
S_1	4	6	5	10
S_2	5	7	6	12
S_3	6	8	7	14
S_4	7	5	6	12
MEAN:	5.5	6.5	6	
GRAND MEAN:			6	

$$[S] = \frac{(\text{subject total}_1)^2 + (\text{subject total}_2)^2 + (\text{subject total}_3)^2 \text{ (and so on)}}{\text{the number of scores making up each of the subject totals}}$$

$$[S] = \frac{(10)^2 + (12)^2 + (14)^2 + (12)^2}{2} \qquad [S] = \frac{100 + 144 + 196 + 144}{2} = \frac{584}{2} = 292$$

$$[T] = \frac{(\text{grand total})^2}{\text{the number of scores that make up the grand total}}$$

$$[T] = \frac{(48)^2}{8} = \frac{2304}{8} = 288$$

$$SS_{SUBJECTS} = [S] - [T] = 292 - 288 = 4$$

$df_{SUBJECTS} = (s - 1)$ therefore, since there are four scores in each level,

$df_{SUBJECTS} = (4 - 1) = 3$

Since the within-group Sum of Squares $(SS_{S/A}) = [Y] - [A]$ and since

$$SS_{S/A} \quad\quad = SS_{SUBJECTS} + SS_{RESIDUAL}$$

$$SS_{RESIDUAL} = SS_{S/A} - SS_{SUBJECTS} \text{ and therefore,}$$

$$SS_{RESIDUAL} = \{[Y] - [A]\} - \{[S] - [T]\} \text{ and therefore,}$$

$$SS_{RESIDUAL} = [Y] - [A] - [S] + [T]$$

Degrees of freedom are also additive so

$$df_{S/A} \quad\quad = df_{SUBJECTS} + df_{RESIDUAL}$$
$$df_{RESIDUAL} = df_{S/A} - df_{SUBJECTS}$$

The highly descriptive subscripts tend to be shortened so that:

$SS_{SUBJECTS}$ is shortened to SS_S; likewise $df_{SUBJECTS}$ is shortened to df_S

$SS_{RESIDUAL}$ is shortened to $SS_{A \times S}$; likewise $df_{RESIDUAL}$ is shortened to $df_{A \times S}$

There is also a formula for calculating the $df_{RESIDUAL}$: $(a-1)(s-1)$. When this formula is used, everything adds up correctly so that

$$df_{TOTAL} = df_{BETWEEN} + df_{RESIDUAL} + df_{SUBJECTS}$$

Box 7.4 completes all of the components for the counting example.

Box 7.4 Computing the components for the counting example

Subject no.	Control	Interference	Subject mean	Subject total
S_1	4	6	5	10
S_2	5	7	6	12
S_3	6	8	7	14
S_4	7	5	6	12
TOTAL:	22	26	24	48
MEAN:	5.5	6.5	6	12

GRAND MEAN: 6   GRAND TOTAL: 48

From Box 7.3: $[S] = 292$ $[T] = 288$

$[Y]$ = the sum of each score squared

$[Y] = (4)^2 + (5)^2 + (6)^2 + (7)^2 + (6)^2 + (7)^2 + (8)^2 + (5)^2$

$[Y] = 16 + 25 + 36 + 49 + 36 + 49 + 64 + 25 = 300$

$$[A] = \frac{\text{(level total of } A_1)^2 + \text{(level total of } A_2)^2}{\text{the number of scores that make up each level}}$$

$$[A] = \frac{(22)^2 + (26)^2}{4} = \frac{484 + 676}{4} = \frac{1160}{4} = 290$$

$SS_{TOTAL} = [Y] - [T] = 300 - 288 = 12$ $df_{TOTAL} = (as - 1) = 8 - 1 = 7$

$SS_A = [A] - [T] = 290 - 288 = 2$ $df_A = (a - 1) = 2 - 1 = 1$

$SS_{S/A} = [Y] - [A] = 300 - 290 = 10$ $df_{S/A} = a(s - 1) = 2(4 - 1) = 2(3) = 6$

But since this is a within-subjects design, the within-group Sum of Squares needs to be broken down into its component parts:

$SS_{SUBJECTS} = [S] - [T] = 292 - 288 = 4$

$SS_{RESIDUAL} = [Y] - [A] - [S] + [T] = 300 - 290 - 292 + 288 = 6$

$df_{SUBJECTS} = (s - 1) = 4 - 1 = 3$

$df_{RESIDUAL} = (a - 1)(s - 1) = (2 - 1)(4 - 1) = (1)(3) = 3$

The ANOVA table

The ANOVA table for this design is similar to the one used for the between-subjects design *except that the within-group Sum of Squares is given as its two component parts*. This time the measure of experimental error, the *error term*, is the *residual variance*. The between-group variance, MS_A, is divided by the residual variance, $MS_{A \times S}$, in order to calculate F. Table 7.11 summarises the component parts of a within-subjects ANOVA. Table 7.12 shows the final ANOVA table for the counting example.

Similarly to the between-subjects design, the degrees of freedom of F are those of the two Mean Squares used to calculate the F ratio. These are the degrees of freedom for the between-group variance followed by the degrees of freedom for the error term. For this particular design the error term is the $A \times S$ Mean Square. Thus, for this experiment, $F(1,3) = 1$. The critical value at the 5%

Table 7.11 Summary of components for within-subjects ANOVA

SOURCE	Sum of Squares	Degrees of freedom	Mean Square	F	p
A	$[A] - [T]$	$(a - 1)$	$\dfrac{[A] - [T]}{(a - 1)}$	$\dfrac{\text{Mean square}_A}{\text{Mean square}_{A \times S}}$	tables
S	$[S] - [T]$	$(s - 1)$	$\dfrac{[S] - [T]}{(s - 1)}$		
A × S	$[Y] - [A] - [S] + [T]$	$(a - 1)(s - 1)$	$\dfrac{[Y] - [A] - [S] + [T]}{(a - 1)(s - 1)}$		
TOTAL	$[Y] - [T]$	$(as - 1)$			

Table 7.12 Summary ANOVA table for the counting example

SOURCE	Sum of Squares	Degrees of freedom	Mean Square	F	p
A (effect)	2.0	1	2.0	1.0	>0.05
S (subjects)	4.0	3	1.3		
A×S (error)	6.0	3	2.0		
TOTAL	12.0	7			

significance level for these degrees of freedom is 10.1, so we cannot conclude that there is a significant difference in counting performance between the two lists.

Planned comparisons and *post-hoc* testing

Like the between-subjects design, within-subjects designs may have more than two levels in a factor. However, this again leads to the problem of how to interpret a significant *F* ratio in this situation. A significant value of *F* means that there are differences somewhere among the means, and again the problem is one of finding out exactly where they are. The most straightforward solution is to use *post-hoc* and planned comparisons, e.g. *t*-tests, contrast analysis, the Tukey test, etc., in exactly the same way as explained in Chapter 6. These would use the identical equations, identical calculations and have identical interpretation, but using the within-subjects error term calculated for the ANOVA tables. This course of action is fine for undergraduate projects. However, there are problems with this, and their consequences are such that if a study *must* be run with three levels or more, readers should at least be aware that the use of follow-up tests in this way is not recommended by some statisticians, and is often disallowed by computer statistical packages. The reason for this will be discussed shortly when we consider an additional assumption necessary in order to analyse data from a within-subjects design. The interested reader should consult more advanced textbooks (e.g. Howell, 1997; Kirk, 1982; Maxwell and Delaney, 1990) where alternative approaches are discussed, and at least consider applying these to any data that are intended for publication.

Additional assumption for a within-subjects design

Three important assumptions for performing a between-subjects ANOVA were discussed in Chapter 5. One of these is that the various groups have variances that do not differ significantly from each other, so that while the treatment may or may not affect the means, it never affects the diversity of the scores. All of the assumptions apply to within-subjects design but, in addition, a further assumption is that of *sphericity*. This assumption is as follows: for a within-subjects design with three or more levels, *the variance of the set of differences between the matched pairs of scores for two levels does not differ significantly from the variances of the difference scores for every other possible pair of levels.*[2] Hence, more specifically, the assumption is that these variances in difference scores do not differ from each other in the general population. However, for a within-subjects design with only two levels in a factor, the sphericity assumption is irrelevant. There are only two groups and so there is only one set of difference scores and only one variance. With only one variance, there are no other values for this to differ from. However, with three or more groups there is scope for the assumption to be violated. Box 7.5 shows the calculated variances of each possible set of difference scores for an imaginary set of data from a one-factor within-subjects ANOVA with three levels.

Box 7.5 shows three sets of difference scores that clearly have quite wide-ranging variances: from 0 to 2.75. One consequence of these differences in the variances is that if we look at individual pairs of groups and their means, while we can be reasonably certain that there really is a difference between levels A_1 and A_3, there is definitely no difference between A_1 and A_2, but we can be much less certain about the other remaining comparison, A_2 versus A_3. If we apply the suggestions for the follow-up tests earlier, we would effectively be using a single, identical error term to test the significance of every difference (i.e. the *Mean Square$_{RESIDUAL}$*). As a result we would be looking at the sizes of differences between pairs of means in order to take these decisions, and would not be taking account of the consistency of the trends in the differences. This is known as the *pooled error term approach*. If the different variances in the sets of difference scores in Box 7.5 mirror differences in the general population, then the use of a pooled error term is incorrect, and separate statistical tests should be applied to each difference (e.g. three entirely separate *t*-tests should be calculated).

Box 7.5 Variances of difference scores

Level	A_1	A_2	A_3	A_1-A_2	A_1-A_3	A_2-A_3
S_1	6	5	7	1	−1	−2
S_2	5	4	6	1	−1	−2
S_3	5	5	6	0	−1	−1
S_4	5	5	6	0	−1	−1
S_5	4	6	5	−2	−1	1
Mean	5.0	5.0	6.0	0	−1	−1
Variance	1.0	1.0	1.0	1.5	0	2.75

However, if the different variances in the sets of difference scores are due to random errors of sampling, and in reality there are no differences in the general population, then the use of pooled error terms *is the most accurate* way to conduct follow-up tests.

The obvious question, therefore, is whether the differences in variances in the example are large enough to be significant, indicating that the sphericity assumption has been violated and that pooled error terms must not be used. Unfortunately, there is no answer to this question, and although several statisticians argue that violations of the sphericity assumption are of major importance, they have proved unable to devise a suitable test in order to determine whether the assumption has been violated (for a discussion see Maxwell and Delaney, 1990; Kirk, 1982). Hence, there is no way of knowing whether the variances in the difference scores deviate from each other more than would be expected by chance, and so whether or not pooled error terms are used is currently a matter of taste. Because of this uncertainty, we therefore recommend the pooled error term approach for undergraduate work. It is simple to perform, by no means automatically gives incorrect answers, and sometimes must be the most accurate approach.

Possible violations of the sphericity assumption also have consequences for overall F ratios on the initial ANOVA table. Normally, the obtained F ratio for a within-subjects design is compared against a critical value which depends upon the degrees of freedom ($df_{BETWEEN}$, df_{ERROR}) or [$(a - 1)$, $(a - 1)(s - 1)$]. It is possible to correct the overall ANOVA for suspected violations of the sphericity assumption by modifying the value of these degrees of freedom so that the obtained F value is tested against a different critical value. The most conservative and simplest suggested correction is to set the $df_{BETWEEN}$ to 1, irrespective of the number of levels, and the df_{ERROR} to the number of subjects minus one, so that the degrees of freedom of the critical value are [1, $(s - 1)$]. As an example, suppose an experiment has three levels and twelve subjects. The degrees of freedom of the obtained F ratio would normally be (2,22) giving a critical value of 3.44 at the 5% significance level. With the degrees of freedom changed to (1,11), the critical value becomes 4.84: a much higher hurdle to cross and this might lead to Type II Errors. However, if the F ratio from a study is so high that it is significant with this correction, then the F ratio will still be significant no matter what other methods of correction are applied.

A slightly different correction, suggested by Greenhouse and Geisser (1991), is less stringent. This approach recommends that the $df_{BETWEEN}$ is set to $\hat{\varepsilon}(a - 1)$, while df_{ERROR} is set to $\hat{\varepsilon}(a - 1)$ $(s - 1)$. The formula to calculate $\hat{\varepsilon}$ is not given here. Today, many computer statistical packages give standard and adjusted p values, taking into account this correction for the obtained F ratios. Table 7.13 shows an example of a one-factor within-subjects ANOVA which might be given by a computer that adjusts p values by applying this correction. Usually, computer software reports revised p values directly rather than adjusted degrees of freedom.

Table 7.13 shows that there would be a significant effect for this study when no correction is applied. However, notice that the uncorrected p value is slightly smaller than the two corrected p values obtained by applying either the Greenhouse and Geisser correction or an alternative called the Huynh–Feldt correction. Notice also that by applying the Greenhouse and Geisser correction the resulting p value is not significant. The Huynh–Feldt correction is always slightly less stringent than the Greenhouse and Geisser correction. However, it has been suggested that this approach is too lenient, thus leading to an increased risk of Type I Errors (see Maxwell and Delaney, 1990). Currently, problems with the sphericity assumption mean that readers should seriously consider using the Greenhouse and Geisser correction. However, note that if the p value obtained from an analysis is extremely low

Table 7.13 Within-subjects ANOVA with correction to *p* values applied

SOURCE	Sum of Squares	Degrees of freedom	Mean Square	F	p
A (Practice)	1464.6	2	732.3	3.99	0.043
S (Subjects)	1240.6	7	177.2		
A × S (Error)	2568.8	14	183.5		
		Greenhouse–Geisser adjusted *p* value:			0.058
		Huynh–Feldt adjusted *p* value:			0.045

(e.g. $p < 0.001$) then the significance is unlikely to be affected no matter what correction is applied.

Non-parametric analysis of variance

For a single-factor within-subjects design with three or more levels, the *Friedman One-Way Analysis of Variance by Ranks* is a useful alternative way to steer clear of possible sphericity violations. A significant test result indicates that the groups differ in their performance. If the design has three or more levels, the significant effect should be followed up by making pairwise comparisons with the Wilcoxon test in order to see exactly which pairs of levels differ (for details, see any introductory statistical book, or an advanced book on non-parametric statistics such as Neave and Worthington, 1988).

Afterword

When planning research, students are often urged to run a within-subjects design study whenever possible. This is because such designs have the benefit of increased sensitivity, and therefore appear to be a more efficient use of resources. However, these benefits come with a cost. For reasons discussed in the previous section, when there are more than two levels in a factor, the application and interpretation of the follow-up tests of the sort discussed in Chapter 6 may become problematic. These difficulties are such that a case can be made for the opposite advice: if an expected effect size is reasonably large, and then if time and resources permit, *always* consider running a between-subjects study. The elegance and simplicity of the underlying mathematics translates into a simpler and more straightforward analysis of the data. Of course, there are exceptions to this advice. If a design is straight-forward, having no more than two levels in any factor, or the numbers of subjects required for a reasonable chance of a significant F ratio for a between-subjects design is too many, then a within-subjects design should be given serious consideration.

Chapter 8

An introduction to factorial designs and interactions

A factorial design is one in which two or more factors are investigated simultaneously in the same study. Although single-factor designs are useful for illustrating the basic mathematics of Analysis of Variance, they probably form a minority of actual research in psychology. The majority of ANOVA analyses reported in journals have at least two and often three factors. This is because, these days, single-factor designs are often inadequate for shedding light upon the complicated research questions that psychologists are trying to answer. This is usually the case even if a single factor has more than two levels. Designs with two or more factors are therefore very common, especially in cognitive psychology. In theory, they could be analysed by using multiple *t*-tests but, similarly to single-factor designs with three or more levels, indiscriminate use of pairwise comparisons is inadvisable due to the sheer number of comparisons necessary. Analysis of Variance is generally a more appropriate way of analysing factorial designs.

An expertise example

The following example of a factorial design is based upon a well-known paradigm in the fields of memory and problem solving. This concerns the relationship between expertise and memory. Suppose expert chess players are shown a chess board with a real mid-game position on it for a brief period of time, say 10 seconds, and each expert is then given an empty chess board along with a set of pieces and asked to reproduce the position from memory. We would expect quite good performance, say 20 out of 32 pieces placed correctly on average. However, if beginners, i.e. novice chess players, are shown the same position, their recollection is much worse: perhaps only 8 out of 32 pieces placed correctly on average. The exact scores would depend upon the expertise of the players and the length of time allowed to look at the board. By itself, this result might show that experts have superior spatial memory to novices. Perhaps this skill was necessary in order to become an expert.

As this design stands, it has a single factor: only the expertise of the player varies: expert versus novice.[1] However, a further factor can be added and this can potentially alter the conclusions. Suppose we also test our experts and novices with an additional position made up by placing chess pieces on a board in random locations. Now we have a second factor, which is hence *position type*, and this has two levels: *real positions* and *random positions*. Now we might find that for random positions, the experts do just as badly as the novices, perhaps with both types of subject placing 8 pieces correctly on average, irrespective of expertise. This shows that the apparent superior memory ability of experts is confined to their own area of expertise, and is therefore unlikely to be due to superior general skill. Overall, adding the second factor means that we can conclude that experts' memory only exceeds novices' memory when experts are tested with material that is compatible with their expertise. This finding is a good example of an *interaction*, a very important statistical topic that will be discussed in detail later in this chapter.

Two factor designs

The simplest factorial design experiments have two factors. Each individual factor may be within subjects or between subjects. Thus, if there are two between-subjects factors, designated A and B in statistical notation, each with two levels (A_1/A_2 and B_1/B_2), then there will be four possible conditions to which subjects could be allocated: A_1B_1; A_1B_2; A_2B_1 and A_2B_2. For example, if you were simultaneously looking at the effects of expertise, *expert* or *novice*, and chess position type, *real* or *random*, on memory performance, and you ran a fully between-subjects design, 1/4 of the subjects would be *experts* tested with *real* positions, 1/4 of the subjects would be *experts* tested with *random* positions, 1/4 of the subjects would be *novices* tested with *real* positions and 1/4 of the subjects would be *novices* tested with *random* positions. Thus, one factor, say factor A, is expertise, and the other, factor

B, is position type. Level A_1 of expertise would be expert, level A_2 would be novice. Level B_1 of position type would be real, level B_2 would be random. This is illustrated in Table 8.1. Because there are two factors, and each factor has two levels, this is referred to as a 2×2 *fully between-subjects design*.

The smallest unit in a factorial experiment is the *cell*. Thus, for a fully between-subjects design using the above example, those subjects whose data are in cell A_1B_1 are experts tested with real positions, and so on. The phrase *cell mean* refers to the mean of a set of scores in a particular cell. The phrase *cell size* refers to the number of scores in a single cell.

Factorial designs can also be fully within-subjects. The most common occurrences of these designs involve memory and word recognition. For example, word type – noun/verb – and word frequency – high/low – could be two factors in such an experiment, with all subjects being given a reading task that involves seeing all four combinations of word types: high frequency nouns; high frequency verbs; low frequency nouns; low frequency verbs. Factorial designs can also be mixed, with at least one between-subjects and at least one within-subjects factor. A study of expertise and memory, as described above, would normally be a mixed design. Expertise must be a between-subjects factor by definition, but each and every expert, and each and every novice should be tested for their memory of *both* real *and* random positions. This comparison will be more sensitive as a within-subjects factor than as a between-subjects factor.

With factorial designs, there is no restriction on the number of levels in a factor, although sticking to two makes a design far

Table 8.1 A 2×2 factorial design

		Factor A: Expertise		
		Level A_1 expert	Level A_2 novice	
Factor B: Position type	Level B_1 real	A_1B_1	A_2B_1	Mean B_1
	Level B_2 random	A_1B_2	A_2B_2	Mean B_2
		Mean A_1	Mean A_2	Grand mean

Table 8.2 A 2×3 factorial design

		Factor A: Expertise		
		Level A_1 expert	Level A_2 intermediate	Level A_3 novice
Factor B: Position type	Level B_1 real	A_1B_1	A_2B_1	A_3B_1
	Level B_2 random	A_1B_2	A_2B_2	A_3B_2

easier to analyse. For example, it would be feasible to study the memory of expert, intermediate and novice subjects. This is illustrated in Table 8.2.

Three-factor designs

With a three-factor design, you move into the third dimension. Figure 8.1 illustrates the simplest possible three-factor design; each factor has two levels giving a 2×2×2 design. This has a total of eight different combinations of conditions, or *cells*. Any combination of within- and between-subjects factors is possible for a design with three or more factors. Hence, the factors can be fully between, fully within, or mixed – with two between-subjects factors and one within-subjects factor, *or* one between-subjects factor and two within-subjects factors. Displaying the cell means of a three-factor design would require at least two separate tables. These designs are somewhat more work to interpret than two-factor designs, and a discussion of them will be left to Chapter 12.

Outcomes of factorial designs

With two factors or more, various combinations of statistical results are possible. The simplest of these are when only the *main effects* are significant. The phrase *main effect* refers to the overall difference between the means of one factor, completely ignoring the other. Thus, if experts remembered more material than novices overall, there would be a *significant main effect* of expertise. If real positions were easier to remember than random positions overall, there would be a *significant main effect* of position type.

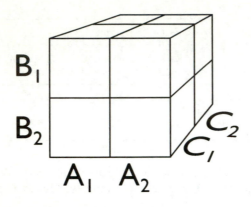

Figure 8.1 A 2×2×2 design

Table 8.3 gives the imaginary data for comparing the performances of experts and novices at remembering real and random chess positions. Position type is a within-subjects factor. Higher scores indicate better memory. Within each cell, the numbers represent the mean number of pieces correctly placed out of 32 (a chess game begins with 32 pieces). This table shows the four *cell means*, the two sets of *level means*, and the *grand mean*.

In this example, the main effect of factor A (expertise) is the difference in overall mean performance between A_1 (experts) and A_2 (novices), ignoring position type. In order to compare these means, factor B (position type) is ignored. To calculate the overall performance at A_1 – expert performance irrespective of position type – it is necessary to combine the mean performance of A_1 at B_1 – experts at real positions – with the mean performance of A_1 at B_2

Table 8.3 Imaginary data for a 2×2 expertise study

			Factor A: Expertise		
			Level A_1 expert	Level A_2 novice	Mean
Factor B: Position type	Level B_1	real	20	8	14
	Level B_2	random	8	8	8
		Mean	14	8	11

– experts at random positions: $(20 + 8)/2 = 14$. By a similar process, the mean overall performance at A_2, novice performance irrespective of position type, is 8. The main effect of B (position type) is comparing the overall mean performance at B_1 (real positions: 14) with the overall mean performance at B_2 (random positions: 8). Hence, overall, experts perform better than novices, and real positions are better remembered than random positions. If either or both of these differences in means were great enough for significance, you would report that there was at least one *significant main effect*. However, this is not the whole story with these data, as you will see when we discuss interactions.

Once studies are conducted with two or more factors, visual methods of data presentation become important and can be extremely helpful for your reader. Tables of means and standard deviations should always be given, but sometimes the addition of figures is also helpful. Figure 8.2 shows two annotated *interaction plots* for the cell means from Table 8.3. The dependent variable is on the vertical axis: the higher a point, the better the memory score. In this example, the plotting of the A_2 scores has a minor distortion because both cell means were the same, but have been separated slightly for clarity on the graph. Interaction plots are the usual way of graphically displaying factorial ANOVA data in a formal report, *but without the annotations, whose only purpose here is to explain the meanings of the various components* (see Appendix A to see how interaction plots should be displayed). Interaction plots are used to illustrate various patterns of effects throughout this chapter. In actual reports, graphs are normally only presented when there is a *significant interaction* although they are always worth inspecting when data are analysed, as they can still be informative when an interaction is non-significant. The meaning of the phrase *interaction* will be explained fully later in the chapter. The various possible ANOVA outcomes will be illustrated by varying the outcomes of the expertise design study described above. To remind you: factor A is *expertise*, level A_1 of expertise is *expert*, level A_2 is *novice*; factor B is *position type*, level B_1 of position type is *real*, level B_2 is *random*.

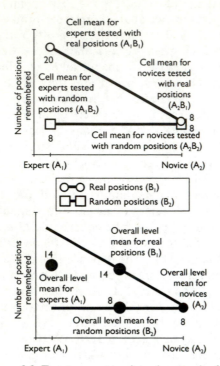

Figure 8.2 Two interaction plots showing the four cell means (top) and, for comparison, the four level means (bottom) taken from Table 8.3

No significant main effects

The simplest, but least interesting, outcome of a 2×2 ANOVA is when there are no significant effects at all. An example of this is given in Figure 8.3 in which the four cell means are plotted and the different factors and levels are identified. Higher data points indicate a greater memory score and better memory performance, but here, all four cell means are nearly identical. Notice that the lines connecting the cell means are flat. This is where the term *flat data* comes from, meaning that nothing of interest has happened. This indicates that there are no significant differences between any of the means. More often, you will see apparent differences between pairs of means which nevertheless your ANOVA tells you are not significantly different. For all graphs

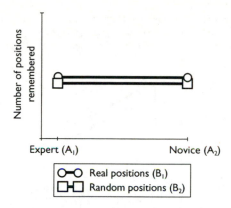

Figure 8.3 Interaction plot showing no significant effects

in this chapter, large difference in means will be assumed to be significant while small differences, where means are so similar as to be almost touching, will be assumed to be non-significant.

One significant main effect

The next most simple outcome of a 2×2 ANOVA is when either one or the other, but not both, of the main effects is significant, and there is no significant interaction. These are illustrated in Figure 8.4. In the left-hand graph, real positions are clearly easier to remember than random positions irrespective of the expertise of the subjects. Novices perform just as well as experts. In other words, there is a significant main effect of position type, factor B; B_1 is clearly greater than B_2 overall. There is no significant main effect of expertise, factor A; A_1 and A_2 are virtually identical overall. The reverse situation is shown in the right-hand graph. Experts remember material better than novices irrespective of position type, and real positions are just as easy to remember as random positions for novices and also for experts. In other words, A_1 is greater than A_2 overall and B_1 is identical to B_2 overall.

Two significant main effects

The next possible outcome is illustrated in Figure 8.5. Here, *both* main effects are significant but not the interaction. Hence, experts

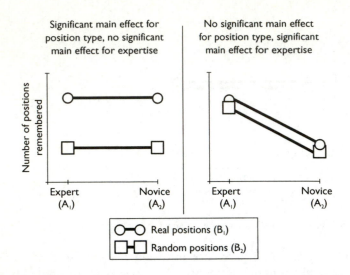

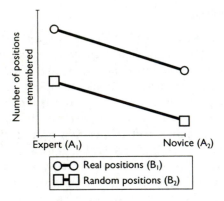

Figure 8.4 Two interaction plots, each showing one significant main effect only

Figure 8.5 Interaction plot showing two significant main effects and no interaction

perform better than novices and real positions are better remembered than random positions. Notice that experts are better than novices both for real and for random positions to exactly the same degree. Thus, the size of the effect of expertise is identical irrespective of position type. In addition, real positions are easier to recall than random positions for both experts and novices to exactly the same degree, and so the size of the effect of position type is identical irrespective of expertise. Overall the independent variables are independently related to performance and their effects are combining in simple additive ways. These effects can therefore be discussed separately. You can talk about the effects of expertise on memory performance, knowing that position type does not matter. You can also talk about the effects of position type on memory performance, knowing that expertise does not matter.

Put more generally, this example shows two significant main effects. A_1 is greater than A_2 overall and B_1 is greater than B_2 overall. Faced with results such as this, we can say that for any given situation, A_1 will always be greater than A_2, whatever the value of B, as the difference between A_1 and A_2 is identical at *both B_1 and B_2*. This is also the case for the main effect of B: B_1 will always be greater than B_2, whatever the value of A, as the difference between B_1 and B_2 is identical at *both A_1 and A_2*. Thus the two factors are related to performance completely independently and there is no *interaction* between the two.

Simple main effects

In Figure 8.5, the two factors were related to performance independently of each other. When thinking about how easy the position was to remember, you could ignore how familiar people were with the domain in general, i.e. their expertise. When comparing the memory of experts and novices, you could ignore the fact that some positions were real while other positions were random. Thus the overall effect of expertise, factor A, in which experts have better memory than novices, was identical to the individual effects of expertise at both B_1 (real positions) and B_2 (random positions). Similarly, the overall effect associated with position type, factor B, in which real positions are easier to remember than random positions, was identical to the individual effects of position type at both A_1 (experts) and A_2 (novices).

When main effects are broken down into component parts and considered separately, they are known as *simple main effects*. In all of the examples above, each pair of simple main effects was identical to the overall main effect from which it was derived. *In other words, for each factor, each pair of simple main effects have always been equivalent in their trends*. They have shown the same size

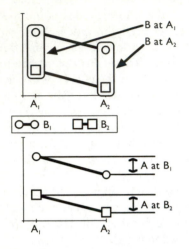

Figure 8.6 Simple main effects illustrated

differences in the same direction and have the same pattern as the overall level means. In other words, *one factor has behaved in exactly the same way whatever the level of the second factor.* Thus, in Figure 8.5, the two simple main effects of expertise were identical both for real positions – experts were *better* than novices – and for random positions – experts were *better* than novices. Likewise, the two simple main effects of position type were identical for experts – real positions were *better* remembered than random positions – and for novices – real positions were *better* remembered than random positions. The pairs of simple main effects are illustrated in Figure 8.6.

Often it will be the case that the simple main effects of one factor will be different at different levels of the second factor. In other words, the way in which one factor is related to performance may depend upon the level of the second factor. When this happens you have an *interaction*. This means that you cannot discuss your results in terms of main effects, you have to consider the ways in which the two factors are working together by looking at each of the simple main effects.

Significant interaction

Figure 8.7 illustrates the originally suggested results for the expertise study (see Table 8.3). This is the most typical pattern of results that is obtained for this type of study. This is an example of an *interaction*. Experts perform better than novices, but only for real positions. The factor of expertise has two *simple main effects*: expertise at real positions and expertise at random positions. There is *no effect* of expertise at random positions, but there is a large effect of expertise at real positions: experts perform better than novices. If two simple main effects are different, for example one very small, one very large, there is an interaction.[2] The simple main effects of position type are also different. There is *no effect* of position type for novices, but there is a large effect of position type for experts: real positions are remembered better than random positions. Hence, overall, memory score depends not just upon whether or not a person is an expert or a novice *or* whether material is real or random but upon *a combination of the two*, and so neither factor can be considered in isolation. The fact that there are main effects both of expertise overall – on average, experts perform better than novices – and of position type overall – real positions are better remembered than random positions – cannot be taken as the best description of the pattern of results and, indeed, may even be misleading.

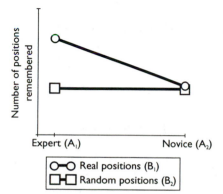

Figure 8.7 The original expertise study cell means from Table 8.3

How to spot an interaction

The basic rule of thumb is that there is an interaction whenever the lines on an interaction plot are not parallel; the lines need not be touching. This indicates that at least one of the pairs of simple main effects is differently significant, e.g. one significant, the other not; or both significant but the difference between means is in the opposite direction. Three different interactions are shown in Figure 8.8. Hence, the conclusions drawn about the meaning of an interaction depend upon the exact pattern of significances of the simple main effects.

At this point, you should be warned that interaction plots can be deceptive. Sometimes, you will 'see' a significant interaction on the plot, but the computer will tell you that the interaction is not significant. Usually this occurs when an exaggerated scale has been used, often chosen by the computer: expanding a scale can have dramatic and deceptive visual effects, as is shown in Figure 8.9. Here, the scale on the left-hand plot has been expanded so that a tiny difference between groups has been magnified visually. The right-hand plot shows the visual effect when a different scale is used. Whenever you believe that a computer has missed an effect that you can clearly see, think about whether the scale on the graph

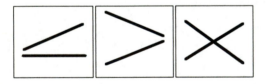

Figure 8.8 Three different interactions: all have non-parallel lines

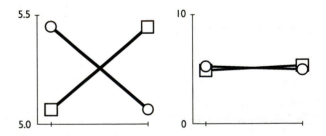

Figure 8.9 The effect of scale on the visual appearance of an interaction plot

is appropriate; is the effect really as large as it appears? Also, remember that highly varied data can cause even a large effect to be non-significant.

The independence of sets of simple main effects

It does not necessarily follow that because some simple main effects of *one* factor are significant and others not, then some simple main effects of the *other* factor will also be significant and others not. Figure 8.10 shows a plot of a 2×3 design in which there is an interaction; but the two simple main effects of factor B are identical: both are significant and have the same pattern. The

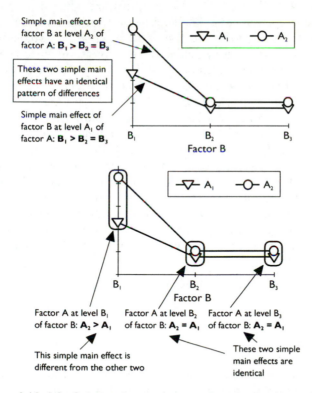

Figure 8.10 A 2×3 design showing an interaction despite the two simple main effects of factor B being identical (upper graph). The interaction is due to the three differently significant simple main effects of factor A (lower graph)

reason for the significant interaction is also shown in Figure 8.10. The three simple main effects of factor A are differently significant: one simple main effect is significant, two are not.

Why do we need to have more than one factor?

The next example illustrates a single-factor experiment that has missed some vital information which only a factorial experiment could show. Suppose the influence of background music on memory performance is to be investigated. The single factor has two levels: classical music and country music. No significant difference in performance is found so the conclusion is that background music has no effect on memory performance. This is shown in the upper half of Figure 8.11. However, this has ignored people's personal music preferences. The above result on its own may be misleading. Suppose people are given a questionnaire in which one of the questions asks them which music they would prefer to listen to if forced to choose between classical or country. On the basis of this question, half of the subjects are given their choice of music while performing the memory task, and the other half are given the opposite to their choice. The experimenter would have to conceal this decision process; otherwise the subjects might behave accordingly, e.g. those who know that they have deliberately been given the opposite to their preference would expect to do worse. This time, we might obtain the results shown in the lower half of Figure 8.11. Thus, the music type factor on its own does not predict behaviour, nor does the music preference factor. Instead the two factors have to be taken together in order to reach a conclusion: people perform better when they listen to the music of their choice.

Managing factorial designs

Planning factorial designs

Although we have not yet discussed the analysis and interpretation of factorial designs, this is a good point at which to give some suggestions about planning factorial research. Although these designs are very powerful, it is possible to make some blunders, and some sensible forward planning can pay dividends later. The advice that follows generally applies whether the designs are fully between-subjects, fully within-subjects, or mixed, but in general, if

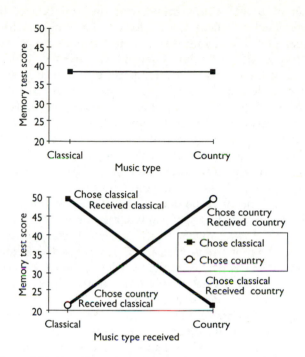

Figure 8.11 No effect of background music on memory test score (upper graph) but this conceals a significant interaction that links performance to music preference (lower graph)

time, resources and statistical power are on your side, then a fully between-subjects design will always be the most straightforward to analyse.

The first points are concerned with group sizes. The number of contributions to each cell should not be too small, otherwise the statistical power will be far too low. Comparing means between small groups of subjects, say fewer than eight per cell, is likely to result in low power and hence Type II Errors. It is also important for between-subjects designs and mixed designs to have equal cell sizes. The data will be more straightforward to analyse and, more importantly, *if your data depart from the usual assumptions that you make in order to run parametric statistical tests, having equal cell sizes means that these departures are less likely to have serious consequences* (see Chapter 5).

The next set of points is concerned with the ambition of a study and associated practical issues. Recall that single-factor experiments may give a false impression as to the importance, or lack of importance, of particular independent variables. Thus, when we looked at the effects of music upon performance in the absence of any consideration of music preference, we were left with a false impression of the relationship between music and performance. The more factors and levels that are included in any study, the less likely that something important is missed. However, there is a trade-off between the complexity of the design and how interpretable its results are, and how practical the study is to run. If you decide that you can only do justice to your field of interest with a 3×3×3 design which needs to be between-subjects, and you wish to have a satisfactory cell size – say eight subjects per cell – then you require $3 \times 3 \times 3 \times 8$ subjects = 216 subjects. If you run this as a within-subjects design, then there are 27 different cells of data to fill, and order effects will be a problem, probably fatigue effects. In addition, as we will see in later chapters, factorial designs are far more straightforward to analyse if the number of levels in each factor is kept as low as possible. Ideally, no factor will have more than two levels. A design in which one factor has two levels, but the other has three levels – a 2×3 design – is manageable (just – especially if fully between-subjects). The practical reason for avoiding multiple levels is that a large number of follow-up tests are required in order to make sense of the outcome, and this is associated with the problem of familywise Type I Error. As a general rule of thumb, avoid any factorial design in which two or more factors have three or more levels.

The final set of points is concerned with the interpretability of complicated designs. *Complicated designs can be difficult to interpret. Avoid designing an experiment that goes beyond your powers of interpretation.* All the examples discussed in this chapter have been of two-factor designs. Any interaction between two factors is called a *two-way interaction.* If you have found these heavy going and continue to do so, then this suggests that you should avoid designing studies with three or more factors. Introducing a third factor gives the possibility of three-way interactions in which all three factors interact with each other. A two-way interaction means that the simple main effects of one factor differ according to the level of the second factor. A three-way interaction means that the two-way interactions between two of the factors differ according to the level of the third factor. For example, the inter-actions between factors *A* and *B* might vary depending upon the level of factor *C*, perhaps giving the three graphs shown in Figure 8.8 if factor *C* has three levels. This sounds nastier than it is, and there are various techniques to disentangle the effects if a three-way interaction is significant.

Three-factor designs are nearly always interpretable with some effort and are often very illuminating, as long as the number of levels in each factor is kept under control. However, by the time you have completed this book, you should know for yourself whether you are in a position to attempt to make sense of such a design. If not, then the best way to avoid a three-way interaction is never to run a three-factor design. The advice to keep designs simple applies even more if designs with four or more factors are being considered. Now potential difficulties multiply, especially if higher order interactions are significant. The interpretability of an unexpected significant four-way interaction ranges from very dif-ficult to interpret to completely impossible. The best strategy to deal with a four-way interaction is to avoid the possibility of it happening to begin with. *If you stick to three-factor experiments then you cannot get a four-way interaction.* This advice is particu-larly aimed at undergraduate students.

Analysing factorial designs

A computer printout will show whether there are significant main effects and/or a significant interaction. If there is a significant interaction, this means that the significance of the main effects – or the lack of them – cannot be taken at face value, and the differences between the cell means that constitute the simple main effects need to be investigated further by testing their sig-nificance directly in order to determine the source and nature of the interaction. *It is not enough merely to find an interaction, as according to the actual patterns of the simple main effects you could reach completely different conclusions* (see Figure 8.8). Although the visual appearance of an interaction is an important component of interpretation, the moral of Figure 8.9, that the scale of a graph can be misleading, must always be remembered. However, even for large differences between means, the visual appearance of graphs can be misleading because whether or not means are significantly different depends not only upon the size of the difference between the pair but also upon the variance of the data and the number of subjects. *Thus lines that appear to be sloping or points that appear to differ may not do so statistically.*

Interactions are analysed by using planned or *post-hoc* tests in order to test the significances of the individual simple main effects. Pairs of means are compared directly in order to find which are significant and which are not. The tests are similar to those used for single-factor designs and work on the same basic principles. The mathematics of analysing factorial designs along with suggestions for interpreting them are discussed in the remaining chapters of this book.

Chapter 9

Calculating *F* ratios for two-factor between-subjects designs

Whenever more than one factor is investigated in an experiment, there is a wide variety of possible outcomes. For a two-factor design, one, both or neither of the main effects and/or the interaction between the two factors may be significant. Figure 9.1 shows the structure of a typical 2×2 fully between-subjects factorial design. There are two factors, each with two levels, giving a total of four cells. Each subject only contributes one single score to the data, hence appearing in only one cell. The example has a total of 36 subjects, 9 per cell. One possible question that can be asked when the data are analysed is: *is either of the main effects significant?* The meaning of this question is also shown in Figure 9.1.

However, as was discussed in the Chapter 8, interpretation of the main effects by themselves is not possible if the interaction between the two factors is significant. An interaction is best interpreted in terms of the *simple main effects*, and the location of the simple main effects for this example is shown in Figure 9.2.

Figures 9.2 and 9.3 show that simple main effects are paired. For example, the difference between the two means A_1 and A_2 at level B_1 is paired with the difference between the two means A_1 and A_2 at level B_2. This makes an interaction easier to define for the purposes of this book. If we take a pair of corresponding simple main effects, there will be a significant interaction if the trends of these simple main effects are not identical statistically. There are two straightforward ways in which a pair of simple main effects might differ in their trend and this is illustrated in Figure 9.3:

1   One of a pair has a significant difference but not the other. For example, the mean of A_1 differs from the mean of A_2 at level B_2 *but not* at level B_1 – see the left-hand graph of Figure 9.3.

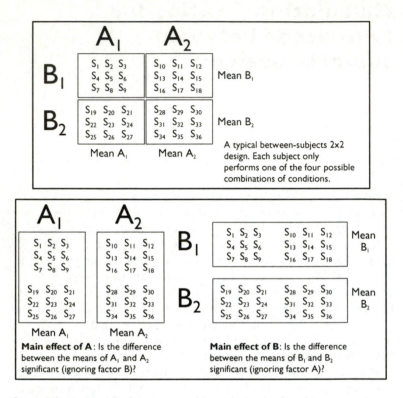

Figure 9.1 A typical 2×2 between-subjects design (top) and its two main effects (bottom)

2   Both simple main effects are significant, but in the opposite direction. For example, the mean of A_1 is greater than the mean of A_2 at level B_1, but the mean of A_2 is greater than the mean of A_1 at level B_2 – see the right-hand graph of Figure 9.3.

Unfortunately, there is a somewhat less straightforward way in which the trend of a pair of simple main effects may differ. This is the comparatively rare occurrence where the interaction and all four simple main effects are significant, but the difference for both members of each pair of simple main effects is in the same direction. One possible occurrence of this is illustrated in Figure 9.4 (assuming that every simple main effect and the interaction are

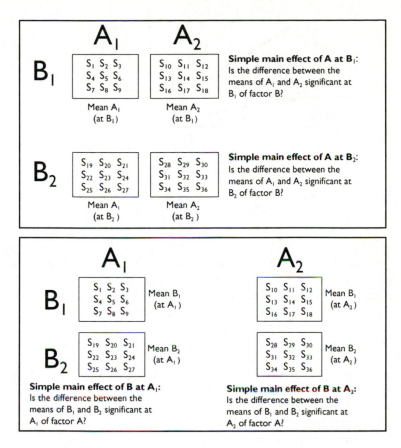

Figure 9.2 The four simple main effects for a typical 2×2 between-subjects design

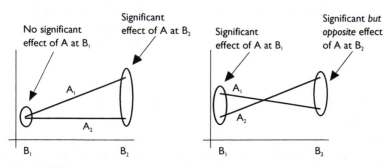

Figure 9.3 Two illustrations of interaction in relation to the simple main effects

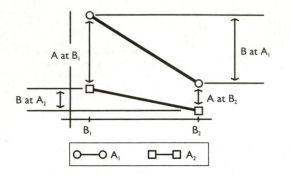

Figure 9.4 An illustration of a less straightforward interaction in relation to the simple main effects

significant). In these circumstances, it is usually the case that for at least one of the pairs of corresponding simple main effects, one simple main effect will be significant (e.g. $p < 0.05$) but the other will be significant at a far more stringent level (e.g. $p < 0.01$). This is effectively showing that a factor has a moderate effect at one level of the other factor, and a much bigger effect at the other level. This is in line with our definition above: the trends are different, a small trend for one effect, a much larger trend for the other, albeit in the same direction. The main problem with this outcome when it does occur is that it is harder to report, as a certain degree of subjective interpretation is required.

Finally, if there is no significant interaction, then both simple main effects of one pair must have an identical trend to each other, and also both simple main effects of the other pair must have the same trend as each other. For example, both simple main effects of one pair might be significant and have a roughly similar difference in the same direction, while both simple main effects in the other pair might be non-significant.

Analysing a 2×2 between-subjects factorial design

In this chapter you will be shown the first stage of analysing a fully between-subjects factorial design. This involves determining which of the two main effects and the interaction are significant. The second stage involves analysing the simple main effects if there is a significant interaction, and will be discussed in Chapter 10.

Although a second factor has been added, the basic mathematical principles are the same, so that:

$$F = \frac{\text{treatment effects + experimental error}}{\text{experimental error}}$$

and as this is a between-subjects design:

$$F = \frac{\text{between-group variance}}{\text{within-group variance}}$$

One major difference is that there are now three F ratios to compute, one for each of the three effects. Some example data for this chapter are given in Box 9.1.

Box 9.1 Example data for a 2×2 between-subjects design

For this example, a group of 12 expert chess players and a group of 12 novice chess players were given a set of chess positions to remember. These were either taken from real games or were created by placing chess pieces on a board at random. If sufficient experts can be recruited, a between-subjects design might be considered, in which some of the experts are given only real positions to remember, and the rest of the experts are only given random positions to remember, likewise for the novices. For this study, each person would be shown a chess position for a set period of time, and then be given an empty board and a set of chess pieces and asked to reproduce the position. Each subject could be given 10 such trials, each trial having the location of, say, 10 pieces on the board to remember. In order to keep the numbers small, and hence keep the calculations manageable, we will use the slightly unusual measure of *the number of boards in which all pieces were placed correctly* as the dependent variable. The more entirely correct boards, the better the memory. If we designate the expertise factor as *A* and the position type factor as *B*, then with six subjects per cell, the two factors combine in the following way:

6 *experts* receive 10 *real* positions (A_1B_1)
6 *experts* receive 10 *random* positions (A_1B_2)
6 *novices* receive 10 *real* positions (A_2B_1)
6 *novices* receive 10 *random* positions (A_2B_2)

Plausible data for such a study might look like this:

		Factor A: Expertise			
		Level A_1 expert		Level A_2 novice	
Factor B: Position type	Level B_1 real positions	S_1	6	S_{13}	2
		S_2	7	S_{14}	3
		S_3	8	S_{15}	4
		S_4	8	S_{16}	4
		S_5	9	S_{17}	5
		S_6	10	S_{18}	6
	Level B_2 random positions	S_7	0	S_{19}	1
		S_8	1	S_{20}	2
		S_9	2	S_{21}	3
		S_{10}	2	S_{22}	3
		S_{11}	3	S_{23}	4
		S_{12}	4	S_{24}	5

And the table of means would be as follows:

	Level A_1 expert	Level A_2 novice	Overall
Level B_1 real	8.0	4.0	6.0
Level B_2 random	2.0	3.0	2.5
Overall	5.0	3.5	4.25

Notation

The two-factor fully between-subjects design requires five basic ratios to compute, three of which you have seen before. As a reminder, these are:

[A]: basic ratio of the level totals, $\dfrac{\text{(level total of } A_1)^2 + \text{(level total of } A_2)^2 \, [\ldots]}{\text{the number of scores that make up each level}}$

[T]: basic ratio of the grand total, $\dfrac{\text{(grand total)}^2}{\text{the number of scores that make up the grand total}}$

[Y]: basic ratio of the scores, $\dfrac{\text{(score}_1)^2 + \text{(score}_2)^2 + \text{(score}_3)^2 + \text{(score}_4)^2 \, [\ldots]}{1 \text{ (only one number make up each individual score)}}$

In order to compute the components of a factorial between-subjects ANOVA, two additional basic ratios will be required:

[B]   By convention, the factors of an ANOVA are labelled alphabetically. Hence, a second factor in any design is normally designated factor B. [B] denotes the basic ratio of the level totals of factor B, or in full, if there are two levels in factor B, then [B] =

$$\frac{\text{(level total of } B_1)^2 + \text{(level total of } B_2)^2}{\text{the number of scores that make up each of the levels}} = \frac{(\sum B_1)^2 + (\sum B_2)^2}{N_B}$$

[AB]   Denotes the basic ratio of the cell totals, where a cell total is the total of all of the scores in any one of the cells. In full, for a 2×2 design, [AB] =

$$\frac{\text{(cell total of } A_1B_1)^2 + \text{(cell total of } A_1B_2)^2 + \text{(cell total of } A_2B_1)^2 + \text{(cell total } A_2B_2)^2}{\text{the number of scores in each cell}}$$

$$= \frac{(\sum A_1B_1)^2 + (\sum A_1B_2)^2 + (\sum A_2B_1)^2 + (\sum A_2B_2)^2}{N_{AB}}$$

(This is the reason why basic ratios are used and not the full notation!)

Box 9.2 shows all the various basic ratios that must be computed in order to analyse the data in the expertise example.

Box 9.2 **Calculating the necessary basic ratios for analysing the example data**

		Factor A: Expertise		
		Level A_1 expert	Level A_2 novice	
Factor B:	Level B_1 real	Total A_1B_1 = 48	Total A_2B_1 = 24	Total B_1 = 48 + 24 = 72
Position type	Level B_2 random	Total A_1B_2 = 12	Total A_2B_2 = 18	Total B_2 = 12 + 18 = 30
		Total A_1 = 48 + 12 = 60	Total A_2 = 24 + 18 = 42	

$$[B] = \frac{72^2 + 30^2}{12} = \frac{5184 + 900}{12} = 507$$

$$[A] = \frac{60^2 + 42^2}{12} = \frac{3600 + 1764}{12} = \frac{5364}{12} = 447$$

Grand total = 102

$$[T] = \frac{102^2}{24} = \frac{10404}{24} = 433.5$$

$$[Y] = 598$$

$$[AB] = \frac{48^2 + 24^2 + 12^2 + 18^2}{6} = \frac{2304 + 576 + 144 + 324}{6} = \frac{3348}{6} = 558$$

Calculating the Sum of Squares for the error term

Within-group variance is a measure of the extent to which people within each of the groups behave differently, despite the fact that they have been treated alike. Suppose that we wanted to test the significance of the main effect of factor A. We could calculate the error term by computing and combining the within-group Sums of Squares and degrees of freedom for A_1 and A_2, ignoring the fact that factor B existed – see Figure 9.5. However, this would be wrong. The error term is supposed to be a measure of the extent to which people behave differently when treated alike, *and this is not true in this case.* Half of the subjects in level A_1 were treated differently from the other half because some were given treatment B_1, while the rest were given treatment B_2. If there was high variability of the data in A_1, this might have been because $A_1 B_1$ subjects behaved very differently from $A_1 B_2$ subjects. In other words, this is variability caused by a treatment effect rather than by experimental error.

For a 2×2 between-subjects design, people have been treated exactly alike *only* within each of the four cells. Thus, in order to calculate the error term, we compute and combine the Sums of Squares and the degrees of freedom using the smallest unit of identically treated subjects – the four cells. This gives one single measure of experimental error that can be used for calculating all of the Fs for all of the effects. This is the overall measure of the extent to which subjects behaved differently despite being treated alike. Again, the homogeneity of variance assumption applies. Because it is assumed that the variances of all four cells are identical, or at least that they do not differ significantly, any differences in variance between cells must be due to error, and so the most accurate measure of within-group variance will be an aggregate of the individual variabilities of the four cells. This is because random errors tend to cancel each other out when aggregated.

The simplest way in which to derive the within-group Sum of Squares is to make use of the fact that:

$$SS_{TOTAL} = SS_{BETWEEN} + SS_{WITHIN}$$

Calculating the total Sum of Squares, which is the measure of total variability for the entire data set irrespective of experimental treatments, is thus the first stage in calculating the error term, and this is performed identically to all previous ANOVAs:

$$SS_{TOTAL} = [Y] - [T]$$

The total between-group Sum of Squares for the individual cells then needs to be calculated. This is a measure of all of the variability due to the various experimental treatments. Only by looking at the four cell means in relation to how distant each is from the grand mean can we see the entire extent to which the treatments caused scores to differ, and so the total between-group Sum of Squares is calculated in the following way. Compare this with the equation in Chapter 4 for the between-group Sum of Squares where there is only one level:

$$SS_{BETWEEN} = [AB] - [T] \qquad SS_{BETWEEN} \text{ will be designated } SS_{AB}$$

Because $SS_{TOTAL} = SS_{BETWEEN} + SS_{WITHIN}$ the within-group Sum of Squares can be found by subtracting SS_{AB} from SS_{TOTAL}:

$$SS_{WITHIN} = SS_{TOTAL} - SS_{BETWEEN}$$
$$SS_{WITHIN} = [Y] - [T] - \{[AB] - [T]\}$$
$$SS_{WITHIN} = [Y] - [T] - [AB] + [T]$$
$$SS_{WITHIN} = [Y] - [AB] \qquad SS_{WITHIN} \text{ will be designated } SS_{S/AB}$$

Thus we now have an equation for the Sum of Squares for the error term that will be used to calculate all of the necessary Fs.

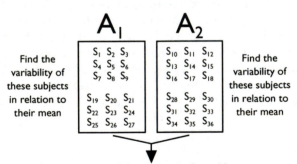

Combine the variability to give the Sum of Squares

Figure 9.5 The wrong way to calculate an error term for a between-subjects factorial design

Calculating the Sums of Squares for the two main effects

For a two-factor design, there are two main effects whose significance needs to be tested. Having calculated the Sum of Squares for the error term above, two between-group Sums of Squares are required, one for each main effect. For the purposes of this calculation, each main effect is treated as being completely independent from the other and so, for example, when calculating the between-group Sum of Squares for the main effect of factor A, the fact that subjects were also treated in different ways at factor B is ignored. This means that the various formulae are identical to all previous designs, hence:

for the between-group Sum of Squares for factor A, $SS_A = [A] - [T]$
for the between-group Sum of Squares for factor B, $SS_B = [B] - [T]$

The calculations for all of the within- and between-group Sums of Squares discussed so far, using the data from the example, are shown in Box 9.3.

Box 9.3 Calculating the Sums of Squares discussed so far, using the example data

Total Sum of Squares:	$SS_{TOTAL} = [Y] - [T] = 598 - 433.5 = 164.5$
Within-group Sum of Squares:	$SS_{S/AB} = [Y] - [AB] = 598 - 558 = 40$
Total between-group Sum of Squares:	$SS_{AB} = [AB] - [T] = 558 - 433.5 = 124.5$
Between-group Sum of Squares for factor A:	$SS_A = [A] - [T] = 447 - 433.5 = 13.5$
Between-group Sum of Squares for factor B:	$SS_B = [B] - [T] = 507 - 433.5 = 73.5$

Calculating the Sum of Squares for the interaction

In order to test the significance of the interaction, a final Sum of Squares is required. In order to see how this is derived, consider again that $SS_{TOTAL} = SS_{BETWEEN} + SS_{WITHIN}$. From the data in Box 9.3, we already have all of these values, and indeed this is the case (SS_{AB} is the component that is equivalent to $SS_{BETWEEN}$). $SS_{BETWEEN}$ can also be split. Some of the total between-group variability in the scores is due to the treatment of factor A, while some is due to the treatment of factor B. However, when we add the two Sums of Squares of these two factors from the example data together (13.5 + 73.5 = 87), we find that *these do not equal the total between-group variability of 124.5*. Something is missing: *some variability between the group means is not accounted for by the main effects.* This residual value is the between-group variability that is *not* accounted for by the two factors *A* and *B* affecting scores independently. It is indicating that a certain amount of variability is due to the two factors interacting with each other. Hence this residual value is the Sum of Squares for the interaction:

$$SS_{AB} \qquad\qquad = SS_A + SS_B + SS_{INTERACTION}$$
$$SS_{INTERACTION} \quad = SS_{AB} - SS_A - SS_B$$

$SS_{INTERACTION}$ will be designated $SS_{A \times B}$

Therefore, $SS_{A \times B} = \{[AB] - [T]\} - \{[A] - [T]\} - \{[B] - [T]\}$

$$SS_{A \times B} \qquad\quad = [AB] - [A] - [B] + [T]$$

This final Sum of Squares calculation for the example data is shown in Box 9.4.

Box 9.4 Calculating the Sum of Squares for the interaction using the example data

$$SS_{A \times B} = [AB] - [A] - [B] + [T]$$
$$SS_{A \times B} = 558 - 447 - 507 + 433.5 = 37.5$$

Calculating the degrees of freedom

Having calculated all of the Sums of Squares, the next step is to calculate the necessary degrees of freedom in order to calculate the variances. For the two main effects, these are as follows.

$$df_A = (\text{number of levels in factor } A - 1) = (a - 1)$$
$$(a \text{ is the number of levels in factor } A)$$
$$df_B = (\text{number of levels in factor } B - 1) = (b - 1)$$
$$(b \text{ is the number of levels in factor } B)$$

For the degrees of freedom for the interaction:

$$df_{A \times B} = df_A \times df_B = (a - 1)(b - 1)$$

For the degrees of freedom for the within-group variance (the error term):

$$df_{S/AB} = \{(\text{number of cells}) \times (\text{number scores in a cell} - 1)\} = ab(s - 1)$$
$$(s \text{ is the number of scores in a cell})$$

And finally, for the total degrees of freedom for all of the data:

$$df_{TOTAL} = (\text{total number of scores} - 1) = (abs) - 1$$

These should all add up so that:

$$df_{TOTAL} = df_A + df_B + df_{A \times B} + df_{S/AB}$$

The various degrees of freedom for the example data are calculated in Box 9.5.

Box 9.5 Calculating the degrees of freedom for the example data

df_A	$= (a - 1)$	$= 2 - 1$	$= 1$ (factor A has two levels)
df_B	$= (b - 1)$	$= 2 - 1$	$= 1$ (factor B has two levels)
$df_{A \times B}$	$= (a - 1)(b - 1)$	$= 1 \times 1$	$= 1$
$df_{S/AB}$	$= ab(s - 1)$	$= 2 \times 2 (6 - 1)$	$= 20$ (six subjects per cell)
df_{TOTAL}	$= (abs) - 1$	$= (2 \times 2 \times 6) - 1$	$= 23$

The ANOVA table for a 2×2 fully between-subjects design

All of the information necessary to perform the first stage of the analysis has now been calculated. To begin with, Table 9.1 summarises the computations necessary to perform the ANOVA.

The error term for this design is the within-group variance; Mean Square$_{S/AB}$. This is used for testing the significance of all three effects of interest. Each of the three F values must be looked up individually to see whether or not it is large enough to be significant. For this design, all Fs have the same degrees of freedom: the degrees of freedom of the between-group variance followed by the degrees of freedom of the error term. For other factorial designs, each F may have different degrees of freedom, so you will need to look up separate critical values. Box 9.6 shows the ANOVA table and interpretation for the example data.

Table 9.1 Summary table for the components of a 2×2 fully between-subjects design ANOVA

Source	Sum of Squares	Degrees of freedom	Mean Square	F	p
A	$[A] - [T]$	$(a - 1)$	$\dfrac{[A] - [T]}{(a - 1)}$	$\dfrac{\text{Mean Square}_A}{\text{Mean Square}_{S/AB}}$	tables
B	$[B] - [T]$	$(b - 1)$	$\dfrac{[B] - [T]}{(b - 1)}$	$\dfrac{\text{Mean Square}_B}{\text{Mean Square}_{S/AB}}$	tables
A×B	$[AB] - [A]$ $- [B] + [T]$	$(a - 1)(b - 1)$	$\dfrac{[AB] - [A] - [B] + [T]}{(a - 1)(b - 1)}$	$\dfrac{\text{Mean Square}_{A \times B}}{\text{Mean Square}_{S/AB}}$	tables
S/AB	$[Y] - [AB]$	$ab(s - 1)$	$\dfrac{[Y] - [AB]}{ab(s - 1)}$		
TOTAL	$[Y] - [T]$	$(abs) - 1$			

As a general rule, if you have a factorial design, you should read your ANOVA table from the bottom up, starting with the most complicated interactions, which must be interpreted first. Only if these are non-significant can you pay close attention to the significance (or lack of this) of the main effects and interpret the meaning of these.

Box 9.6 ANOVA table and interpretation for the example data

As a reminder, this was the table of means for the data that was calculated earlier – there is little point in attempting to interpret ANOVA without a table of means. The units of the dependent variable are the *numbers of positions correctly reproduced*:

	Level A_1 expert	Level A_2 novice	Overall
Level B_1 real	8.0	4.0	6.0
Level B_2 random	2.0	3.0	2.5
Overall	5.0	3.5	4.25

And here is the completed ANOVA table:

SOURCE	Sum of Squares	Degrees of freedom	Mean Square	F	p
A (expertise)	13.5	1	13.5	6.75	<0.05
B (position)	73.5	1	73.5	36.75	<0.01
A×B	37.5	1	37.5	18.75	<0.01
S/AB (error)	40.0	20	2.0		
TOTAL	164.5	23			

The critical value of F at the 5% level of significance for degrees of freedom (1,20) is 4.35. Thus, there was a significant main effect of factor A, a difference between overall means of 5 and 3.5 positions remembered correctly, showing that experts appear to have better memories than novices. There was also a significant main effect of factor B, a difference between overall means of 6 and 2.5, showing that real chess positions appear to be easier to recall than random chess positions.

We could conclude from this that experts always remember more than novices irrespective of material and that real chess positions are easier to remember than random chess positions irrespective of previous experiences. However, the significant interaction tells us that this is not the whole story, and that if we draw these conclusions then we are missing something important. We cannot simply talk about the overall difference in performance between level A_1 and level A_2 of factor A, or between level B_1 and level B_2 of factor B. Instead we need to use further tests to investigate the simple main effects. The simple main effects for these data will be analysed in Chapter 10.

Factorial between-subjects ANOVA: unequal cell sizes

Chapter 5 discussed some of the assumptions that underlie Analysis of Variance, and warned that the procedures are far less robust if any of the assumptions are violated *and* group sizes are not equal. These details are particularly important for a factorial between-subjects design, and unequal cell sizes can be so disruptive that readers are strongly advised never to conduct an unbalanced study if there is any way around this. The problem with an unbalanced design is that the interaction and the main effects are not orthogonal; in other words, there is a correlation between them, so that knowing the level of one factor, we can predict the level of another factor. Overall, the separate factors do not account for independent proportions of variability in the data. The result of this is that, if there is a significant main effect for both factors, we cannot know whether the factors are related to performance independently or whether either factor by itself could account for just as much variability as the two combined.

In order to demonstrate the problem of non-orthogonality, consider a fictitious 2×2 fully between-subjects study in which the relationship between gender, age of car, and driving performance was investigated. The greater the means, the better the driving performance. Unfortunately, the subjects were allowed to provide their own cars, and this has resulted in an unbalanced design. As Table 9.2 shows, the factors are not independent, and knowing the value of one factor, e.g. *female*, it is possible to predict the value of the other factor, *older car*.

The actual effects of the study appear to depend upon how the

Table 9.2 Data from a driving study with non-orthogonal factors

	Level A_1 male	Level A_2 female	Weighted mean	Unweighted mean
Level B_1 older car	$N = 5$ $\bar{X} = 3.0$	$N = 15$ $\bar{X} = 5.0$	4.5	4.0
Level B_2 newer car	$N = 15$ $\bar{X} = 8.6$	$N = 10$ $\bar{X} = 10.0$	9.2	9.3
Weighted mean	7.2	7.0		
Unweighted mean	5.8	7.5		

data are summarised. The weighted means take account of the numbers of scores in each cell, and underlying this is the assumption that means with more scores as their basis are likely to give a truer reflection of the population value, and hence should be given more weight. Hence, for male drivers:

$$\text{weighted mean of performance} = \frac{5(3.0) + 15(8.6)}{20} = \frac{15 + 129}{20} = \frac{144}{20} = 7.2$$

Alternatively, the use of unweighted means assumes that each cell reflects the correct population performance and so sample size need not be taken into account. Hence, for male drivers:

$$\text{unweighted mean of performance} = \frac{3.0 + 8.6}{2} = \frac{11.6}{2} = 5.8$$

The difficulty is that we have conflicting data and it is not clear what has actually happened. If we weight the means, then the men are slightly better performers. If we look at the unweighted means, then the women are considerably better. However, the situation is clear for age of car; older cars are associated with much worse performance than newer cars. Overall, the problem is that when weighted means are considered, the variability due to car age appears to have contributed to the main effect of gender, changing *both* the direction *and* the magnitude of the difference in driving performance between males and females. Expressing the same idea in a slightly different way, more women were tested with older than newer cars, thus their weighted mean of performance is a reflection of extensive testing with older cars, while more men were tested with newer cars, thus their weighted mean of performance reflects this unbalance. Hence the main effects of gender and car age are not independent.

In order to analyse the data in the example, it is necessary to take account of the fact that the car age has made a different contribution to male driving scores than to female driving scores. In order to do so, it is necessary to use a statistical test that compares the unweighted means rather than the weighted means. This will remove the effect of the differences in cell sizes from the statistical test of the main effects. In practical terms this assumes that each cell mean reflects its population mean equally well, ignoring the fact that larger sample sizes tend to be linked to more accurate estimates. Thus, in the above example, rather than comparing a mean for females of 7.0 with a mean for males of 7.2 – males obtaining the better score – a test is required that will compare a mean for females of 7.5 with a mean for males of 5.8 – females obtaining the better score. The computational approach that achieves this is an approximation of the general linear model approach to ANOVA designs using Type III Sums of Squares (for a description see Kirk, 1982). When faced with an unbalanced design, most computer packages automatically calculate an ANOVA based upon unweighted means. Rather than demonstrate a computation by hand, Table 9.3 shows an ANOVA table that a suitable computer package might produce for this example.

The ANOVA findings should be reported and interpreted as usual, with degrees of freedom and F values taken from the table in the normal way. However, the important point to remember is that this ANOVA reflects an analysis of the *unweighted means*. Therefore a significant effect of gender shows that women out-performed men, with unweighted means of 7.5 versus 5.8 respectively, and not that men outperformed women, with weighted means of 7.2 and 7.0 respectively. This fact provides a trap for the unwary who are performing ANOVA by computer. Many computer programs adopt the unweighted mean approach. A few give the user the option of whether to do so. Some programs not only give the user no option but also give no warning that this has taken place. This is particularly a problem if a table of weighted means is generated as a default option by a computer package, and the unweighted means either have to be searched for or, worse still, are not offered at all. The unwary user could misinterpret the results in this situation. In the example used here, a user could easily see the significant effect for gender, and look at the weighted means, perhaps failing to look any further than this, and conclude

Table 9.3 ANOVA table using unweighted means

SOURCE	Sum of Squares	Degrees of freedom	Mean Square	F	p
A (gender)	26.67	1	26.67	5.07	<0.05
B (car age)	259.28	1	259.28	49.31	<0.01
A×B	0.83	1	0.83	0.16	>0.05
S/AB (error)	215.60	41	5.26		

that men had outperformed women, when the opposite is the case. This trap alone is enough reason to assert that computer packages should be used to aid the understanding of Analysis of Variance, and are not a substitute for understanding.

Chapter 10

Following up a two-factor between-subjects ANOVA

With any factorial design, one possible outcome of the analysis is a significant interaction. If this occurs, it must not be ignored. Whether or not the main effects are significant, these will be unable to provide an adequate summary of the results by themselves. In addition, interpreting an interaction by eye is also inadequate. This is illustrated in Figure 10.1. Suppose that you were predicting the pattern of data on the top left-hand side, but instead obtained the data on the top right-hand side. The circled cell means were predicted not to be significantly different, but appear to be different on the graph. The only way to determine whether or not this unexpected difference is significant is to conduct the follow-up tests to be described in this chapter. As a further example, consider that a

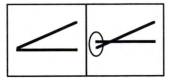

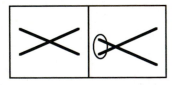

Figure 10.1 A predicted outcome (top left) but with an unexpected difference (top right), and a predicted outcome (bottom left) but one of the actual differences is unexpectedly small (bottom right)

large expected difference on the bottom left-hand graph in Figure 10.1 has turned out to be slightly smaller than expected, as shown by the circled cell means on the bottom right-hand graph. Again, without further statistical tests, there is no way of knowing whether or not the outcome has gone against the prediction.

In both cases, the unexpected results may be trivial, merely irritating, or may suggest that a revision is necessary for an important theory. Whatever the theoretical implications, drawing conclusions from an interaction by eye only makes no sense. Why go to the bother of performing any statistical tests at all if the final judgements are going to be subjective? Papers in journals in which interactions are not analysed are rarer than they used to be, but you should still be wary of them. Unless some sort of attempt has been made to make sense of the interaction, then the conclusions of the paper are at best incomplete, at worst they are wrong.

Analysing an interaction for a 2×2 between-subjects design

One way to analyse an interaction is directly to test the significance of each of the four simple main effects. For a 2×2 design, these will simply be pairwise comparisons, analogous to using four t-tests – one to compare each pair of means for each simple main effect – and these are shown in Figure 10.2. This process requires the calculation of the between-group variance for each simple main effect, dividing each variance by a suitable error term to give four F ratios. This is most straightforward for the between-subjects design ANOVA, where there is only one measure of experimental error and this has already been calculated for the main ANOVA table. This error term is used to test the significance of both main effects and the interaction. It is also used to test the significance of the simple main effects.

Thus, for the simple main effect of factor B at A_1, we will be comparing the mean of A_1B_1 with the mean of A_1B_2: number 1 on the graph, for which we need to find a suitable between-group variance. For the simple main effect of factor B at A_2 we will be comparing the mean of A_2B_1 with the mean of A_2B_2: number 2 on the graph, for which we will need to find another between-group variance value. However, the error term will be the same for all comparisons. Similarly, for the simple main effect of factor A at B_1,

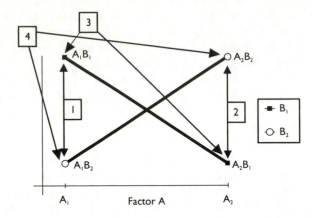

Figure 10.2 Four pairwise comparisons to test the simple main effects of a 2×2 ANOVA

we will be comparing the mean of A_1B_1 with the mean of A_2B_1: number 3 on the graph. Finally, for the simple main effect of factor A at B_2, we will be comparing the mean of A_1B_2 with the mean of A_2B_2: number 4 on the graph. Each of the four between-group variances can then be divided by the same error term to give four separate F values.

Calculating the between-group Sums of Squares and the degrees of freedom

Calculating the between-group variances for the simple main effects uses exactly the same techniques as in previous chapters. We will need to calculate appropriate between-group Sums of Squares, and divide these by degrees of freedom. As before, the size of each between-group Sum of Squares will depend upon the difference between the means: the greater the difference, the greater this variability. *However, unlike calculating the between-group Sums of Squares for the main effects, the between-group Sums of Squares for the simple main effects are not calculated by comparing the cell means with the grand mean* (see Figure 10.3, top).

For each simple main effect, its Sum of Squares between groups is calculated from the difference between the individual means of the simple main effect *in relation to the overall mean of these cells*

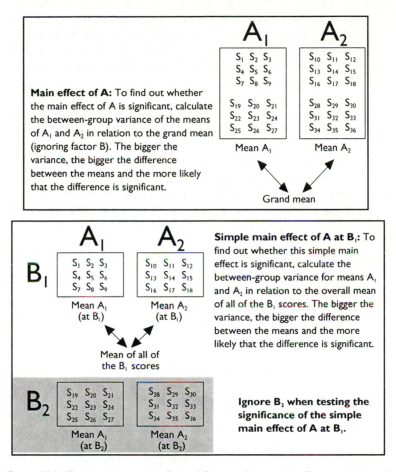

Figure 10.3 The between-group Sum of Squares for a main effect is calculated from the sizes of the level means in relation to the grand mean (top) but the between-group Sum of Squares for a simple main effect is calculated from the sizes of the cell means in relation to the mean of these cell means only (bottom)

only. This is also shown in Figure 10.3 (bottom). In effect, for calculating between-group variance, each simple main effects analysis is a miniature Analysis of Variance in which only those cells for the simple main effect are considered and the values of all others are ignored.

The formula for calculating a straightforward between-group

Sum of Squares is the basic ratio of the group totals of interest, minus the basic ratio of the total of these totals. Hence, the formula for calculating the $SS_{BETWEEN}$ for the main effect of factor A is $[A] - [T]$. The basic ratios that we will use to calculate the variances of the simple main effects are directly analogous to these. For example:

$[A_{B_1}]$ is the basic ratio of factor A, but only for the B_1 scores: square the total for A_1B_1, square the total for $A_2 B_1$, add the squares together and divide by the number of scores that make up each cell.

$[T_{B_1}]$ is the basic ratio of the total of the scores at level B_1 of factor B: take the total of all of the scores in level B_1 and square the total, divide the square by the number of scores making up this total.

Eight basic ratios are required in order to test the four simple main effects of a 2×2 design. These then give four between-group Sums of Squares. As we will see, for a 2×3 design, there is an extra simple main effect and hence 10 basic ratios are required. Box 10.1 shows the calculations for testing the main effects for the expertise example discussed in the previous chapter.

Sum of Squares between groups of factor A at level B_1 ($SS_{A \text{ at } B_1}$): $[A_{B_1}] - [T_{B_1}]$

Sum of Squares between groups of factor A at level B_2 ($SS_{A \text{ at } B_2}$): $[A_{B_2}] - [T_{B_2}]$

Sum of Squares between groups of factor B at level A_1 ($SS_{B \text{ at } A_1}$): $[B_{A_1}] - [T_{A_1}]$

Sum of Squares between groups of factor B at level A_2 ($SS_{B \text{ at } A_2}$): $[B_{A_2}] - [T_{A_2}]$

In order to calculate the variances, all that is now needed are the degrees of freedom for each of the simple main effects. All of the degrees of freedom are equal to the ([*number of levels in each simple main effect*] $- 1$). Hence, for the two simple main effects of A, both at B_1 and at B_2, the degrees of freedom are given as $(a - 1)$ where a is the number of levels in factor A. For the two simple main effects of B, the degrees of freedom are given as $(b - 1)$ where b is the number of levels in factor B.

Box 10.1 Calculating between-group Sums of Squares for the expertise example

As a reminder, the cell and level means were as follows:

	Level A_1 expert	Level A_2 novice	Overall
Level B_1 real	8.0	4.0	6.0
Level B_2 random	2.0	3.0	2.5
Overall	5.0	3.5	4.25

These are the various necessary cell and level totals:

		Factor A: Expertise		
		Level A_1 expert	Level A_2 novice	
Factor B: Position type	Level B_1 real	Total A_1B_1 = 48	Total A_2B_1 = 24	Total B_1 = 48 + 24 = 72
	Level B_2 random	Total A_1B_2 = 12	Total A_2B_2 = 18	Total B_2 = 12 + 18 = 30
		Total A_1 = 48 + 12 = 60	Total A_2 = 24 + 18 = 42	

And these are the calculations for the between-group Sums of Squares:

Expertise (expert versus novice) for real positions (A at B_1):

$$[A_{B_1}] = \frac{48^2 + 24^2}{6} = 480 \quad [T_{B_1}] = \frac{72^2}{12} = 432 \quad [A_{B_1}] - [T_{B_1}] = 48$$

Expertise (expert versus novice) for random positions (A at B_2):

$$[A_{B_2}] = \frac{12^2 + 18^2}{6} = 78 \quad [T_{B_2}] = \frac{30^2}{12} = 75 \quad [A_{B_2}] - [T_{B_2}] = 3$$

Position type (real versus random) for experts (B at A_1)

$$[B_{A_1}] = \frac{48^2 + 12^2}{6} = 408 \quad [T_{A_1}] = \frac{60^2}{12} = 300 \quad [B_{A_1}] - [T_{A_1}] = 108$$

Position type (real versus random) for novices (B at A_2)

$$[B_{A_2}] = \frac{24^2 + 18^2}{6} = 150 \quad [T_{A_2}] = \frac{42^2}{12} = 147 \quad [B_{A_2}] - [T_{A_2}] = 3$$

Summary tables

Table 10.1 is a summary of all of the various components necessary to test the four simple main effects of a 2×2 between-subjects design. As we will see later, extra rows are required if either or both factors have more than two levels. Box 10.2 completes the analysis for the expertise example, and interprets the interaction in the light of the patterns of significances.

Table 10.1 Summary of procedures for calculating simple main effects for a 2×2 fully between-subjects design

SOURCE	Sum of Squares	Degrees of freedom	Mean Square	F	p
A at B_1	$[A_{B_1}] - [T_{B_1}]$	$(a - 1)$	$\dfrac{[A_{B_1}] - [T_{B_1}]}{(a - 1)}$	$\dfrac{\text{Mean Square}_{A \text{ at } B_1}}{\text{Mean Square}_{S/AB}}$	tables
A at B_2	$[A_{B_2}] - [T_{B_2}]$	$(a - 1)$	$\dfrac{[A_{B_2}] - [T_{B_2}]}{(a - 1)}$	$\dfrac{\text{Mean Square}_{A \text{ at } B_2}}{\text{Mean Square}_{S/AB}}$	tables
B at A_1	$[B_{A_1}] - [T_{A_1}]$	$(b - 1)$	$\dfrac{[B_{A_1}] - [T_{A_1}]}{(b - 1)}$	$\dfrac{\text{Mean Square}_{B \text{ at } A_1}}{\text{Mean Square}_{S/AB}}$	tables
B at A_2	$[B_{A_2}] - [T_{A_2}]$	$(b - 1)$	$\dfrac{[B_{A_2}] - [T_{A_2}]}{(b - 1)}$	$\dfrac{\text{Mean Square}_{B \text{ at } A_2}}{\text{Mean Square}_{S/AB}}$	tables
S/AB	$[Y] - [AB]$	$ab(s - 1)$	$\dfrac{[Y] - [AB]}{ab(s - 1)}$		

Box 10.2 Completing the expertise example

Below is the main ANOVA table from Chapter 9. Note the value of the error term: this is needed in order to complete the simple main effects analysis.

SOURCE	Sum of Squares	Degrees of freedom	Mean Square	F	p
A (expertise)	13.5	1	13.5	6.75	<0.05
B (position)	73.5	1	73.5	36.75	<0.01
A×B (interaction)	37.5	1	37.5	18.75	<0.01
S/AB (error)	40.0	20	2.0		
TOTAL	164.5	23			

Because the interaction was significant in the original analysis, including an interaction plot in a formal report is justified. We have constructed one below, note how the interaction is clearly shown by the non-parallel lines.

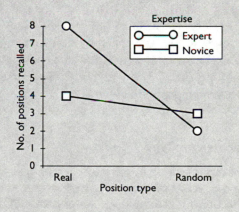

Below is the simple main effects table:

SOURCE	Sum of Squares	Degrees of freedom	Mean Square	F	p
A at B_1 (expertise/ real positions)	48	1	48	24	<0.01
A at B_2 (expertise/ random positions)	3	1	3	1.5	>0.05
B at A_1 (position type/experts)	108	1	108	54	<0.01
B at A_2 (position type/novices)	3	1	3	1.5	>0.05
S/AB (error)	40	20	2		

The critical value of F at the 5% level of significance for degrees of freedom (1,20) is 4.35. Thus, only two simple main effects are significant. Note that these significances have not been corrected for multiple comparisons.

Overall, the significant simple main effects show that (i) experts remember real positions better than novices ($F(1,20) = 24.0$, $p < 0.01$) and also that (ii) experts remember real positions more easily than random positions ($F(1,20) = 54.0$, $p < 0.01$). These results therefore replicate the classic expertise findings: the memory of experts is superior to the memory of novices, but only for material that makes sense to the experts. The data have now been fully analysed and a specimen results section is given in Appendix A.

A note on familywise Type I Error

One important point to note is that when testing the significance of the simple main effects, we made no corrections to the significance level to take account of the multiple comparisons. With four pairwise comparisons tested at the 5% level of significance, in theory we are working to a familywise Type I Error rate of 5% times 4 equals 20%, one Type I Error for every five experiments. However, in practice the problem is not quite as severe as this. The testing of simple main effects is usually *protected*. This means that their significance is not normally tested unless the interaction is significant,[1] and this protection considerably reduces the familywise Type I Error rate.

Consider a 2×2 design. Suppose that an interaction is found to be significant, but this is mistaken and there are no differences between any of the means for the actual populations from which the samples in the four cells were drawn. A Type I Error has therefore been made. Because of the way in which effects are linked, an interaction is unlikely to be significant unless at least one of the simple main effects is also significant. Given that in reality there are no differences between means in the population, any significant simple main effects are also Type I Errors. However, the familywise Type I Error has already been made in finding the significant interaction, and any significant simple main effects merely duplicate this. Given that the familywise Type I Error rate is the probability of making *at least one* Type I Error in a set of comparisons, the familywise error rate in this example has not been increased by testing the four simple main effects after finding the significant interaction, despite the number of comparisons made.

Alternatively, suppose that an interaction is found that is genuinely significant. Again, an interaction is unlikely to be significant unless at least one of the simple main effects is genuinely significant, and this means that if all four simple main effects are found to be significant, no more than three could possibly be significant due to a Type I Error (giving a familywise Type I Error rate of no more than 15%). Similarly, if both of the main effects are significant, then the familywise Type I Error rate is likely to fall still further. However, although intuitively sensible, a formal mathematical proof of the effects of protecting the simple main effects by the *F* ratio of the interaction is far from straightforward. In addition, with more levels and more factors, the familywise Type I Error rate can creep up in any case, and some caution is necessary. The problem is that most statistics textbooks are somewhat evasive about the correct procedures necessary for caution, and this is a problem whose solution is largely at the discretion of the reader. For example, some books may advise readers not to perform an excessive number of comparisons, with no indication as to what an 'excessive' figure might be.

The easiest way to exercise some caution is to use the Bonferroni adjustment when making pairwise comparisons. Although the t-test described in Chapter 6 can be used to make these, where simple main effects have only two levels this outcome will be identical to the simple main effects analysis. This is because, for any comparison with two levels, t is the same as the square root of F. However, if the use of follow-up tests is to be protected by a significant interaction, and the design has no more than two levels per factor, then for the reasons discussed above, it is debatable whether any correction is required at all. Hence, the suggestion is as follows: for a two-factor design with two levels per factor, if the interaction is significant then test the simple main effects. For any larger design, if the interaction is significant then make pairwise comparisons with the t-test – or linear contrasts if necessary – applying the Bonferroni adjustment to control for their number. The fewer the number of comparisons made, the more powerful the analysis. If the comparisons were genuinely planned in advance of the data analysis, and one less comparison than the number of cells is intended, the analysis may proceed in the absence of a significant interaction. The Bonferroni adjustment is only recommended for planned comparisons if five or more are intended.

An alternative way of following up an interaction is to apply the Tukey test to make pairwise comparisons if the interaction is significant. However, caution should be exercised here. For a 2×2 design, there are four cells and six possible pairs of means that could be compared, four of these pairs correspond to the simple main effects, but the additional two correspond to comparing A_1B_1 versus A_2B_2 and A_1B_2 versus A_2B_1. Such comparisons rarely make sense, but the Tukey test will assume that they are being made and will correct for them. Because of this, making four out of six pairwise comparisons with the t-test, and then applying the Bonferroni adjustment to the significance level to correct for four comparisons is actually less stringent than making the same four comparisons with the Tukey test, because this will automatically correct for all six possible comparisons.

Two-factor designs with more than two levels

Suppose you had run an experiment with more than two levels in one of the factors. In theory, it is still possible to test the significance of the simple main effects if the interaction is significant. In practice, the number of comparisons made, given no correction to the significance level, is becoming excessive even if protected by a significant interaction. In addition, the outcome of the simple main effects analysis will not necessarily be helpful, in the same way that a significant F ratio for a single-factor design with three or more factors is uninformative, leading to the requirement for more follow-up tests. Here, the Tukey HSD test is recommended for following up a significant three-level simple main effect on a 2×3 design, unless specific comparisons are planned. In the example to be discussed, a researcher is investigating the focus of attention of people who suffer from various symptoms of anxiety. One theory of anxiety is that such people show an information processing bias which causes them to focus excessively on unpleasant or threatening information at the expense of pleasant or neutral information, thus sustaining, perhaps even causing, their anxiety.

In order to test for this, a study has been devised in which factor A, subject type, has two levels: level A_1, a control group of people who suffer from no detectable anxiety disorders; and level A_2, people who suffer from chronic anxiety problems. Factor B is information type and has three levels: level B_1 – threatening words (e.g. *death, fail*); level B_2 – positive words (e.g. *smile, laughter*); and level B_3 – neutral words (e.g. *think, walk*). The threatening words will be referred to as *negative* words for this example. The actual task is a modified Stroop experiment in which the subject sees a list of words printed in a variety of ink colours, and the task is to completely ignore the words and name the ink colour that each word is printed in, as fast as possible. For one list, the words will be entirely negative words, for another list, the words will be entirely positive words, while the final list will be entirely neutral words. If people with anxiety have an attentional bias towards unpleasant information, they will find it hard to ignore the unpleasant words on the negative word list, thus interfering with, and slowing down, their ink naming time. This study is a fully between-subjects design in which each subject sees only one type of word. The dependent variable is the average time taken to name the ink colour of each word in the list (in tenths of a second). Box 10.3 summarises the major components of the analysis up to the main ANOVA table.

The analysis in Box 10.3 shows that there is a significant interaction in the example. At this point, there are various strategies

Box 10.3 Data and preliminary analysis for the anxiety study

Here are the raw data that might be obtained for the study described. The dependent variable is the average time in tenths of a second to name the ink colours of a list of words. For example, if the score is 3, this corresponds to a time per word of 0.3 seconds.

		Factor A: Subject			
		Level A_1 control		Level A_2 anxious	
Factor B: List type	Level B_1 negative words	S_1	2	S_{16}	6
		S_2	3	S_{17}	7
		S_3	5	S_{18}	9
		S_4	3	S_{19}	7
		S_5	2	S_{20}	6
	Level B_2 positive words	S_6	3	S_{21}	3
		S_7	4	S_{22}	4
		S_8	5	S_{23}	5
		S_9	4	S_{24}	5
		S_{10}	3	S_{25}	3
	Level B_3 neutral words	S_{11}	3	S_{26}	5
		S_{12}	4	S_{27}	4
		S_{13}	6	S_{28}	5
		S_{14}	4	S_{29}	4
		S_{15}	4	S_{30}	4

This gives the following table of means:

	Factor A: Subject		
	Level A_1 control	Level A_2 anxious	Overall
B_1 negative words	3.0	7.0	5.0
B_2 positive words	3.8	4.0	4.0
B_3 neutral words	4.2	4.4	4.3
Overall	3.7	5.1	4.4

Below is a typical ANOVA table as would be expected if a computer package had been used to analyse these data. Note that the main effect of word type is not significant (just) but that there is a significant main effect of factor *A*. This indicates that the mean performance for anxious subjects (5.1 seconds) is slower than the mean performance for control subjects (3.7 seconds). Although this might imply that anxious people are generally slower than non-anxious people, this interpretation may not be justified and the significant interaction must be investigated properly.

SOURCE	Sum of Squares	Degrees of freedom	Mean Square	F	p
A (subject type)	16.13	1	16.13	15.61	0.001
B (word type)	6.20	2	3.10	3.00	0.069
A×B	24.07	2	12.03	11.65	0.000
S/AB (error)	24.80	24	1.03		

Finally, here is an interaction plot for these data, again clearly showing the non-parallel lines.

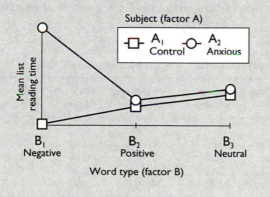

possible for follow-up tests depending on whether or not specific planned comparisons are intended. For example, if the researcher is only interested in how anxious people differ from normal people, then the three pairs of means for anxious versus controls for negative, positive and neutral words should be compared. These correspond to the three simple main effects of factor A at levels B_1, B_2 and B_3, and the square root of these F ratios will be the same as the t values in any case, and so no further calculations are necessary. *Hence, the simple main effect F values may be reported as planned comparisons.* With six cells, carrying out three comparisons is easily within the limit of the number of cells minus one, and hence these tests could have been performed even in the absence of a significant interaction. In addition, with only three comparisons, the Bonferroni adjustment is not necessary. Table 10.2 shows a simple main effects analysis that a computer program should produce for the example data. Note that the table has calculated all five simple main effects, but you are only interested in three. In a formal report, the writer should make it clear that as far as the hypothesis was concerned, it was only necessary to test three simple main effects, and why, and only to report these three in the results section and no others. Starting from the top of the table, the simple main effects of interest show there is a significant difference of subject type for negative words ($F(1,24) = 38.71$, $p < 0.01$) with anxious subjects being slower than control subjects. There are no significant differences for neutral or positive words

Table 10.2 Simple main effects analysis for the example data

Source of variation	Sum of Squares	Degrees of freedom	Mean Square	F	p
Subject at					
negative	40.00	1	40.00	38.71	0.000
positive	0.10	1	0.10	0.10	0.758
neutral	0.10	1	0.10	0.10	0.758
Error term	24.80	24	1.03		
Word type at					
control	3.73	2	1.87	1.81	0.186
anxious	26.53	2	13.27	12.84	0.000
Error term	24.80	24	1.03		

$(F(1,24) = 0.10, p > 0.05$ for both). Figure 10.4 shows the location of these simple main effects on the interaction plot.

The above planned comparisons are probably not the best to make, because often, in the literature, it is found that anxious subjects are generally slower at these sorts of tasks than control subjects. The actual hypothesis is that anxious people have a tendency selectively to attend to threatening information, hence we need to know whether anxious people are slower for negative words than for positive words, and slower for negative words than for neutral words. The equivalent comparisons would also have to be performed for control subjects. Non-significant differences for the controls would show that negative words are not attention grabbing in general, only attention grabbing for anxious people. The analysis of the two simple main effects of factor B, at A_1 and at A_2, can shed some light on this, but in practice this is not the whole story. The simple main effect of word type for control subjects is helpful. There is no significant difference, $F(2,24) = 1.87, p > 0.05$, showing that control subjects have no particular tendency to focus on any particular types of word. On the other hand, the significant simple main effect for word type for anxious subjects tells us nothing about whether the pairwise differences would correspond with our prediction, and although the visual appearance of the data is reasonably certain in this respect, the outcome of real research will usually be less clear cut. *We are now*

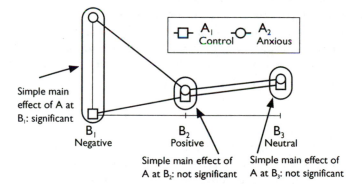

Figure 10.4 Interaction plot showing the location of the specific simple main effects of interest for the example data

in a similar situation to that when we have a single-factor experiment with three or more levels. The significant F tells us that there are some significant differences somewhere among the three means for anxious subjects, but not exactly where. In this circumstance, the Tukey test can be used to compare the three means in the significant simple main effect only, applying the same procedure as described in Chapter 6, setting the value of r to three, and using the error term from the main ANOVA table in order to calculate the critical differences. Alternatively, rather than following up this simple main effects analysis with more follow-up tests, our clear prediction is better tested with planned pairwise comparisons right from the start. Four comparisons are within the limit for no adjustment, but here, pairwise t-tests will have to be performed because the equivalent F values are not available on the simple main effects table.

For a fully between-subjects design, in order to test to see whether anxious subjects with negative words are slower than anxious subjects with positive words and neutral words, and then make the similar comparisons for control subjects, we simply apply the t-test formula given in Chapter 6. The error term is taken from the original ANOVA table, and has 24 degrees of freedom in this example. If a hypothesis requires composite comparisons or, alternatively, a trend analysis, then these techniques should be applied (also described in Chapter 6), treating this design as a single-factor design with six levels and five subjects per level when calculating weights and performing calculations. Box 10.4 shows the calculations for the selected planned comparisons on the example data.

Finally, if a hypothesis is particularly intricate, or you are genuinely uncertain what to expect, then all five simple main effects may be tested. Here we are reaching numbers where the Bonferroni adjustment probably should be applied. Hence, if the usual per-comparison significance level is 5%, then to keep the familywise Type I Error rate at 5%, it is necessary to divide the 5% significance level by 5 comparisons to give a new per-comparison significance level of 1%. Any significant simple main effects with three or more levels may then be individually followed up with the Tukey test, in which r is set to the number of means in the simple main effect under test and the error term and its degrees of freedom are taken from the main ANOVA table. Alternatively a *post-hoc* test may be

Box 10.4 Performing the planned comparisons on the selected data

$$t = \frac{\bar{A}_1 - \bar{A}_2}{\sqrt{(\text{Mean Square}_{ERROR})\left(\dfrac{2}{N_A}\right)}}$$

For the example data, the Mean Square$_{ERROR}$ from the ANOVA table is 1.03 and has 24 degrees of freedom. The critical value of t for 24 degrees of freedom at the 5% significance level is 2.064. N_A, the number of scores in a cell, is 5 and so:

$$t = \frac{\bar{A}_1 - \bar{A}_2}{\sqrt{1.03\left(\dfrac{2}{5}\right)}} = \frac{\bar{A}_1 - \bar{A}_2}{\sqrt{0.42}} = \frac{\bar{A}_1 - \bar{A}_2}{0.65}$$

For anxious/negative word versus anxious/ positive word subjects:

$$t = \frac{7.0 - 4.0}{0.65} = 4.62, \, p < 0.01$$

For anxious/negative word versus anxious/neutral word subjects:

$$t = \frac{7.0 - 4.4}{0.65} = 4.0, \, p < 0.01$$

For control/negative word versus control/positive word subjects:

$$t = \frac{3.0 - 3.8}{0.65} = 1.23, \, \text{NS}$$

For control/negative word versus control/neutral word subjects:

$$t = \frac{3.0 - 4.2}{0.65} = 1.85, \, \text{NS}$$

(Note that t values do not need a sign.)

Hence, the outcome is in line with our predictions. Anxious people have a selective bias towards attending to negative information, compared with positive and neutral information. Control people have no such bias.

used right from the start in order to analyse a significant inter-action. The standard formula from Chapter 6 may again be applied:

$$W = q_{(r, df_{ERROR})} \sqrt{\frac{\text{Mean Square}_{ERROR}}{N_A}}$$

where r is the number of means being compared. With 24 degrees of freedom in the error term and six means, this gives a value for q of 4.37 at the 5% significance level.

When applied to the equation with 1.03 as the error term, the critical difference between means for significance (W) is 1.98 tenths of a second. As shown in Figure 10.5, the three differences previously identified as important when discussing the simple main effects and planned comparisons above are significant. Anxious people are slower than normal people for negative words and are not significantly different for neutral or positive words. Also, comparing the three word types for anxious people, they are slower for negative words than for either positive or neutral words. Control subjects do not differ for any of the three types of word, showing no bias. The difference between neutral and positive words for anxious subjects is also non-significant. These state-ments encompass nine different pairwise comparisons. However, it is important to note that there are a further six possible pairs of means, whose differences can also be tested by planned compar-isons or the Tukey test, which are not only not interesting but do not make sense. For example, while technically the difference between anxious/neutral word and control/positive word subjects will also be significant with the test, this comparison makes no sense and tells us nothing about our hypothesis. As a general rule of thumb, one of the levels should be present in each of a pair of means under comparison. For example, A_2B_2 and A_2B_3 may be compared, as both contain A_2. Also A_1B_2 and A_2B_2 may be com-pared, as both contain B_2, but A_2B_1 and A_1B_2 should not be compared. *There is little point in performing or reporting compar-isons that make no sense. Statistical tests should be focused with respect to a hypothesis, but if this is not possible, then statistical comparisons should never be attempted if they will make no sense whatever their outcome.* The problem is that the correction that the Tukey test applies assumes that for a 2×3 design, all 15 possible pairwise comparisons will be made, when only 9 of these at the

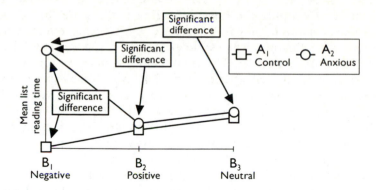

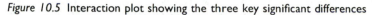

Figure 10.5 Interaction plot showing the three key significant differences

very most make sense, and this correction is very stringent indeed. The solution is to make the 9 pairwise comparisons with the *t*-test, and apply the Bonferroni adjustment to the standard per-comparison significance level.

Some pitfalls in interpreting interactions

Interactions are not always straightforward to interpret. When a factorial design is run, a very wide range of performance is likely to be sampled. Because of this, there is ample opportunity for floor and ceiling effects to occur. The consequence of either of these is that the limits of a scale have prevented a measure from being a true reflection of performance. In practice, restricting the measurement scale can either give the impression of an interaction where there should have been none, or conceal the presence of one. Consider an experiment in which a researcher is looking at the distractibility of adults and children. Performance is measured by having the subjects work through a booklet of 100 arithmetic problems to solve in a set time. The measure of performance is the number of problems solved in this time. Some subjects solve the problems in a quiet room, while others solve the problems while roadworks are taking place in the street outside the room.

The left-hand graph in the top of Figure 10.6 shows one possible outcome of this experiment, and the interaction implies that the performance of children is more susceptible to distraction than the performance of adults. However, consider the possibility that the problems were too easy for the adults, and they completed them all well within the time limit. Hence, the score for adults in quiet conditions might be affected by a ceiling effect. One way around this problem would be simply to add another 100 problems to the booklet. The right-hand graph shows that there is no trace of any ceiling effect for adults with these extra items, but the consequence of this is that the interaction has vanished, and adults are just as susceptible to distraction as children. Overall, the interaction in the left-hand graph is a spurious artefact of the measurement scale, rather than representing a genuine phenomenon.

Unfortunately, problems with the measurement scale can conceal an interaction just as easily as they can create one. In the lower half of Figure 10.6, another plausible pattern of results is shown

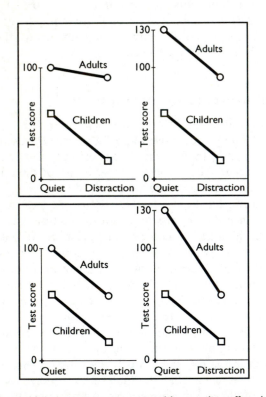

Figure 10.6 An interaction created by a ceiling effect (top) and an interaction concealed by a ceiling effect (bottom)

on the left-hand graph. Here, there appears to be no interaction, and the performance of adults is just as susceptible to distraction as the performance of children. However, with only 100 items in the test book, again the adult performance under quiet conditions may be being underestimated due to the ceiling effect. This time, the right-hand graph shows that, by adding items, extending the scale shows that an interaction had previously been concealed. Now, adults are more susceptible to distraction than children. However, even here, the score for children may well be a result of a floor effect for the distraction condition.

The advice here is simply that you should be aware that this problem is possible, especially for error or accuracy data. If scores are clustering towards either end of a scale, then this could represent a floor or ceiling effect that will distort the outcome of the data analysis. Error data can be more prone to this problem than response time data, and so you should collect both where possible.

Chapter 11

Interpreting two-factor mixed and within-subjects designs

In this chapter, two-factor mixed and within-subjects designs and their interpretation will be discussed. Although you will be shown the basic calculations for analysing these designs, the emphasis will shift from detailed discussions of how and why Analysis of Variance is calculated, to which procedures should be chosen and how various ANOVA tables and graphs should be interpreted. You have been shown the three most mathematically straightforward designs in earlier chapters, and there is little new to learn from analysing more complicated designs by hand. The following have been illustrated so far:

1 Splitting total variability into between-group and within-group variability – one-factor between-subjects designs (Chapters 3 and 4).
2 Splitting within-group variability into between-subject variability and residual variability – one-factor within-subjects designs (Chapter 7).
3 Splitting between-group variability into main effect and interaction variability – 2×2 between-subjects designs (Chapter 9).

For more complicated designs, there are no new concepts to be learned. We will begin with the analysis of a two-factor mixed design.

A two-factor mixed design

Mixed design ANOVAs are particularly versatile and are often used in psychology. These designs have at least one between-subjects factor and at least one within-subjects factor. A simple expertise study of memory would normally use this design (see

Chapters 9 and 10). Expertise would be the between-subjects factor out of necessity, while position type, for a chess study, can be a within-subjects factor in order to increase the sensitivity of the experiment and save on the number of subjects. Recall that a between-subjects design uses the within-group variance as its error term, while a within-subjects design uses the residual variance as its error term. It therefore follows that a mixed design ANOVA will need at least two error terms; one for the between-subjects main effect and one for the within-subjects main effect. The imaginary experiment to be described will be the same task as described in Chapter 9. Hence, there are two factors: expertise (expert versus novice) and position type (real versus random). This time, each subject is briefly shown twenty chess positions one at a time. There are ten real positions and ten random positions, each with ten pieces on the board. After the

---

Box 11.1 Preliminary analysis for the expertise data

Below is a table of raw data for this experiment. The dependent variable is the number of positions recalled correctly:

			Factor B: Position type (within subjects)	
			Level B_1 real	Level B_2 random
Factor A: Expertise (between–ss)	Level A_1 expert	S_1	8	3
		S_2	10	1
		S_3	9	2
		S_4	9	5
		S_5	7	4
	Level A_2 novice	S_6	3	4
		S_7	5	4
		S_8	4	5
		S_9	2	2
		S_{10}	3	2

Next is the table of cell and level means:

	Level B₁ real	Level B₂ random	Overall
Level A₁ expert	8.6	3.0	5.8
Level A₂ novice	3.4	3.4	3.4
Overall	6.0	3.2	4.6

Finally, here is the ANOVA table for these data:

SOURCE	Sum of Squares	Degrees of freedom	Mean Square	F	p
A (expertise)	28.80	1	28.80	16.46	0.0036
Error S/A (Bet-ss)	14.00	8	1.75		
B (position type)	39.20	1	39.20	23.06	0.0014
A×B	39.20	1	39.20	23.06	0.0014
Error B×S/A	13.60	8	1.70		

subject has been shown each, the task is to reproduce it from memory. The dependent variable is the number of boards remembered entirely correctly for each subject for each position type. Box 11.1 shows possible raw data, a table of means and an ANOVA table for the data (the end of this section gives the details of the actual calculations).

The first point to note from Box 11.1 is that there are two separate error terms. One is labelled *Error S/A (Bet-ss)* and this has been used to calculate the *F* ratio for the between-subjects factor. *Error B×S/A* has been used to calculate the *F* ratio for every component linked to factor *B*, i.e. the within-subjects factor and the interaction. You need to know which is which when reporting the degrees of freedom of *F* ratios, and also if these error terms are to be used for testing simple main effects. Unfortunately, not all computer software is as helpful as this in labelling and setting out tables, and so some care in navigation may be required.

The next point to note is that the interaction (designated $A \times B$ on the table) is significant. Since neither factor has more than two levels, the interaction should be investigated by testing the significance of the simple main effects. Among applied statisticians, there are different opinions on how the testing of simple main effects in mixed ANOVA designs should be carried out (for discussions see Howell, 1997; Kirk, 1982; Maxwell and Delaney, 1990). The simplest method, using *pooled error terms*, will be described here (see Chapter 7). This approach is adequate for undergraduate work, and arguably is no worse than alternatives for professional research.

In order to test the significance of the simple main effects by using the pooled error term approach, it is first necessary to calculate the between-group variances for each effect. The actual calculations are identical to those used for the between-subjects design in Chapter 10 and will not be repeated here. For each pair of simple main effects, for example the two within-subjects effects, the difference between the means for both should then be tested for significance by using the same error term (hence pooled error term approach). The error term for testing the significance of the between-subjects effects is the pooled between-group variance aggregated across the cells, calculated identically to a fully between-subjects design. This is used to test the significance of the two simple main effects for the between-subjects factor, i.e. the simple main effects of expertise at real positions (A at B_1) and at random positions (A at B_2). The other error term is used to test the significance of the two within-subjects simple main effects – position type for experts and for novices – and this is the within-subjects factor error term taken straight from the ANOVA table in Box 11.1 (i.e. *Error B×S/A*). The outcome of such a simple main effects analysis is shown in Table 11.1. The alternative to this approach is to calculate a separate *t*-test for the data, making up each pair of means to be compared, not using a common error term (i.e. using the appropriate equation in Chapter 2, not Chapter 6). This approach might be considered for work intended for publication, but lack of space precludes any further discussion of the pros and cons of this alternative approach (see Chapter 7).

Where there is a significant interaction, an interaction plot is always helpful for interpretation and one for these data is shown in Figure 11.1.

Table 11.1 Simple main effects analysis for the expertise data

Source of variation	Sum of Squares	df	Mean Square	F	p
Expertise at					
real pos	67.60	1	67.60	39.19	0.0000
random pos	0.40	1	0.40	0.23	0.6367
Error term	27.60	16	1.73		
Position type at					
expert	78.40	1	78.40	46.11	0.0001
novice	0.00	1	0.00	0.00	1.0000
Error term	13.60	8	1.70		

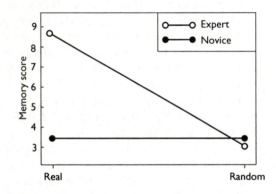

Figure 11.1 Plot showing the interaction between expertise and position type for the example data

Once you have a graph and a simple main effects table, the first step in interpreting an interaction is to identify the various effects. Starting from the top of the table, there is a significant simple main effect of expertise for real positions: $F(1,16) = 39.2$, $p < 0.01$. This shows that the experts' mean for real positions, 8.6, is significantly greater than the novices' mean for real positions, 3.4. The next F ratio – expertise for random positions – is not significant: $F(1,16) = 0.23$, $p > 0.05$. This in turn shows that the experts' mean for random positions, 3.0, is not significantly different from the novices' mean for random positions, 3.4. Next, there is a significant simple main effect of position type for experts: $F(1,8) = 46.1, p < 0.01$. This effect shows that experts have a better recall of real positions than of random positions, i.e. the mean of 8.6 is greater than the mean of 3.0. Finally, there is no significant effect of position type for novices: $F(1,8) = 0, p > 0.05$. Novices find real positions just as difficult to recall as random positions, with means of 3.4 and 3.4. Once the significant effects have been identified, they must be interpreted. Just a couple of sentences will suffice in order to state what has happened: experts only have a better memory than novices for material that is meaningful to their field of expertise, in other words real positions. Again, the expected findings have been replicated.

As a final note, if the design has three or more levels in either factor then, as for the between-subjects design, the analysis becomes less straightforward because the outcome of the simple main effects analysis will be far less meaningful. The Tukey test could in theory be used to follow up each significant simple main effect which has more than two levels. This would utilise the error term and its degrees of freedom for testing the significance of that simple main effect. The number of means in that effect and the cell size would be the other values to use for the equation given in Chapter 6. The within-subjects design example below shows how to use the Tukey test to follow up a significant simple main effect with three levels or more, and the logic is the same whether the simple main effect being followed up is within or between subjects. However, in such circumstances, planned comparisons or linear contrasts will often be preferable, although again there is a debate about which is the most appropriate error term. Taking appropriate pooled error terms directly from ANOVA tables is fine for undergraduate work, and if the computer package which you are using will let you analyse an interaction for a mixed design by using *post-hoc* tests, then it is safe to assume that the analysis is making a reasonable choice of error term.

Calculating the F ratios for the mixed design ANOVA

If you are curious, or ever without a computer, Table 11.2 summarises the necessary calculations for a two-factor mixed design in the basic ratio format. Box 11.2 applies these calculations to the expertise example data.

Table 11.2 Individual calculations for a 2×2 mixed design ANOVA

Source	Sum of Squares	Degrees of freedom	Mean Square	F	p
A (between)	$[A] - [T]$	$(a - 1)$	$\dfrac{[A] - [T]}{(a - 1)}$	$\dfrac{\text{Mean Square}_A}{\text{Mean Square}_{S/AB}}$	tables
S/A (error)	$[S] - [A]$	$a(s - 1)$	$\dfrac{[S] - [A]}{a(s - 1)}$		
B (within)	$[B] - [T]$	$(b - 1)$	$\dfrac{[B] - [T]}{(b - 1)}$	$\dfrac{\text{Mean Square}_B}{\text{Mean Square}_{B \times S/A}}$	tables
A×B	$[AB] - [A] - [B] + [T]$	$(a - 1)(b - 1)$	$\dfrac{[AB] - [A] - [B] + [T]}{(a - 1)(b - 1)}$	$\dfrac{\text{Mean Square}_{A \times B}}{\text{Mean Square}_{B \times S/A}}$	tables
B×S/A (error)	$[Y] - [AB] - [S] + [A]$	$a(b - 1)(s - 1)$	$\dfrac{[Y] - [AB] - [S] + [A]}{a(b - 1)(s - 1)}$		
TOTAL	$[Y] - [T]$	$(abs - 1)$			

Box 11.2 Performing ANOVA on the expertise data

The necessary cell and subject totals are given in the following table.

			Factor B: Position type (within-subjects)		
			Level B_1 real	Level B_1 random	Ss totals
Factor A: expertise (between-ss)	Level A_1 expert	S_1	Cell total A_1B_1	Cell total A_1B_1	11
		S_2			11
		S_3	43	15	11
		S_4			14
		S_5			11
	Level A_2 novice	S_6	Cell total A_2B_1	Cell total A_2B_1	7
		S_7			9
		S_8	17	17	9
		S_9			4
		S_{10}			5

For the Sums of Squares:

$[A]$ (basic ratio of the two level A totals) $= \dfrac{(43 + 15)^2 + (17 + 17)^2}{10} = 452$

$[B]$ (basic ratio of the two level B totals) $= \dfrac{(43 + 17)^2 + (15 + 17)^2}{10} = 462.4$

$[AB]$ (basic ratio of the cell totals) $= \dfrac{43^2 + 17^2 + 15^2 + 17^2}{5} = 530.4$

$[S]$ (basic ratio of the subject totals)

$$= \dfrac{11^2 + 11^2 + 11^2 + 14^2 + 11^2 + 7^2 + 9^2 + 9^2 + 4^2 + 5^2}{2} = 466$$

$[T]$ (basic ratio of the grand total) $= \dfrac{(43 + 15 + 17 + 17)^2}{20} = 423.2$

$[Y]$ (basic ratio of the individual scores) $= 558$

$SS_A = [A] - [T] = 28.8$ $SS_B = [B] - [T] = 39.2$

$SS_{A \times B} = [AB] - [A] - [B] + [T] = 39.2$ $SS_{S/A} = [S] - [A] = 14.0$

$SS_{B \times S/A} = [Y] - [AB] - [S] + [A] = 13.6$ $SS_{TOTAL} = [Y] - [T] = 138.4$

For the degrees of freedom:

$df_A = (a - 1) = 1$ $df_B = (b - 1) = 1$ $df_{A \times B} = (a - 1)(b - 1) = 1$

$df_{S/A} = a(s - 1) = 8$ $df_{B \times S/A} = a(b - 1)(s - 1) = 8$

$df_{TOTAL} = (abs - 1) = 19$

For testing the simple main effects, the individual between-group variances for each simple main effect should be calculated as shown in Chapter 10. The within-subjects error term from the main ANOVA table should be used for the two within-subjects simple main effects (position type for novices and for experts). For the two between-subjects simple main effects (expertise for real and random positions), the pooled within-group variance for the four cells should be calculated. This is identical to the calculation for the error term used for the fully between-subjects design, and the logic behind its use is the same. The within-group Sums of Squares are therefore required. The calculations are identical to those in Chapter 10, hence:

$SS_{S/AB} = [Y] - [AB] = 558 - 530.4 = 27.6$

$df_{S/AB} = ab(s - 1) = 16$

It should now be possible to take all of these calculated values and see how they fit into the ANOVA tables above.

A two-factor fully within-subjects design

Two-factor within-subjects designs are also frequently used in psychology. An element of caution is required for this type of design, however. Every subject is experiencing at least four different conditions, and so great care must be taken to make sure that performance on some conditions is not affecting performance on others, unless of course this is explicitly being tested for. In addition, the problems with analysing within-subjects designs discussed in Chapter 7 are amplified for factorial designs, particularly when there are more than two levels in any factor. Although the example to be shown is a 2×3 design, the problems with the use of follow-up tests mean that we would urge people not to utilise factorial designs with more than two levels in any within-subjects factor if possible. Like the mixed design ANOVA, there is also more than one error term to contend with. It is therefore again necessary to ensure that the correct degrees of freedom are read from the various tables.

Suppose we are interested in whether people identify words as single units or on a letter by letter basis. If people identify words as a whole, they might be less sensitive to individual letters, and more likely to miss them while reading a passage of text. This could be tested by a task in which subjects have to read passages of text and delete certain target letters while doing so. For this experiment, subjects looked at passages of text and deleted all occurrences of the letter 't'. There were two types of passage: one with real words, the prose passage, and one with the same words and each letter t in the same position but the rest of the letters in each word scrambled so that, for example, *the* becomes *teh*. This was the scrambled passage. If subjects were to miss more letters in the prose passage than the scrambled passage, then this might indicate they were seeing real words as whole units rather than as the individual letters that make them up. Hence, in full, the passage type factor, factor A, had two levels: level A_1 was prose and level A_2 was scrambled. The word frequency in the prose passage was also varied. This was factor B: level B_1 was high, level B_2 was medium and level B_3 was low word frequency. If more letters were missed for high frequency words than low frequency words, then this would show that high frequency words were being read as whole units, but not low frequency words. There were ten instances of the letter *t* for each word type; a total of 30 *t*s in each passage. All subjects were given both prose and scrambled passages in a random order. Box 11.3 gives some imaginary data and the preliminary analysis. Scores are the number of letters missed by each subject.

Box 11.3 Preliminary analysis for the letter deletion data

Raw data are given in the following table:

| | A_1 prose passage | | | A_2 scrambled passage | | |
	B_1 high	B_2 med	B_3 low	B_1 high	B_2 med	B_3 low
S_1	7	5	3	2	3	3
S_2	5	5	4	3	2	1
S_3	8	2	3	3	4	3
S_4	4	3	2	0	2	1
S_5	5	2	3	2	0	3
S_6	7	1	3	1	1	4
Means	6.0	3.0	3.0	1.8	2.0	2.5

Examples of words in each condition would be as follows (means are also given):

	High frequency words	Medium frequency words	Low frequency words
Prose passage	6.0 **the**	3.0 **through**	3.0 **tannin**
Scrambled passage	1.8 **teh**	2.0 **trghhuo**	2.5 **tninna**

Here is the ANOVA table that you might expect for these data:

SOURCE	Sum of Squares	Degrees of freedom	Mean Square	F	p
A (passage)	32.11	1	32.11	62.83	0.0005
Error A×S	2.56	5	0.51		
B (frequency)	13.72	2	6.86	3.90	0.0561
Error B×S	17.61	10	1.76		
A×B	23.72	2	11.86	7.598	0.0098
Error A×B×S	15.61	10	1.56		
S (subjects)	16.56	5	3.31		

Notice that each effect has its own error term directly underneath it, which makes locating the appropriate degrees of freedom particularly easy. Not all computer statistics packages are this helpful, so some searching may be necessary. The letters with each error term denote the factor that each applies to. Hence *error A×S* is used to calculate the *F* ratio of factor *A* and so on. Also note that there is a significant interaction, so now we need to analyse the data in more depth and do not need to worry about the main effects.

Although it is possible to test the simple main effects in this example, this is not necessarily helpful because of the extra level in the word frequency factor. Thus, while it is recommended that simple main effects are always tested if there is a significant interaction for a 2×2 design, the use of planned comparisons, linear contrasts or *post-hoc* tests is recommended if any factor has more than two levels. If simple main effects are to be tested, then the between-group variances for the individual effects should be calculated as shown in Chapter 10. The error terms to use are those from the original ANOVA table. Hence, for the simple main effects of factor *A*, at B_1, B_2 and B_3, the error term for testing the significance of factor *A* on the original ANOVA table could be used. This is shown as *Error A×S* on the table. If such a simple main effects analysis were conducted, then the outcome should be similar to Table 11.3.

Table 11.3 Simple main effects analysis for the letter deletion data

Source of variation	Sum of Squares	df	Mean Square	F	p
Passage at					
high freq	52.08	1	52.08	101.90	0.0002
med freq	3.00	1	3.00	5.87	0.0599
low freq	0.75	1	0.75	1.47	0.2799
Error term	2.56	5	0.51		
Frequency at					
prose	36.00	2	18.00	10.22	0.0038
scrambled	1.44	2	0.72	0.41	0.6743
Error term	17.61	10	1.76		

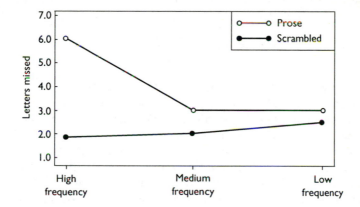

Figure 11.2 Plot showing the interaction between passage type and word frequency for the example data

Where there is a significant interaction, an interaction plot is always helpful for interpretation and one for these data is shown in Figure 11.2.

Looking at the simple main effects in order on the table, significantly more *t*s are missed for high frequency prose words than their scrambled equivalents, but there are no differences between prose words and their scrambled equivalents for medium and low frequency words. Looking at the other pair of effects, there is at least one significant difference between the three prose word means and so, even after the analyses completed so far, additional tests are required in order to find out exactly where. Again, the Tukey test may be used. As a reminder, the equation to calculate the critical difference is:

$$W = q_{(r, df_{ERROR})} \sqrt{\frac{\text{Mean Square}_{ERROR}}{N_A}}$$

If we use this test to compare the three means for the significant simple main effect of word frequency for the prose passage, r, the number of means is 3 and not 6 – we are ignoring the other three means for the other simple main effect. The value for the degrees of freedom for the error term from the ANOVA table is 10, and the value for the Mean Square$_{ERROR}$ is 1.76. The cell size is 6. From studentized range statistic tables, the value of q for 3 means and 10 degrees of freedom is 3.88. Hence,

$$W = 3.88 \sqrt{\frac{1.76}{6}} = 3.88 \sqrt{0.29} = 2.10$$

For the three prose means of 6 (high frequency), 3 (medium frequency) and 3 (low frequency), only differences of 2.1 or bigger are large enough to be significant. Hence, the most failures to delete letters were for high frequency words, suggesting that these are recognised as whole units. There were significantly fewer errors for medium and low frequency words, implying that these are identified on a letter by letter basis. The simple main effect for word frequency for the scrambled passage was not significant, showing that for scrambled words, letters were just as easily deleted irrespective of the frequency of their prose equivalent. No further testing is necessary in order to follow up the scrambled words. Alternatively, we could have made various planned comparisons using the equation given in Chapter 6, choosing the appropriate error term from the main ANOVA table. For example, if we wished to compare the mean of $A_1 B_1$ with the mean of $A_2 B_1$, then the error term for testing the significance of factor A should be used, and if we wished to compare the mean of $A_1 B_1$ with the mean of $A_1 B_2$, then the error term for testing the significance of factor B should be used in the t-test equation. Again, if comparisons are planned in advance and one fewer than the number of cells is intended, then significant F ratios are not required in order to proceed with them, but if five or more are planned then the Bonferroni adjustment should be applied to the significance level.

Finally, note that we did not apply any correction for multiple comparisons when testing the five simple main effects. We probably should have applied the Bonferroni adjustment to each, giving a per-comparison significance level of 1%. However, all of the significant simple main effects were significant to $p < 0.01$ in any case, and so applying the adjustment would have made no difference to the interpretation of this example.

Calculating the F ratios for the within-subjects ANOVA

If you are curious, or ever without a computer, Table 11.4 summarises the necessary calculations for a two-factor within-subjects design in the basic ratio format (see also formula on p. 210). Box 11.4 applies these calculations to the letter deletion example data.

Table 11.4 Individual calculations for a 2×2 fully within-subjects design ANOVA

Source	Sum of Squares	Degrees of freedom	Mean Square	F	p
A	$[A] - [T]$	$(a - 1)$	$\dfrac{[A] - [T]}{(a - 1)}$	$\dfrac{\text{Mean Square}_A}{\text{Mean Square}_{A \times S}}$	tables
A×S (error)	$[AS] - [A]$ $- [S] + [T]$	$(a - 1)(s - 1)$	$\dfrac{[AS] - [A] - [S] + [T]}{(a - 1)(s - 1)}$		
B	$[B] - [T]$	$(b - 1)$	$\dfrac{[B] - [T]}{(b - 1)}$	$\dfrac{\text{Mean Square}_B}{\text{Mean Square}_{B \times S}}$	tables
B×S (error)	$[BS] - [B]$ $- [S] + [T]$	$(b - 1)(s - 1)$	$\dfrac{[BS] - [B] - [S] + [T]}{(b - 1)(s - 1)}$		
A×B	$[AB] - [A]$ $- [B] + [T]$	$(a - 1)(b - 1)$	$\dfrac{[AB] - [A] - [B] + [T]}{(a - 1)(b - 1)}$	$\dfrac{\text{Mean Square}_{A \times B}}{\text{Mean Square}_{A \times B \times S}}$	tables
A×B×S (error)	$[Y] - [AB]$ $- [AS] - [BS]$ $+ [A] + [B]$ $+ [S] - [T]$	see p. 210	see p. 210		
S	$[S] - [T]$	$(s - 1)$	$\dfrac{[S] - [T]}{(s - 1)}$		
TOTAL	$[Y] - [T]$	$(abs - 1)$			

Box 11.4 Performing ANOVA on the letter deletion data

In order to calculate the within-subjects ANOVA, two new basic ratios are required. These are derived from the level totals for each subject. Thus, for the first subject in the table below, we need to find the total for the three A_1 scores: A_1B_1, A_1B_2 and A_1B_3; the three A_2 scores, and also the total of each pair of B_1, B_2 and B_3 scores. These totals are shown for the letter deletion example in the tables below.

	A_1B_1	A_1B_2	A_1B_3	A_2B_1	A_2B_2	A_2B_3	Overall subject total	A_1 subject total	A_2 subject total
S_1	7	5	3	2	3	3	23	15	8
S_2	5	5	4	3	2	1	20	m14	6
S_3	8	2	3	3	4	3	23	13	10
S_4	4	3	2	0	2	1	12	9	3
S_5	5	2	3	2	0	3	15	10	5
S_6	7	1	3	1	1	4	17	11	6
Cell total	36	18	18	11	12	15			

	A_1B_1	A_1B_2	A_1B_3	A_2B_1	A_2B_2	A_2B_3	B_1 subject total	B_2 subject total	B_3 subject total
S_1	7	5	3	2	3	3	9	8	6
S_2	5	5	4	3	2	1	8	7	5
S_3	8	2	3	3	4	3	11	6	6
S_4	4	3	2	0	2	1	4	5	3
S_5	5	2	3	2	0	3	7	2	6
S_6	7	1	3	1	1	4	8	2	7

The first new basic ratio that we need is [AS] which is the basic ratio of the subject totals for each level of factor A. Hence, we need to take each of the 12 A_1 and A_2 subject totals, square these, and divide the total of the squares by the number of scores which made up each subject total (three). Hence:

$$[AS] = \frac{15^2 + 14^2 + 13^2 + 9^2 + 10^2 + 11^2 + 8^2 + 6^2 + 10^2 + 3^2 + 5^2 + 6^2}{3} = 387.3$$

The other new basic ratio that we need is $[BS]$ which is the basic ratio of the subject totals for each level of factor B. Hence, we need to take each of the 18 B_1, B_2 and B_3 subject totals, square these and divide the total of the squares by the number of scores which made up each subject total (two). Hence $[BS] =$

$$\frac{9^2 + 8^2 + 11^2 + 4^2 + 7^2 + 8^2 + 8^2 + 7^2 + 6^2 + 5^2 + 2^2 + 2^2 + 6^2 + 5^2 + 6^2 + 3^2 + 6^2 + 7^2}{2}$$

$$= 384$$

The remaining basic ratios are calculated in the normal way:

$[A]$ (basic ratio of the two level A totals) $= \dfrac{72^2 + 38^2}{18} = 368.2$

$[B]$ (basic ratio of the three level B totals) $= \dfrac{47^2 + 30^2 + 33^2}{12} = 349.8$

$[AB]$ (basic ratio of the cell totals) $= \dfrac{36^2 + 18^2 + 18^2 + 11^2 + 12^2 + 15^2}{6} = 405.7$

$[S]$ (basic ratio of the subject totals) $= \dfrac{23^2 + 20^2 + 23^2 + 12^2 + 15^2 + 17^2}{6} = 352.7$

$[T]$ (basic ratio of the grand total) $= \dfrac{110^2}{36} = 336.1$

$[Y]$ (basic ratio of the individual scores) $= 458$

$SS_A \quad = [A] - [T] = 32.1 \qquad\qquad SS_B = [B] - [T] = 13.7$

$SS_{A \times B} \quad = [AB] - [A] - [B] + [T] = 23.8$

$SS_{A \times S} \quad = [AS] - [A] - [S] + [T] = 2.5 \qquad SS_{B \times S} = [BS] - [B] - [S] + [T] = 17.6$

$SS_{A \times B \times S} = [Y] - [AB] - [AS] - [BS] + [A] + [B] + [S] - [T] = 15.6$

$SS_S \quad = [S] - [T] = 16.6 \qquad\qquad SS_{TOTAL} = [Y] - [T] = 121.9$

For the degrees of freedom ($a = 2$, $b = 3$ and $s = 6$):

df_A $= (a - 1) = 1$ df_B $= (b - 1) = 2$ $df_{A \times B}$ $= (a - 1)(b - 1) = 2$

$df_{A \times S}$ $= (a - 1)(s - 1) = 5$ $df_{B \times S}$ $= (b - 1)(s - 1) = 10$

$df_{A \times B \times S} = (a - 1)(b - 1)(s - 1) = 1$ df_S $= (s - 1) = 5$ df_{TOTAL} $= (abs - 1) = 35$

It should now be possible to take all of these calculated values and see how they fit into the ANOVA tables above. Small discrepancies are due to rounding errors.

From Table 11.4:

$$\text{df}_{A \times B \times S} = (a - 1)(b - 1)(s - 1)$$

$$\text{Mean Square}_{A \times B \times S} = \frac{[Y] - [AB] - [AS] - [BS] + [A] + [B] + [S] - [T]}{(a - 1)(b - 1)(s - 1)}$$

In the examples above, we have discussed the simplest procedures for analysing and following up two-factor mixed and within-subjects designs. These methods are satisfactory for undergraduate project work. However, because these designs contain within-subjects factors, both are subject to the same difficulties potentially faced by all within-subjects designs. These were introduced in Chapter 7. The solutions to the problems are broadly similar to those for single-factor designs, and should be considered for any work which is intended for publication. The interested reader on this topic should consult more advanced textbooks (e.g. Howell, 1997; Kirk, 1982; Maxwell and Delaney, 1990).

It should be noted that the analysis in Box 11.3 does not include the Greenhouse and Geisser correction for possible violations of the sphericity assumption (see Chapter 7). In the letter deletion example, both the Mean Square$_{BETWEEN}$ (i.e. Mean Square$_{EFFECT}$) for the word frequency factor and that for the interaction have more than one degree of freedom. Had this correction been performed by a computer package and applied to these two effects, we would have obtained larger p values for the word frequency main effect, $F = 3.90$, but now $p = 0.081$, and for the interaction, $F = 7.60$, but now $p = 0.022$ (although this has had no effect on the significances of either effect). Notice that no correction is required for the passage main effect since it is based on a single pair of means, and hence $df_{BETWEEN}$ (i.e. df_{EFFECT}) has one degree of freedom for its between-group variance.

Chapter 12

Interpreting a three-factor ANOVA

Three-factor ANOVAs are encountered reasonably often in psychology, and their complexity means that the first few designs you will see will require considerable effort before the effects are understood. These designs need to be treated with great respect and should never be attempted for project work if there are any difficulties in understanding the meaning of a *three-way interaction* – the most complicated outcome of a three-factor design. The mathematics of performing a three-factor ANOVA will not be demonstrated in this chapter. There is nothing new to learn, and without a computer to perform calculations, the chance of making an error at some stage is so great that there is nothing to gain in performing an analysis by hand.

The basic design principles outlined in other chapters apply equally here. The fully between-subjects design is still comparatively simple, with just a single error term for all effects. However, with eight subjects per cell minimum, a $2\times2\times2$ design will require at least 64 subjects in order to have a satisfactory cell size, but if the resources are available, the reward is a design that is very straightforward to analyse. The problems discussed with mixed and fully within-subjects designs apply equally to three-factor designs, especially if any factors have three or more levels. Readers are urged never to exceed two factors per level unless absolutely necessary, and not to contemplate a four-factor design, especially for undergraduate work, unless confidence is high.

The most straightforward outcome for a three-factor design is when the three-way interaction is not significant. These outcomes will not be discussed in this chapter. Where this occurs, one or more of the two-way interactions may be significant. In which case, each significant interaction should be investigated independently of the others, ignoring the non-interacting factor. The exact techniques for interpreting each interaction are the same as those described in Chapters 9, 10 and 11, depending on whether the interacting factors are mixed, fully between- or fully within-subjects. If two or three of the two-way interactions are significant but not the three-way interaction, then each may be investigated completely independently of the other(s). For example, if factors A and B interact significantly, but the three-way interaction is not significant, factor C may be ignored and the simple main effects of A at B and B at A investigated. An even simpler outcome of a three-factor design is if none of the interactions is significant. In which case, the outcome must be interpreted in terms of the main effects if any of these are significant. If nothing is significant, then unless specific pairwise comparisons or other linear contrasts are planned, the analysis is complete.

For a significant *three-way interaction*, there are different two-way interactions between two of the factors according to the level of the third factor. This is not as unpleasant as it sounds, and many even quite simple-sounding psychological findings have a three-way interaction as their basis. Where a three-way interaction is significant, there are two possible strategies for performing follow-up tests.

1 One possibility is to split the design and reanalyse it as a series of two-factor ANOVAs. This strategy is particularly recommended if there are more than three levels in any factor. However, this is less suited to a design that is fully between subjects, which will lose sensitivity. The degrees of freedom for df_{ERROR} will decline for each of the two-factor ANOVAs and more stringent critical value(s) of F will result.

2 The other possibility is to test the significance of each of the simple main effects against a suitable error term. These are occasionally called *simple simple main effects* because they are at a third level of depth, and could otherwise be confused with the simple main effects of the two-way interactions. This terminology will be adopted here. As we shall see, it is best to be selective when testing for these effects, but if this is not possible, then some sort of correction for multiple comparisons will be inevitable. For any design with three or more levels in any one factor, testing the significance of these simple simple main effects and then following up significant, but

ambiguous, *F* values can be a very cumbersome procedure. In which case, splitting the design may be better for mixed and fully within-subjects designs, although pairwise comparisons will be better for fully between-subjects designs.

In the two examples that follow, we will demonstrate the procedures for following up a three-way interaction for two 2×2×2 designs: fully within subjects and mixed. Interpreting a between-subjects design is similar, but far simpler mathematically. As before, we will use the *pooled error term approach* when testing the significance of the simple simple main effects (see Chapters 7 and 11). We will not discuss a design with three or more levels in any factor.

Memory and context: a 2×2×2 fully within-subjects design

I wish to see whether memory is better if material is tested in the same context as it is learnt in, compared with being tested in a different context. I also wish to see whether recall and recognition are equally context dependent. To do so, I run a fully within-subjects design with three factors in which the subjects are divers. Each factor has two levels, making a 2×2×2 design; *memory task* (*recall* or *recognition*), *learning context* (*land* or *under water*) and *testing context* (*land* or *under water*). Subjects are given words to remember in a learning context and then their memory for the words is tested, either by having to recall the material by reciting a list of answers, or having to recognise the material by choosing the correct word from several alternatives. The dependent variable is the number of words remembered correctly. The design is fully within subjects, so subjects will have to be tested with eight different lists of words in all combinations of context. Raw data are given in Table 12.1 and cell means in Table 12.2. The first point to note for a three-factor design is that, in order to display cell means, two tables are needed. Most three-factor experiments have a natural divide in this respect. Here, it makes most sense to split the data by factor *A*. This will show the pattern of results for recall on the one hand, and the pattern of results for recognition on the other. Later, two separate graphs will be used in order to show the results visually. Three-dimensional graphs should always be avoided as it is difficult to read their values accurately.

Table 12.1 Raw data for the memory and context study

Factor A: Task	Level A_1 recall				Level A_2 recognition			
Factor B: Learning	Level B_1 under		Level B_2 land		Level B_1 under		Level B_2 land	
Factor C: Testing	C_1 under	C_2 land	C_1 under	C_2 land	C_1 under	C_2 land	C_1 under	C_2 land
S_1	8	5	3	7	5	5	7	6
S_2	9	6	3	8	7	6	5	8
S_3	7	5	4	6	6	7	5	6
S_4	8	4	4	5	7	5	6	5
S_5	6	3	3	8	5	4	6	4

Table 12.2 Cell and level means for the memory and context study

	Level A_1 recall task			Level A_2 recognition task		
	Level B_1 under water	Level B_2 land	Overall	Level B_1 under water	Level B_2 land	Overall
Level C_1 under water	7.6 (same context)	3.4	5.5	6 (same context)	5.8	5.9
Level C_2 land	4.6	6.8 (same context)	5.7	5.4	5.8 (same context)	5.6
Overall	6.1	5.1	5.6	5.7	5.8	5.8

Table 12.3 shows the ANOVA summary table. There are seven different F ratios, each with its own error term, but the only effect that matters is the significant three-way interaction ($A \times B \times C$ near the bottom of the table). The consequence of this is that we should ignore the significant two-way interaction between factors B and C, and any main effects had they been significant. The three-way interaction must be understood first and foremost. For this example, the interaction will be analysed by testing the significance of the simple simple main effects. Table 12.4 shows a simple simple main effects analysis for the memory data.

Each simple simple main effect is analogous to the simple main

Table 12.3 ANOVA table for the memory and context study

SOURCE	Sum of Squares	Degrees of freedom	Mean Square	F	p
A (memory task)	0.23	1	0.23	1.00	0.3739
Error A×S	0.90	4	0.23		
B (learning context)	2.03	1	2.03	1.59	0.2761
Error B×S	5.10	4	1.28		
C (testing context)	0.03	1	0.03	0.01	0.9113
Error C×S	7.10	4	1.78		
A×B	3.03	1	3.03	2.95	0.1609
Error A×B×S	4.10	4	1.03		
A×C	0.63	1	0.63	0.71	0.4456
Error A×C×S	3.50	4	0.88		
B×C	30.63	1	30.63	27.22	0.0064
Error B×C×S	4.50	4	1.13		
A×B×C	21.03	1	21.03	27.13	0.0065
Error A×B×C×S	3.10	4	0.78		
S (subjects)	10.90	4	2.73		

Table 12.4 Simple simple main effects table for the memory and context study

Source of variation	Sum of Squares	df	Mean Square	F	p
Memory task at					
learn under, test under	6.400	1	6.400	28.444	0.0060
learn under, test land	1.600	1	1.600	7.111	0.0560
learn land, test under	14.400	1	14.400	64.000	0.0013
learn land, test land	2.500	1	2.500	11.111	0.0290
Error term (error A×S)	0.900	4	0.225		
Learning at					
recall, test under	44.100	1	44.100	34.588	0.0042
recall, test land	12.100	1	12.100	9.490	0.0369
recognition, test under	0.100	1	0.100	0.078	0.7933
recognition, test land	0.400	1	0.400	0.314	0.6053
Error term (error B×S)	5.100	4	1.275		
Testing at					
recall, learn under	22.500	1	22.500	12.676	0.0236
recall, learn land	28.900	1	28.900	16.282	0.0157
recognition, learn under	0.900	1	0.900	0.507	0.5158
recognition, learn land	0.000	1	0.000	0.000	1.0000
Error term (error C×S)	7.100	4	1.775		

effects discussed in Chapters 10 and 11. Each effect thus represents a between-group variance – the measure of the size of the difference between two means – divided by an error term. When first seen, the table can appear daunting, even though it has been fully labelled so that the effects can be identified. In effect, twelve pairwise comparisons have been carried out. For example, the first effect of all is labelled *Memory task at learn under, test under*. This indicates that the performances for recall and for recognition are being compared when the subjects learnt the words under water, and then were tested under water (i.e. same context for learning and testing). The exact means being compared are shown in Table 12.5. There is a significant difference between these means: $F(1,4) = 28.4, p < 0.05$. The next three comparisons correspond to the other three cross-table comparisons which are possible. In fact, none of the first four effects is very important. We are interested in whether context affects recall, and whether context affects recognition. Comparing recall with equivalent recognition performance will not answer this question, and it is not clear whether these comparisons would make sense anyway. For this reason, although the computer has calculated all twelve simple simple main effects, only the last eight are of interest, and only these should be interpreted and reported.

Figure 12.1 shows two graphs for this study. These have been split so that one graph gives the recall data while the other gives the recognition data. We can thus see the meaning of a three-way interaction. For the recognition data, there appears to be no interaction at all, while for the recall data, there appears to be a clear interaction – the lines are not parallel. In other words, there are different interactions between factors B and C according to the level of factor A. It is important to note here that both graphs have

Table 12.5 Cell means compared by the first simple simple main effect in Table 12.4

	Level A_1 recall task		Level A_2 recognition task	
	Level B_1 learn under	Level B_2 learn land	Level B_1 learn under	Level B_2 learn land
Level C_1 test under	7.6 (same context)		6 (same context)	
Level C_2 test land				

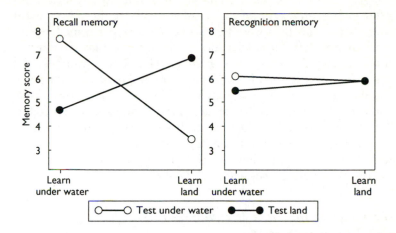

Figure 12.1 Two interaction plots for recall data showing an effect of context for recall memory but not for recognition memory

the same scale on the y-axis. Without this, a visual comparison would be meaningless. Using these graphs and the tables above, it should be possible to pick out all of the simple simple main effects, seeing which are significant and which are not. Of the eight effects of interest, the four significant effects are all located on the recall memory graph, while the four non-significant effects are located on the recognition memory graph.

Overall, we can see that there are no context effects for recognition memory. People remembered just as many words, irrespective of where they were learnt and where they were tested. However, for recall memory, performance is significantly better when people were tested in the same context as when they learnt the information, e.g. they learnt the material on land, and then were tested on land, and significantly worse if they were tested in a different context, e.g. they learnt the material on land, and then were tested under water. However, we have tested the significance of eight simple simple main effects without making any correction in order to control for the familywise Type I Error rate, and this number of comparisons is becoming somewhat excessive. The only really robust correction to apply in such circumstances is the Bonferroni adjustment, in which the significance level, 0.05, is divided by the number of comparisons, 8, to give the new significance level,

0.00625. This correction prevents us from finding any significant differences at all except for the recall task, where those who learnt under water and then were tested under water performed significantly better than those who learnt on land and then were tested under water: $F(1,4) = 34.6$, $p = 0.0042$. This highlights the unsatisfactory nature of the Bonferroni adjustment with small sample sizes: despite several very large F ratios indeed, the correction is too ferocious and has rendered the findings uninterpretable. The alternatives in this situation are either to run more subjects, or to split the data, so that on finding a significant three-way interaction, the recall data and recognition data are analysed as two completely separate two-factor ANOVAs.

Learning to pronounce irregular words: a 2×2×2 mixed design

A less involved way of analysing a significant three-way interaction is to split the data in half and analyse it as two separate two-factor experiments. Bear in mind that you will lose some of the possible comparisons, and hence information, if you do this. In the memory example above, the data could have been split by memory task with the recognition memory data analysed separately from the recall data, *but then it would not have been possible to make the first four comparisons in Table 12.4.* On the other hand, these may not have been comparisons which were interesting or made sense. In the example below, the data also have a natural divide, and the three-way interaction will be analysed in this way.

The following study is intended to investigate the development in children's ability to pronounce regular and irregular words. This is a mixed three-factor 2×2×2 design. Age, factor A, is a between-subjects factor; level A_1 is 7 years old, level A_2 is 9 years old. Word frequency, factor B, is a within-subjects factor; level B_1 is high frequency, level B_2 is low frequency. Word type, factor C, is also a within-subjects factor; level C_1 is regular words, level C_2 is irregular words. Subjects are given 10 words to pronounce in each word category, a total of 40 words. Raw data are given in Table 12.6. The dependent variable is the number of errors of pronunciation. Table 12.7 shows the cell and level means, while Table 12.8 shows the main ANOVA table for these data.

Note that there are only four different error terms for this design. Some error terms have been used twice. From Table 12.8,

Table 12.6 Raw data for the word pronunciation study

Factor A: Age	*Level A_1 7-years-old*					*Level A_2 9-years-old*			
Factor B: Frequency	*Level B_1 high*		*Level B_2 low*			*Level B_1 high*		*Level B_2 low*	
Factor C: Word type	*C_1 reg*	*C_2 irr*	*C_1 reg*	*C_2 irr*		*C_1 reg*	*C_2 irr*	*C_1 reg*	*C_2 irr*
S_1	6	7	5	6	S_6	4	4	3	6
S_2	7	5	6	7	S_7	3	4	4	7
S_3	5	6	7	6	S_8	4	3	5	9
S_4	6	7	5	7	S_9	5	5	3	8
S_5	6	6	5	7	S_{10}	3	4	3	7

Table 12.7 Cell and level means for the word pronunciation study

	Level A_1 7-years-old				*Level A_2 9-years-old*		
	Level B_1 high	*Level B_2 low*	*Overall*		*Level B_1 high*	*Level B_2 low*	*Overall*
Level C_1 regular	6	5.6	5.8	Level C_1 regular	3.8	3.6	3.7
Level C_2 irregular	6.2	6.6	6.4	Level C_2 irregular	4.0	7.4	5.7
Overall	6.1	6.1	6.1	Overall	3.9	5.5	4.7

Between error S/A is used to test the significance of the between-subjects effect – the main effect of factor *A*. *Error* $B \times C \times S/A$ is used to test the significance of all within-subjects effects with *both* factor *B and* factor *C* in them: namely the $A \times B \times C$ interaction and the $B \times C$ interaction. *Error* $C \times S/A$ is used to test the significance of all within-subjects effects with *only* factor *C* and *not* factor *B* in them: namely the $A \times C$ interaction and the main effect of factor *C*. *Error* $B \times S/A$ is used to test the significance of all within-subjects effects with *only* factor *B* and *not* factor *C* in them: namely the $A \times B$ interaction and the main effect of factor *B*. This time, the significant three-way interaction will be analysed by splitting the data by factor *A*, and analysing the 7-years-old group and the 9-years-old

Table 12.8 ANOVA table for the word pronunciation study

Source of variation	Sum of Squares	df	Mean Square	F	p
A (age)	19.600	1	19.600	34.844	0.0004
Between error S/A	4.500	8	0.562		
B (frequency)	6.400	1	6.400	5.885	0.0415
Error B×S/A	8.700	8	1.087		
C (word type)	16.900	1	16.900	36.541	0.0003
Error C×S/A	3.700	8	0.462		
A×B	6.400	1	6.400	5.885	0.0415
Error B×S/A	8.700	8	1.087		
A×C	4.900	1	4.900	10.595	0.0116
Error C×S/A	3.700	8	0.462		
B×C	12.100	1	12.100	17.600	0.0030
Error B×C×S/A	5.500	8	0.688		
A×B×C	4.900	1	4.900	7.127	0.0284
Error B×C×S/A	5.500	8	0.688		

Table 12.9 ANOVA table for 7-year-old children

Source of variation	Sum of Squares	df	Mean Square	F	p
A (frequency)	0.000	1	0.000	0.000	1.0000
Error A×S	2.500	4	0.625		
B (word type)	1.800	1	1.800	2.667	0.1778
Error B×S	2.700	4	0.675		
A×B	0.800	1	0.800	0.865	0.4050
Error A×B×S	3.700	4	0.925		
S (subjects)	0.300	4	0.075		

group separately as two 2×2 fully within-subjects ANOVAs. Table 12.9 shows the main ANOVA table for 7-year-old children.

This outcome is very straightforward; there are no significant differences at all. Seven-year-olds make the same numbers of errors irrespective of whether the words are high or low frequency or regular or irregular. Table 12.10 shows the main ANOVA table for 9-year-old children. Here, the interaction is significant, and Table 12.11 shows the results of testing the significance of the simple main effects. These effects are shown on the graph in Figure 12.2.

Table 12.10 ANOVA table for 9-year-old children

Source of variation	Sum of Squares	df	Mean Square	F	p
A (frequency)	12.800	1	12.800	8.258	0.0453
Error A×S	6.200	4	1.550		
B (word type)	20.000	1	20.000	80.000	0.0009
Error B×S	1.000	4	0.250		
AxB	16.200	1	16.200	36.000	0.0039
Error A×B×S	1.800	4	0.450		
S (subjects)	4.200	4	1.050		

Table 12.11 Simple main effects table for 9-year-old children

Source of variation	Sum of Squares	df	Mean Square	F	p
Word frequency at					
regular words	0.100	1	0.100	0.065	0.8120
irregular words	28.900	1	28.900	18.645	0.0125
Error term	6.200	4	1.550		
Word type at					
high frequency	0.100	1	0.100	0.400	0.5614
low frequency	36.100	1	36.100	144.400	0.0003
Error term	1.000	4	0.250		

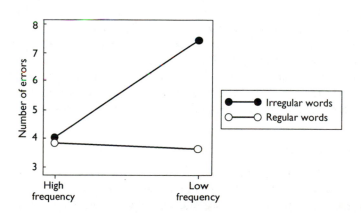

Figure 12.2 Interaction plot for 9-year-olds showing that many errors are made pronouncing low frequency irregular words

From Table 12.11 and the graph in Figure 12.2, we can see that for 9-year-olds, there is a significant simple main effect of word frequency for irregular words: significantly more mispronunciations are made for low frequency irregular words, with a mean of 7.4, than high frequency irregular words, with a mean of 4.0; $F(1,4) = 18.65, p < 0.01$. There is a significant simple main effect of word type for low frequency words: significantly more mispronunciations are made for irregular low frequency words, with a mean of 7.4, than regular low frequency words, with a mean of 3.6; $F(1,4) = 144.4$, $p < 0.01$. Neither of the other two simple main effects is significant.

The overall results for the 9-year-olds show that high frequency irregular words are subject to as few pronunciation errors as high frequency regular words. Presumably these irregular words have been learnt on an individual basis. Low frequency regular words are subject to as few pronunciation errors as high frequency regular words. Presumably, pronunciation rules for regular words have been learnt and can be applied to high frequency regular words. However, more errors are made for low frequency irregular words. It is likely that they have not yet been learnt on an individual basis, and when the rules for regular words are applied, errors are made. Compare these results with the 7-year-olds, whose results suggest that pronunciation rules have not yet been learnt, resulting in frequent errors all round whatever the word type. Note that by splitting the data in this way, you cannot directly compare 7-year-old performance with 9-year-old performance. If you wished to compare performance across ages as well, then splitting the data is not possible. However, the original summary ANOVA table provides a pointer towards this. The main effect of age was significant showing that on average, 9-year-old children perform better than 7-year-old children. Although the three-way interaction means that this conclusion should be treated with caution, it does show that main effects are not entirely irrelevant when interpreting a factorial design with a significant interaction.

General points

As always, the general rule of a three-factor ANOVA is to start at the bottom of the ANOVA table and work your way up. If the three-way interaction is significant then this must be analysed, if not then each of the significant two-way interactions should be analysed independently using the techniques discussed in Chapters

10 and 11. If none of the two-way interactions is significant, the ANOVA results may be described in terms of main effects, again with follow-up tests for the significant main effects with three or more levels. The two designs discussed in detail only had two levels per factor. If three or more levels in any one factor are necessary, then the analysis of an experiment is far less straightforward. If it is absolutely necessary for a design not to be split, then using pairwise comparisons to follow up significant effects with three or more means is an acceptable alternative. These follow-up tests could either be individual t-tests corrected by the Bonferroni adjustment if necessary, or the Tukey test could be applied, but the problem with applying this is, again, that it assumes that all possible comparisons between a set of means will be performed. It is unlikely that all of these will be needed, some comparisons may not even make any sense. The Tukey test will hence be the far more stringent of the two alternatives, and should be avoided. Linear contrast analysis is also possible for effects with more than two levels, and if these are to be used, then the total within-group variance should be used as the error term for between-subjects factors, while the error terms recommended in Chapters 7 and 11 should be used for within-subjects factors.

Chapter 13

Summary and frequently asked questions

This chapter will begin with a summary of the options for analysing various experimental designs when using ANOVA. These have been spread throughout the book, and bringing them all together will be useful. We will then complete this chapter by answering some frequently asked questions, which hopefully will clarify some issues that may have been troubling readers.

A summary of follow-up tests for Analysis of Variance

When no tests are necessary

Sometimes, when Analysis of Variance is performed, the first summary table gives all of the information necessary and no follow-up tests at all are required. The trivial case is where no F ratios are significant and no planned comparisons were intended. However, this can also apply where there are significant F ratios, but only if there are no more than two factors per level. Specifically:

1   A significant F for a one-factor two-level design indicates that the level means are different. No further analysis is possible.
2   For factorial designs (e.g. 2×2, $2\times2\times2$), if none of the interactions is significant, then the outcome should be interpreted in terms of the main effects. Each has only two levels, and so the significant differences are between pairs of means.

How should different designs be analysed?

If planned comparisons are to be used, whether these are pairwise or linear contrasts, we recommend that they are applied in the following way: if $(a - 1)$ comparisons are intended, where a is the number of levels in the factor, then these comparisons may be applied without the need for a significant F ratio for the factor. If four or fewer planned comparisons are intended, then the significance level need not be corrected, but if five or more comparisons are planned, then the Bonferroni adjustment is recommended. You are never obliged to make every possible comparison, and the fewer that you make, the more powerful the statistical test. An analysis with planned comparisons will always be more powerful than the alternatives. However, if there is *no intention of using planned comparisons*, we suggest that you analyse the following designs in the following ways:

1 *Single factor designs.* If the F ratio is significant, then for three-level designs use the Newman–Keuls test to compare each mean with each other mean. For four levels or more, use the Tukey test.
2 *Two factors each with two levels (2×2).* If the interaction is significant, then test the significance of the four simple main effects. If the interaction is not significant, interpret the outcome in terms of main effects if any are significant.
3 *Two factors with at least one having more than two levels (2×3, 2 ×4, 3×3 etc.).* If the interaction is significant, various analyses are possible:

   i Test all possible simple main effects, but apply the Bonferroni adjustment to control for the problem of a high familywise Type I Error rate. Follow up those simple main effects with three or more levels with the Tukey test.
   ii For fully between-subjects designs, use the Tukey test to make all pairwise comparisons. This will be more stringent than (iii) below because the Tukey test will assume that you will wish to make, say, all 15 possible pairwise comparisons for a 2×3 design. Only 9 of these will make any sense, and the other 6 should not be reported (see Chapter 10).
   iii Use t-tests to make the all of the pairwise comparisons which make sense, applying the Bonferroni adjustment to control for their number.

If the interaction is not significant, but any main effect(s) with more than two levels are, then use either the Newman–Keuls test or the Tukey test to locate the significant differences among the pairs of means. The exact choice of test depends upon the number of levels in the factor – see (1) above.

4   *Three factors, each with two levels (2×2×2).* If only the two-way interactions are significant, then separately test the four simple main effects for each interaction as for (2) above. If the three-way interaction is significant, then there are two possible courses of action:

   i   Split the design in half by one of the factors, and conduct separate ANOVAs on the two data sets. This is not recommended for fully between-subjects designs.
   ii Test the 12 simple simple main effects, applying the Bonferroni adjustment as necessary.

If no interactions are significant, interpret the analysis in terms of the main effects.

5   *Three factors, with at least one having more than two levels (e.g. 2×2×3, 2×3×4).* If only the two-way interactions are significant, then separately test the simple main effects for each interaction as for (2) and (3) above. If the three-way interaction is significant, then either:

   i   Split the design by one of the factors, preferably the factor with three or more levels, and conduct separate two-way ANOVAs on the data sets. This is particularly recommended for mixed and fully within-subjects designs, but it is not recommended for fully between-subjects designs.
   ii Test the simple simple main effects, applying the Bonferroni adjustment. Follow up any significant simple simple main effects with three levels or more with the Tukey test.

If no interactions are significant, interpret the analysis in terms of the main effects.

Planned comparisons using pairwise *t*-tests or linear contrasts may be performed on any design. All that is required for the linear contrasts is a suitable set of weights in order to make the comparisons. You should specify in advance which effects are to be tested, and keep the number of comparisons as small as possible. The reward for this is that significant *F* ratios are not required in order to perform the analyses, and as long as the number of comparisons does not exceed the number of levels minus one, for a single-factor design, or the number of cells minus one, for a factorial design, then no correction is necessary. However, with five or more comparisons, the Bonferroni adjustment should be applied.

Frequently asked questions

We are sure that many readers will be wanting to ask at least some of the questions below. For some, there will be no hard and fast answers. In such instances, the advice of instructors and project supervisors will be important.

What exactly do I need to understand?

The level of mathematical understanding taught in this book is unlikely to be necessary to survive a psychology degree – although this will depend on the statistics requirement of individual degrees. If research projects are straightforward then a strategy of letting the computer do everything, coupled with a state of blissful ignorance, is just about enough, *but total ignorance is not*. Computers have massively simplified the process of analysing data, but even the best software cannot interpret outputs yet. If you cannot understand ANOVA tables, then sooner or later you will run into trouble. In addition, you should bear in mind that, if you have any intention of choosing a career that involves psychological research methods, poor understanding of statistical techniques will put you at a disadvantage. If you choose one of the research areas where knowledge of statistical methods may be poor, then the possession of a deeper understanding than average will give you a considerable advantage over others. The final answer to this question is thus: if you do not wish to pursue psychology as a career, then an overall deep understanding of ANOVA is not necessary. However, for a successful career in psychology, especially if research is involved, a sound understanding of *all of the material* in the book will be essential in the long run.

*Why demonstrate the ANOVA equations at all? There are
plenty of computer programs that will do the work for me.*

When analysing data, there is no point to performing ANOVA by
hand if there is computer software available, but only by seeing the
equations used can the underlying principles be made apparent.
Performing ANOVA by computer protects you from all of the
nastier mathematics of the process. A good package will always
calculate the Sums of Squares correctly, choose the best error term,
and so on. Unfortunately, lurking inside many programs, even
expensive commercial packages, are occasional bugs. Only with a
full understanding of the underlying principles of ANOVA can you
be in a position to spot them. *Pay close attention to your ANOVA
printout, look for any results that seem absurd.* As a general rule of
thumb, beware of any amateur software or public domain software. Getting a package to work satisfactorily involves many years
of development.

More often an ANOVA will produce an absurd result due to
incorrect data entry, and you need to be able to spot these errors
too. To shield yourself from this problem, always calculate cell
means by hand. Compare your means with the computer output.
If they match, you are safe, if they do not then something has gone
wrong somewhere. In particular, be careful not to mix up within-
subjects and between-subjects factors. You will have noticed that
the tables used throughout this book usually have the factors and
levels fully labelled. Whenever you use computer software it is
important that you make use of these facilities where available.
Only when everything is clearly labelled can you hope to be able to
make sense of results.

Help, I feel a bit lost, what do I do?

If you are in this position, the golden rule is that complicated
designs can be difficult to interpret, and you must avoid designing
an experiment that goes beyond your powers of interpretation. If
you do not like the look of three-way interactions, then do not use
a three-factor design, and don't be persuaded to use one by an
enthusiastic project supervisor. Keep the levels in each factor
under control. Avoid having three or more levels in any factor
unless you really have to. It is better to have simple data that
you can understand rather than complicated data that you cannot.

There are still plenty of research questions that can be answered by straightforward experimental designs and statistical tests. There is much to be said for using the simplest possible design and analysis in order to answer the questions of interest, whatever your level of understanding.

Whatever your design of project, think about how you intend to analyse it before you launch into collecting data. A couple of hours extra invested at the beginning could save you weeks of difficulty. Otherwise, you could find yourself in the awful position of having genuinely unanalysable data. More often, data turn out to be awkward to analyse, perhaps resulting in wasted time, having to learn new statistical tests at short notice that you did not realise you would need, or not being able to make use of data in the way that was intended. None of these is a satisfactory outcome, but with a bit of care and thought at the right time, you can completely protect yourself from them.

Finally, keep in mind the fact that despite some of the mathematics, deep down ANOVA is simply about deciding whether means are different. Big consistent differences are more likely to be real than small inconsistent differences; everything else is just window dressing. There is one important consequence of this: *the purpose of ANOVA is to compare means. If you don't know what the means are, then why are you using ANOVA?* Hence, a reader of a formal report is unlikely to be impressed by F ratios, degrees of freedom and error terms if the summary statistics are not presented.

Why have you mentioned one-tailed statistical tests only occasionally?

With a factorial ANOVA, one- and two-tailed tests often do not make any sense. Suppose you have a one-factor design with three levels. You expect A_1 to be greater then A_2 and you expect A_1 to be greater than A_3, but you are not sure about A_2 and A_3. One theory predicts that A_3 will be greater than A_2, the other predicts that A_2 will be greater than A_3. You cannot possibly have an F ratio that is both one- and two-tailed, and so all F ratios automatically test two-tailed hypotheses; you are looking for differences, and differences in any direction will be found to be significant. This does not stop you from making predictions of the direction of effects, it is just that these predictions will be tested with two-tailed tests.

You have not been consistent with your significance levels.
What are you working to – p < 0.05 or p < 0.01?

The advice to students is usually that they should choose a significance level before the data are collected and stick to it. They should either be conservative ($p < 0.01$) or lenient ($p < 0.05$). However, brief perusal through the journals will reveal that, typically, both levels may be reported in the same paper. The rationale behind this is that some differences are more crucial to a theory than others, and that some people prefer to be stringent while others prefer to be lenient. By reporting the exact significance level, a reader is being kept fully informed of the situation and can reach his or her own conclusions about the trustworthiness of the data. This means that, in general, psychologists report the level at which each difference is significant rather than adopting a criterion right from the start.

For within-subjects factors, you keep hinting at a choice
between pooled and individual error terms for following up
ANOVA: can I really get away with only using pooled error
terms?

This is a current controversy in ANOVA which is unlikely to be resolved in the near future. Psychology journals appear to be agnostic on this issue, but, like all other areas, opinions change with time. The pooled error term approach is simple, especially for follow-up tests, and most of the time gives the same overall answer as the individual error term approach. It is possible to find data where the choice of error term does make a difference, but it is not clear how often the two approaches will give different answers, nor is it clear, when answers differ, which is correct. Overall, we recommend the pooled error term approach for undergraduate project work, unless computer software prohibits this, or makes the individual error term approach easy. For ANOVA by hand, the pooled error term approach is almost essential, although a good spreadsheet package can simplify the work. Opinions vary as to just how inaccurate the pooled approach is likely to be in real life. The extent to which the use of pooled error terms raises the likelihood of making a statistical error to an unacceptable degree, if at all, is far from clear. Even if two individually calculated error terms differ from each other, it is hard to tell whether or not this is a genuine difference which exists in the population. If the difference is not genuine then, in fact, the individual error terms are *less accurate* than a pooled error term.

My tutor disagrees with one of your rules of thumb, who is right?

The problem with many statistics books is that they often flip rapidly from mathematical precision to subjective opinions, and an inexperienced reader can find this disorientating. For example, when discussing limits on planned comparisons, many books simply advise readers 'not to make too many' – whatever this means! This is not helpful to readers, and we have tried to make clear suggestions whenever possible. These are not objective truths, but at least they ensure consistency between pieces of work. Instructors are welcome to disagree with our suggestions, and the best strategy for students is to accept the advice of the instructor and also try to understand why different people disagree with each other on which statistical technique to use.

Why haven't you included the XXX test?

Lack of space prevents a full discussion of every single ANOVA technique as applied to every possible design, and readers without computers may find themselves having to make educated guesses from time to time. This book cannot give the right answer to every question, but aims for a level of understanding at which readers will be able to make their own decisions. For some topics, it is not clear that all the possible options are even necessary; there are very many *post-hoc* tests, for example. We have also excluded more involved ANOVA techniques such as Multivariate Analysis of Variance (MANOVA) and Analysis of Covariance (ANCOVA). These are all topics for another book and another research methods course.

Which computer packages do you recommend?

One of the major findings in the problem-solving literature is that people are more likely to draw analogies to solve new problems if they have had several different related past experiences. In other words, the more packages that you become familiar with, the more likely that you will be able to adapt to a new piece of software quickly. Sticking to a single package is unlikely to be a good idea; packages tend to have a range of strengths and weaknesses. Performing the same analysis twice on an important piece of data with two different packages will do much to confirm that the analysis has in fact been performed correctly. Computer packages do get things wrong, it is not always possible to test every combination of options, and so you should always be wary of new packages and shareware. However, even the major programs have been known to make occasional errors. The answer to this question is therefore somewhat vague: we recommend as many different packages as possible!

In one chapter, you urge readers not to run an experiment with a cell size fewer than eight scores, but most of your examples break your own advice. Why?

For all of the worked examples in this book, we have used designs with small numbers of scores. With real data, Sums of Squares can often reach ten digits or more, and the effort required to be accurate at calculations distracts people from how and why the calculations are working. In terms of sample size, the examples therefore do not represent good experimental practice, and readers should not treat them as such. With small sample sizes, single subjects can make the difference between a significant and a non-significant effect, and this is not a satisfactory state of affairs.

Appendix A

Writing up the results of Analysis of Variance

Before giving suggestions about writing up the results of Analysis of Variance, the following point needs to be emphasised: the purpose of ANOVA is to help you decide whether or not a set of means differs due to treatment effects (as opposed to experimental error). Thus, if you (or the reader) do not know what the means are, there is no point in reporting any ANOVA findings. *F*s are not a substitute for means, so always calculate and scrutinise cell and level means and their standard deviations before you interpret your data.

Reporting the results of an ANOVA: preliminaries

Before reporting the results of any statistical test, remember that the results section *must* begin with a description of how you treated your data. For example, did you exclude certain types of response or exclude certain subjects, did you transform the data, did you analyse means or medians of individuals? This must always be followed by descriptive statistics – means *and* standard deviations for each of the levels or cells. *Descriptive statistics should always be included before the statistical tests.*

When talking about the actual levels, give them meaningful names. Only statisticians use notation like A_1, A_2, A_3, and so on. For a real experiment, your report will be far easier to follow if you talk about, for example, the difference between the means of the mnemonic group and the no-mnemonic group rather than the difference between the means of levels A_1 and A_2. Hence you are not advised to use *any* statistical notation in a report.

Reporting the results of a single-factor design

Whether your factor was within or between subjects, the overall formatting of the results section will be the same. Between-subjects designs have been used for the examples here. After beginning with a general description of data treatment followed by the table of means and standard deviations, Box A1 shows how to state the main ANOVA finding. The first paragraph describes a significant effect, the second paragraph describes a non-significant effect.

Note that you *must* include the degrees of freedom – the figures in brackets – your F value and the significance level. Some journals require writers to include the error terms used to test each F ratio, and the way in which to format these will be shown later. This is particularly important for within-subjects factors where there is sometimes disagreement on which is the best error term to use.

If your ANOVA has just one factor with only two levels, no further analysis would be required after the initial F ratio, and you would round off with a sentence saying what the statistical results mean in English. For example, that subjects in one condition were on average faster (or slower or better) than subjects in the other. *The ANOVA table itself should not appear in the body of the report.*

If you used planned comparisons to follow up the initial ANOVA finding, then after giving a description of how you treated the data, the means and standard deviations and your preliminary ANOVA findings, you would report the results of the planned comparisons. The third paragraph in Box A1 shows this and is based upon the Computer Aided Learning data discussed in Chapter 6. For any study in which planned comparisons are to be conducted, whether linear contrast analysis or pairwise comparisons, it is essential that the reader has some form of prior warning of which tests to expect. This expectation can come from ending an introduction section with an explicit outline of the tests to be performed, or, at the very least, a clear description of predictions so that the reader knows implicitly what to expect.

After giving all of the relevant analyses, you then need to round off the results section by saying what the results of the statistical tests mean in English (fourth paragraph in Box A1). You would discuss the implications of your results and why they came out the way that they did, etc., in the *discussion* section.

If you used *post-hoc* tests (e.g. Tukey or Newman–Keuls) to follow up the ANOVA, you would start off with a description of preliminary treatment of your data as before, including the table of means and standard deviations, then give your preliminary ANOVA result, and next give the results of the *post-hoc* test and say what they mean in English. This is shown in the fifth paragraph in Box A1, the figures are based upon the cough mixture study described in Chapter 6.

Box A1 Writing up a single-factor ANOVA

Begin with data treatment and summary statistics, then:

1 For a significant effect

Using a single-factor between-subjects ANOVA, the differences between the means were found to be significant: $F(2,27) = 8.44$, $p < 0.05$.

2 For a non-significant effect

Using a single-factor between-subjects ANOVA, the differences between the means were found to be non-significant: $F(2,27) = 1.44$, $p > 0.05$.

If the ANOVA has more than two levels, then follow-up tests will be required.

3 For planned comparisons

Using t-tests to make the planned comparisons described in the introduction, the difference in means between the LT and LCAL conditions was found to be non-significant ($t(27) = 0.28$, $p > 0.05$) while the difference in means between the LCAL and L conditions was significant ($t(27) = 2.12$, $p < 0.05$). An additional *Scheffé* test was performed to compare the means of the LCAL and LT conditions, but this difference was found not to be significant ($p > 0.05$).

4 The results should then be translated into English

Thus, there was no difference in exam marks between the Lectures/Tutorial support group and the Lectures/Computer Aided Learning group, but the exam marks of the Lectures/Computer Aided Learning group were higher than the Lectures only group. There was not sufficient evidence to show that the Lectures/Tutorial support group was superior to the Lectures only group.

5 If a post-hoc test has been used

Using a single-factor between-subjects ANOVA, the differences between the means were found to be significant: $F(3,36) = 10.2, p < 0.05$. The Tukey test was used to make pairwise comparisions between all of the means. All means differed from all other means ($p < 0.05$) except for the means of the placebo group and the drug 1 group ($p > 0.05$). Hence, drug 2 degraded performance the most, followed by drug 3. Drug 1 degraded performance the least, if at all, and was equivalent to the placebo.

Reporting the results of a two-factor design

Two-factor designs should be written up in a similar way irrespective of whether they are fully between subjects, fully within subjects or mixed, *but make sure that you do not mix up the degrees of freedom.* The overall format is to begin with the data preliminaries and the table of means/standard deviations, then to continue with the three F values – for the two main effects and their interaction – and next, if the interaction is significant, to describe the results of analysing the simple main effects, etc. If you have tested all simple main effects when analysing an interaction, all these should be reported, including the non-significant ones. You must not pick your favourite results from the analyses performed, unless they were planned in advance. Although graphs can help make a pattern of results clearer, you should not include an interaction plot in your results section unless the interaction is significant.

Box A2 shows a full results section for the expertise example discussed in Chapter 11; note that error terms have been reported for each *F* ratio. This is important so that the reader can see whether or not pooled error terms have been used.

Box *A2* **Specimen results section for the expertise study in Chapter 11**

Results

For each subject, the total memory scores for real and random positions were calculated separately. Means and standard deviations for the four conditions are given in Table 1.

Table 1 Mean number of board conditions correctly reconstructed

	Real positions	Random positions
Expert	8.6 (2.4)	3.0 (1.6)
Novice	3.4 (1.1)	3.4 (1.3)

Standard deviations are shown in brackets

A 2×2 mixed design Analysis of Variance was used to analyse the data. There was a significant main effect of expertise ($F(1,8) = 16.5$, $MS_e = 1.75$, $p < 0.01$) and a significant main effect of position type ($F(1,8) = 23.1$, $MS_e = 1.70$, $p < 0.01$). However, the interaction was also significant ($F(1,8) = 23.1$, $MS_e = 1.70$, $p < 0.01$).

Looking at the simple main effects, there was a significant effect of expertise for real positions showing that experts performed better than novices ($F(1,16) = 39.2$, $MS_e = 1.73$, $p < 0.01$) but not for random positions

($F(1,16) = 0.23$, $MS_e = 1.73$, $p > 0.05$). There was also a significant effect of material type for experts showing that real positions were easier to remember than random positions ($F(1,8) = 46.1$, $MS_e = 1.70$, $p < 0.01$) but not for novices ($F(1,8) = 0$, $MS_e = 1.70$, $p > 0.05$).

Hence, experts were found to have a better memory than novices only for real positions, and only the experts found real positions easier to remember than random positions. This is illustrated in Figure 1.

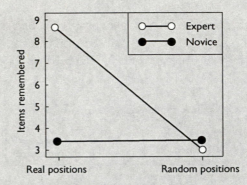

Figure 1 Graph of mean performance at the memory task

Box A3 shows a full results section for the letter deletion example discussed in Chapter 11. Note that we have not mentioned any corrections to the significance level due to making multiple comparisons, the reason for this is that every single effect is significant at the 1% level of significance, so that in effect the comparisons have corrected themselves.

***Box A3* Specimen results section for the letter deletion study in Chapter 11**

Results

For each subject, the total number of *t*s that were failed to be deleted were found for each of the six conditions.

Overall mean performance and standard deviations are given in Table 1.

Table 1 Mean number of missed letters for each condition

	High frequency words	Medium frequency words	Low frequency words
Prose passage	6.0 (1.6)	3.0 (1.7)	3.0 (0.6)
Scrambled passage	1.8 (1.2)	2.0 (1.4)	2.5 (1.2)

Standard deviations are shown in brackets

A 2×3 within-subjects Analysis of Variance was used to analyse the data. There was a significant main effect of passage type ($F(1,5) = 62.8$, $MS_e = 0.51$, $p < 0.01$) and no significant main effect of word frequency ($F(2,10) = 3.90$, $MS_e = 1.76$, $p > 0.05$). The interaction was significant ($F(2,10) = 7.60$, $MS_e = 1.56$, $p < 0.01$).

Looking at the simple main effects, there was a significant effect of passage type for high frequency words showing that more letters were missed for these prose words than their scrambled controls ($F(1,5) = 101.9$, $MS_e = 0.51$, $p < 0.01$) but not for medium or low frequency words ($F(1,5) = 5.90$ and 1.47 respectively, $MS_e = 0.51$, $p > 0.05$). There was a significant effect of word frequency for the prose passage, showing that different word frequencies were related to different numbers of errors ($F(2,10) = 10.2$, $MS_e = 1.76$, $p < 0.01$) but there was no significant effect for the scrambled passage ($F(2,10) = 0.41$, $MS_e = 1.76$, $p > 0.05$).

Tukey HSD pairwise comparisons were used to compare the means for the prose passage. Significantly more letters were missed for high frequency words than for medium frequency words ($p < 0.01$) and for high frequency words than for low frequency words ($p < 0.01$). There was no significant difference between medium and low frequency words for the prose passage ($p > 0.05$).

Hence, more letters were missed for high frequency words than medium or low frequency words in the prose passage. There were no differences between prose and scrambled passages except for the high frequency words, where significantly fewer letters were deleted in the prose passage compared with their controls in the scrambled passage. These patterns of performance are shown in Figure 1.

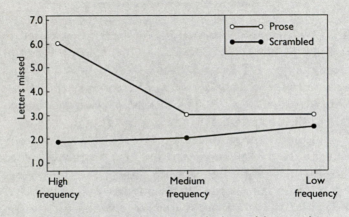

Figure 1 Graph of mean performance at the letter deletion task

Writing up the results of a three-factor design

Three-factor designs are potentially more complicated and need more care than two-factor designs. However, the overall style is similar, so that significance tests for main effects and interactions must all be reported with F ratios, degrees of freedom, p values and, if required, error terms. Again, the order of description is the same, so begin with summary statistics, then summarise the main ANOVA table, next describe follow-up tests for interactions, then report graphs, and finally translate the results into English.

Reporting the effects from the main ANOVA table is cumbersome rather than difficult. A three-factor design has seven different F values on the main ANOVA table: three main effects, three two-way interactions and one three-way interaction. Although you can report all these if you wish, if the three-way interaction is significant you can probably get away with reporting only the three main effects and the three-way interaction, ignoring the two-way interactions, which the three-way interaction renders superfluous.

You would then report the results of follow-up tests, either on the different two-way interactions, if the three-way interaction is not significant, or on everything if the three-way interaction is significant. The reader will require considerable help in understanding this section, so you should be careful to be explicit as to exactly which differences were tested with which follow-up tests. Visual presentation of interactions is particularly important for a three-way ANOVA. A three-way interaction will always need at least two graphs to display it. It is helpful to the reader if both graphs have the same scale.

Reporting a results section with transformed data

Reporting an experiment in which transformed data are analysed needs some care, and again the reader will need to know exactly what is happening. To illustrate this, we will analyse some imaginary problem solving data for a between-subjects design in which

Table A1 Imaginary data for a reasoning experiment

	A_1	A_2
	1	5
	2	10
	3	15
	3	15
	4	20
	5	25
Mean (minutes)	3.0	15.0
Standard deviation	1.41	7.07
Variance	2.0	50.0
Degrees of freedom	4	4
Mean ÷ variance	1.5	0.3
Mean ÷ standard deviation	2.12	2.12

the dependent variable is the time in minutes necessary to solve a reasoning task. The raw data are given in Table A1. As you can see, the variances differ somewhat between the groups, so that if we apply the test of homogeneity of variance discussed in Chapter 5, we find that dividing the larger variance by the smaller variance gives an F value of 25, which with (4,4) degrees of freedom is significant, $p < 0.01$. The groups differ significantly in their variance, and violate the homogeneity of variance assumption quite badly as a result. In one condition, people are much more similar to each other than in the other. If we divide the mean by the standard deviation for each group, we can see that the answer is the same in both cases. As discussed in Chapter 5, the most appropriate transformation in such circumstances is to take the logarithm of each data point and perform Analysis of Variance on these values. This is shown in Table A2.

Analysis of Variance should be performed on the new values, but tables of means should report the anti-log of the mean of the transformed data as well; this will be helpful to the reader. Box A4 shows a suitable results section for these data. In fact, transforming these data made no difference to the outcome: ANOVA on the original scores would give an F value of 16.6 with (1,10) degrees of freedom, and so transforming the data for this particular experiment does not really help and so it is not necessary. However, sometimes transforming data will make a difference and it is essential that, if this is performed, the reader is kept informed of what is happening.

Table A2 Transformed data for the reasoning experiment

	A_1	$log(A_1)$	A_2	$log(A_2)$
	1	0	5	0.70
	2	0.30	10	1.00
	3	0.48	15	1.18
	3	0.48	15	1.18
	4	0.60	20	1.30
	5	0.70	25	1.40
Mean (log_{10}(minutes))		0.42		1.13
Standard deviation		0.25		0.25
Variance		0.06		0.06
Anti-log(mean) (minutes)		2.7		13.3

Box A4 Specimen results section for the transformed data

Results

A preliminary analysis of the data showed that there was a large and significant difference in variance between the groups, $F(4,4) = 25.0$, $p < 0.01$. The data clearly violated the homogeneity of variance assumption. For the two groups, it was found that dividing the mean by the standard deviation gave a constant value, and this suggested that a logarithmic transform of the data would be appropriate. Table 1 shows means and standard deviations for the natural data, means and standard deviations for the transformed data, and means of the transformed data after conversion back to the original scale of measurement.

Table 1 Summary statistics for performance at the reasoning task. Original units are minutes, transformed units are $\log_{10}$(minutes)

	Easy problems	Hard problems
Mean of natural data	3.0	15.0
SD	1.41	7.07
Mean of transformed data	0.42	1.13
SD	0.25	0.25
Mean of transformed data (original scale)	2.7	13.3

A between-subjects Analysis of Variance was performed on the transformed data points. There was a significant difference between the means, $F(1,10) = 24.0$, $p < 0.01$. Hence, the prediction that certain types of problem should be harder than others was confirmed.

Appendix B
Statistical tables

F tables	245
t table	252
Weights (coefficients) for orthogonal polynomial trend contrasts	254
Studentized range statistic (q) tables, e.g. for the Tukey test	255
Z table	256

F tables

The tables below give the critical values of F for significance levels of $p = 0.05$ and $p = 0.01$. The null hypothesis is rejected if the obtained value of the F ratio is larger than the critical value for the appropriate number of degrees of freedom. Numerator (effect) degrees of freedom are displayed along the top row. Denominator (error term) degrees of freedom are displayed in the first column on the left-hand side.

Significance level of $p = 0.05$

df denominator	df numerator									
	1	2	3	4	5	6	7	8	9	10
1	161.4	199.5	215.7	224.6	230.2	234.0	236.8	238.9	240.5	241.8
2	18.5	19.0	19.2	19.2	19.3	19.3	19.4	19.4	19.4	19.40
3	10.1	9.55	9.28	9.12	9.01	8.94	8.89	8.85	8.81	8.79
4	7.71	6.94	6.59	6.39	6.26	6.16	6.09	6.04	6.00	5.96
5	6.61	5.79	5.41	5.19	5.05	4.95	4.88	4.82	4.77	4.74
6	5.99	5.14	4.76	4.53	4.39	4.28	4.21	4.15	4.10	4.06
7	5.59	4.74	4.35	4.12	3.97	3.87	3.79	3.73	3.68	3.64
8	5.32	4.46	4.07	3.84	3.69	3.58	3.50	3.44	3.39	3.35
9	5.12	4.26	3.86	3.63	3.48	3.37	3.29	3.23	3.18	3.14
10	4.96	4.10	3.71	3.48	3.33	3.22	3.14	3.07	3.02	2.98
11	4.84	3.98	3.59	3.36	3.20	3.09	3.01	2.95	2.90	2.85
12	4.75	3.89	3.49	3.26	3.11	3.00	2.91	2.85	2.80	2.75
13	4.67	3.81	3.41	3.18	3.03	2.92	2.83	2.77	2.71	2.67
14	4.60	3.74	3.34	3.11	2.96	2.85	2.76	2.70	2.65	2.60
15	4.54	3.68	3.29	3.06	2.90	2.79	2.71	2.64	2.59	2.54
16	4.49	3.63	3.24	3.01	2.85	2.74	2.66	2.59	2.54	2.49
17	4.45	3.59	3.20	2.96	2.81	2.70	2.61	2.55	2.49	2.45
18	4.41	3.55	3.16	2.93	2.77	2.66	2.58	2.51	2.46	2.41
19	4.38	3.52	3.13	2.90	2.74	2.63	2.54	2.48	2.42	2.38
20	4.35	3.49	3.10	2.87	2.71	2.60	2.51	2.45	2.39	2.35

(cont.)

21	4.32	3.47	3.07	2.84	2.68	2.57	2.49	2.42	2.37	2.32
22	4.30	3.44	3.05	2.82	2.66	2.55	2.46	2.40	2.34	2.30
23	4.28	3.42	3.03	2.80	2.64	2.53	2.44	2.37	2.32	2.27
24	4.26	3.40	3.01	2.78	2.62	2.51	2.42	2.36	2.30	2.25
25	4.24	3.39	2.99	2.76	2.60	2.49	2.40	2.34	2.28	2.24
26	4.23	3.37	2.98	2.74	2.59	2.47	2.39	2.32	2.27	2.22
27	4.21	3.35	2.96	2.73	2.57	2.46	2.37	2.31	2.25	2.20
28	4.20	3.34	2.95	2.71	2.56	2.45	2.36	2.29	2.24	2.19
29	4.18	3.33	2.93	2.70	2.55	2.43	2.35	2.28	2.22	2.18
30	4.17	3.32	2.92	2.69	2.53	2.42	2.33	2.27	2.21	2.16
31	4.16	3.30	2.91	2.68	2.52	2.41	2.32	2.25	2.20	2.15
33	4.14	3.28	2.89	2.66	2.50	2.39	2.30	2.23	2.18	2.13
35	4.12	3.27	2.87	2.64	2.49	2.37	2.29	2.22	2.16	2.11
37	4.11	3.25	2.86	2.63	2.47	2.36	2.27	2.20	2.14	2.10
39	4.09	3.24	2.85	2.61	2.46	2.34	2.26	2.19	2.13	2.08
40	4.08	3.23	2.84	2.61	2.45	2.34	2.25	2.18	2.12	2.08
41	4.08	3.23	2.83	2.60	2.44	2.33	2.24	2.17	2.12	2.07
43	4.07	3.21	2.82	2.59	2.43	2.32	2.23	2.16	2.11	2.06
45	4.06	3.20	2.81	2.58	2.42	2.31	2.22	2.15	2.10	2.05
47	4.05	3.20	2.80	2.57	2.41	2.30	2.21	2.14	2.09	2.04
50	4.03	3.18	2.79	2.56	2.40	2.29	2.20	2.13	2.07	2.03

(cont.)

Significance level of $p = 0.05$ cont.

df denominator	df numerator 1	2	3	4	5	6	7	8	9	10
55	4.02	3.16	2.77	2.54	2.38	2.27	2.18	2.11	2.06	2.01
60	4.00	3.15	2.76	2.53	2.37	2.25	2.17	2.10	2.04	1.99
65	3.99	3.14	2.75	2.51	2.36	2.24	2.15	2.08	2.03	1.98
70	3.98	3.13	2.74	2.50	2.35	2.23	2.14	2.07	2.02	1.97
75	3.97	3.12	2.73	2.49	2.34	2.22	2.13	2.06	2.01	1.96
80	3.96	3.11	2.72	2.49	2.33	2.21	2.13	2.06	2.00	1.95
85	3.95	3.10	2.71	2.48	2.32	2.21	2.12	2.05	1.99	1.94
90	3.95	3.10	2.71	2.47	2.32	2.20	2.11	2.04	1.99	1.94
95	3.94	3.09	2.70	2.47	2.31	2.20	2.11	2.04	1.98	1.93
100	3.94	3.09	2.70	2.46	2.31	2.19	2.10	2.03	1.97	1.93
120	3.92	3.07	2.68	2.45	2.29	2.18	2.09	2.02	1.96	1.91
140	3.91	3.06	2.67	2.44	2.28	2.16	2.08	2.01	1.95	1.90
160	3.90	3.05	2.66	2.43	2.27	2.16	2.07	2.00	1.94	1.89
180	3.89	3.05	2.65	2.42	2.26	2.15	2.06	1.99	1.93	1.88
200	3.89	3.04	2.65	2.42	2.26	2.14	2.06	1.98	1.93	1.88
250	3.88	3.03	2.64	2.41	2.25	2.13	2.05	1.98	1.92	1.87
300	3.87	3.03	2.63	2.40	2.24	2.13	2.04	1.97	1.91	1.86
400	3.86	3.02	2.63	2.39	2.24	2.12	2.03	1.96	1.90	1.85
500	3.86	3.01	2.62	2.39	2.23	2.12	2.03	1.96	1.90	1.85
1000	3.85	3.00	2.61	2.38	2.22	2.11	2.02	1.95	1.89	1.84

Significance level of $p = 0.01$

df denominator	df numerator									
	1	2	3	4	5	6	7	8	9	10
1	4052	4999	5404	5624	5764	5859	5928	5981	6022	6056
2	98.5	99.0	99.2	99.3	99.3	99.3	99.4	99.4	99.4	99.4
3	34.1	30.8	29.5	28.7	28.2	27.9	27.7	27.5	27.3	27.2
4	21.2	18.0	16.7	16.0	15.5	15.2	15.0	14.8	14.7	14.5
5	16.3	13.3	12.1	11.4	11.0	10.7	10.5	10.3	10.2	10.1
6	13.7	10.9	9.78	9.15	8.75	8.47	8.26	8.10	7.98	7.87
7	12.2	9.55	8.45	7.85	7.46	7.19	6.99	6.84	6.72	6.62
8	11.3	8.65	7.59	7.01	6.63	6.37	6.18	6.03	5.91	5.81
9	10.6	8.02	6.99	6.42	6.06	5.80	5.61	5.47	5.35	5.26
10	10.0	7.56	6.55	5.99	5.64	5.39	5.20	5.06	4.94	4.85
11	9.65	7.21	6.22	5.67	5.32	5.07	4.89	4.74	4.63	4.54
12	9.33	6.93	5.95	5.41	5.06	4.82	4.64	4.50	4.39	4.30
13	9.07	6.70	5.74	5.21	4.86	4.62	4.44	4.30	4.19	4.10
14	8.86	6.51	5.56	5.04	4.69	4.46	4.28	4.14	4.03	3.94
15	8.68	6.36	5.42	4.89	4.56	4.32	4.14	4.00	3.89	3.80
16	8.53	6.23	5.29	4.77	4.44	4.20	4.03	3.89	3.78	3.69
17	8.40	6.11	5.19	4.67	4.34	4.10	3.93	3.79	3.68	3.59
18	8.29	6.01	5.09	4.58	4.25	4.01	3.84	3.71	3.60	3.51
19	8.18	5.93	5.01	4.50	4.17	3.94	3.77	3.63	3.52	3.43
20	8.10	5.85	4.94	4.43	4.10	3.87	3.70	3.56	3.46	3.37

(cont.)

Significance level of $p = 0.01$ cont.

df denominator	df numerator 1	2	3	4	5	6	7	8	9	10
21	8.02	5.78	4.87	4.37	4.04	3.81	3.64	3.51	3.40	3.31
22	7.95	5.72	4.82	4.31	3.99	3.76	3.59	3.45	3.35	3.26
23	7.88	5.66	4.76	4.26	3.94	3.71	3.54	3.41	3.30	3.21
24	7.82	5.61	4.72	4.22	3.90	3.67	3.50	3.36	3.26	3.17
25	7.77	5.57	4.68	4.18	3.85	3.63	3.46	3.32	3.22	3.13
26	7.72	5.53	4.64	4.14	3.82	3.59	3.42	3.29	3.18	3.09
27	7.68	5.49	4.60	4.11	3.78	3.56	3.39	3.26	3.15	3.06
28	7.64	5.45	4.57	4.07	3.75	3.53	3.36	3.23	3.12	3.03
29	7.60	5.42	4.54	4.04	3.73	3.50	3.33	3.20	3.09	3.00
30	7.56	5.39	4.51	4.02	3.70	3.47	3.30	3.17	3.07	2.98
31	7.53	5.36	4.48	3.99	3.67	3.45	3.28	3.15	3.04	2.96
33	7.47	5.31	4.44	3.95	3.63	3.41	3.24	3.11	3.00	2.91
35	7.42	5.27	4.40	3.91	3.59	3.37	3.20	3.07	2.96	2.88
37	7.37	5.23	4.36	3.87	3.56	3.33	3.17	3.04	2.93	2.84
39	7.33	5.19	4.33	3.84	3.53	3.30	3.14	3.01	2.90	2.81
40	7.31	5.18	4.31	3.83	3.51	3.29	3.12	2.99	2.89	2.80
41	7.30	5.16	4.30	3.81	3.50	3.28	3.11	2.98	2.87	2.79
43	7.26	5.14	4.27	3.79	3.48	3.25	3.09	2.96	2.85	2.76
45	7.23	5.11	4.25	3.77	3.45	3.23	3.07	2.94	2.83	2.74
47	7.21	5.09	4.23	3.75	3.43	3.21	3.05	2.92	2.81	2.72

(cont.)

50	7.17	5.06	4.20	3.72	3.41	3.19	3.02	2.89	2.78	2.70
55	7.12	5.01	4.16	3.68	3.37	3.15	2.98	2.85	2.75	2.66
60	7.08	4.98	4.13	3.65	3.34	3.12	2.95	2.82	2.72	2.63
65	7.04	4.95	4.10	3.62	3.31	3.09	2.93	2.80	2.69	2.61
70	7.01	4.92	4.07	3.60	3.29	3.07	2.91	2.78	2.67	2.59
75	6.99	4.90	4.05	3.58	3.27	3.05	2.89	2.76	2.65	2.57
80	6.96	4.88	4.04	3.56	3.26	3.04	2.87	2.74	2.64	2.55
85	6.94	4.86	4.02	3.55	3.24	3.02	2.86	2.73	2.62	2.54
90	6.93	4.85	4.01	3.53	3.23	3.01	2.84	2.72	2.61	2.52
95	6.91	4.84	3.99	3.52	3.22	3.00	2.83	2.70	2.60	2.51
100	6.90	4.82	3.98	3.51	3.21	2.99	2.82	2.69	2.59	2.50
120	6.85	4.79	3.95	3.48	3.17	2.96	2.79	2.66	2.56	2.47
140	6.82	4.76	3.92	3.46	3.15	2.93	2.77	2.64	2.54	2.45
160	6.80	4.74	3.91	3.44	3.13	2.92	2.75	2.62	2.52	2.43
180	6.78	4.73	3.89	3.43	3.12	2.90	2.74	2.61	2.51	2.42
200	6.76	4.71	3.88	3.41	3.11	2.89	2.73	2.60	2.50	2.41
250	6.74	4.69	3.86	3.40	3.09	2.87	2.71	2.58	2.48	2.39
300	6.72	4.68	3.85	3.38	3.08	2.86	2.70	2.57	2.47	2.38
400	6.70	4.66	3.83	3.37	3.06	2.85	2.68	2.56	2.45	2.37
500	6.69	4.65	3.82	3.36	3.05	2.84	2.68	2.55	2.44	2.36
1000	6.66	4.63	3.80	3.34	3.04	2.82	2.66	2.53	2.43	2.34

The values entered in these tables were computed by the authors.

t table

The table below gives the critical values of *t* for various significance levels (one-tailed or two-tailed). The null hypothesis is rejected if the observed *t* score is larger than the critical value for the appropriate number of degrees of freedom. Degrees of freedom are displayed in the first column on the left-hand side.

df	$p = 0.05$ (one-tail) $p = 0.10$ (two-tail)	$p = 0.025$ (one-tail) $p = 0.05$ (two-tail)	$p = 0.0125$ (one-tail) $p = 0.025$ (two-tail)	$p = 0.005$ (one-tail) $p = 0.01$ (two-tail)
1	6.31	12.71	25.45	63.66
2	2.92	4.30	6.21	9.92
3	2.35	3.18	4.18	5.84
4	2.13	2.78	3.50	4.60
5	2.02	2.57	3.16	4.03
6	1.94	2.45	2.97	3.71
7	1.89	2.36	2.84	3.50
8	1.86	2.31	2.75	3.36
9	1.83	2.26	2.69	3.25
10	1.81	2.23	2.63	3.17
11	1.80	2.20	2.59	3.11
12	1.78	2.18	2.56	3.05
13	1.77	2.16	2.53	3.01
14	1.76	2.14	2.51	2.98
15	1.75	2.13	2.49	2.95
16	1.75	2.12	2.47	2.92
17	1.74	2.11	2.46	2.90
18	1.73	2.10	2.45	2.88
19	1.73	2.09	2.43	2.86
20	1.72	2.09	2.42	2.85
21	1.72	2.08	2.41	2.83
22	1.72	2.07	2.41	2.82
23	1.71	2.07	2.40	2.81
24	1.71	2.06	2.39	2.80
25	1.71	2.06	2.38	2.79
26	1.71	2.06	2.38	2.78
27	1.70	2.05	2.37	2.77
28	1.70	2.05	2.37	2.76
29	1.70	2.05	2.36	2.76
30	1.70	2.04	2.36	2.75

(cont.)

df	p = 0.05 (one-tail) p = 0.10 (two-tail)	p = 0.025 (one-tail) p = 0.05 (two-tail)	p = 0.0125 (one-tail) p = 0.025 (two-tail)	p = 0.005 (one-tail) p = 0.01 (two-tail)
31	1.70	2.04	2.36	2.74
33	1.69	2.03	2.35	2.73
35	1.69	2.03	2.34	2.72
37	1.69	2.03	2.34	2.72
39	1.68	2.02	2.33	2.71
40	1.68	2.02	2.33	2.70
41	1.68	2.02	2.33	2.70
43	1.68	2.02	2.32	2.70
45	1.68	2.01	2.32	2.69
47	1.68	2.01	2.32	2.68
50	1.68	2.01	2.31	2.68
55	1.67	2.00	2.30	2.67
60	1.67	2.00	2.30	2.66
65	1.67	2.00	2.29	2.65
70	1.67	1.99	2.29	2.65
75	1.67	1.99	2.29	2.64
80	1.66	1.99	2.28	2.64
85	1.66	1.99	2.28	2.63
90	1.66	1.99	2.28	2.63
95	1.66	1.99	2.28	2.63
100	1.66	1.98	2.28	2.63
120	1.66	1.98	2.27	2.62
140	1.66	1.98	2.27	2.61
160	1.65	1.97	2.26	2.61
180	1.65	1.97	2.26	2.60
200	1.65	1.97	2.26	2.60
300	1.65	1.97	2.25	2.59
400	1.65	1.97	2.25	2.59
500	1.65	1.96	2.25	2.59
1000	1.65	1.96	2.24	2.58

The values entered in this table were computed by the authors.

Weights (coefficients) for orthogonal polynomial trend contrasts

Number of levels	Type of trend	Ordered levels of the experimental design							
		1	2	3	4	5	6	7	8
2	Linear	−1	1						
3	Linear	−1	0	1					
	Quadratic	1	−2	1					
4	Linear	−3	−1	1	3				
	Quadratic	1	−1	−1	1				
5	Linear	−2	−1	0	1	2			
	Quadratic	2	−1	−2	−1	2			
6	Linear	−5	−3	−1	1	3	5		
	Quadratic	5	−1	−4	−4	−1	5		
7	Linear	−3	−2	−1	0	1	2	3	
	Quadratic	5	0	−3	−4	−3	0	5	
8	Linear	−7	−5	−3	−1	1	3	5	7
	Quadratic	7	1	−3	−5	−5	−3	1	7

Studentized range statistic (q) tables, e.g. for the Tukey test

Entries are the critical values for the relevant number of means (the r value) and the degrees of freedom.

Table 1 Significance level of $p = 0.05$

df error	Number of means 2	3	4	5	6	7	8	9	10
8	3.26	4.04	4.53	4.89	5.17	5.40	5.60	5.77	5.92
10	3.15	3.88	4.33	4.65	4.91	5.12	5.31	5.46	5.60
12	3.08	3.77	4.20	4.51	4.75	4.95	5.12	5.26	5.40
14	3.03	3.70	4.11	4.41	4.64	4.83	4.99	5.13	5.25
16	3.00	3.65	4.05	4.33	4.56	4.74	4.90	5.03	5.15
18	2.97	3.61	4.00	4.28	4.50	4.67	4.82	4.96	5.07
20	2.95	3.58	3.96	4.23	4.44	4.62	4.77	4.90	5.01
24	2.92	3.53	3.90	4.17	4.37	4.54	4.68	4.81	4.92
30	2.89	3.49	3.84	4.10	4.30	4.46	4.60	4.72	4.82
40	2.86	3.44	3.79	4.04	4.23	4.39	4.52	4.64	4.74
60	2.83	3.40	3.74	3.98	4.16	4.31	4.44	4.55	4.65
120	2.80	3.36	3.69	3.92	4.10	4.24	4.36	4.47	4.56
Infinity	2.77	3.31	3.63	3.86	4.03	4.17	4.29	4.39	4.47

Table 2 Significance level of $p = 0.01$

df error	Number of means 2	3	4	5	6	7	8	9	10
8	4.75	5.64	6.20	6.62	6.96	7.24	7.47	7.68	7.86
10	4.48	5.27	5.77	6.14	6.43	6.67	6.88	7.06	7.21
12	4.32	5.05	5.50	5.84	6.10	6.32	6.51	6.67	6.81
14	4.21	4.90	5.32	5.63	5.88	6.09	6.26	6.41	6.54
16	4.13	4.79	5.19	5.49	5.72	5.92	6.08	6.35	5.15
18	4.07	4.70	5.09	5.38	5.60	5.79	5.94	6.08	6.20
20	4.02	4.64	5.02	5.29	5.51	5.69	5.84	5.97	6.09
24	3.96	4.55	4.91	5.17	5.37	5.54	5.69	5.81	5.92
30	3.89	4.46	4.80	5.05	5.24	5.40	5.54	5.65	5.76
40	3.83	4.37	4.70	4.93	5.11	5.27	5.39	5.50	5.60
60	3.76	4.28	4.60	4.82	4.99	5.13	5.25	5.36	5.45
120	3.70	4.20	4.50	4.71	4.87	5.00	5.12	5.21	5.30
Infinity	3.64	4.12	4.40	4.60	4.76	4.88	4.99	5.08	5.16

The entries in these tables were adapted from L. H. Harter (1960) 'Tables of range and studentized range', *Annals of Mathematical Statistics* 31: 1122–1147, with the permission of the publisher.

Z table

The table below gives the cumulative probability values for normal Z standard deviation scores. The cumulative probability attached to each Z score is equivalent to the area underneath the normal curve from minus infinity to each Z score. The critical values of Z for a significant level of $p = 0.05$ (two-tailed) are -1.96 and $+1.96$. The critical values of Z for a significant level of $p = 0.01$ (two-tailed) are -2.576 and $+2.576$.

Z score	Cumulative p value	Z score	Cumulative p value
−4.768	0.000001	−0.915	0.18
−4.265	0.00001	−0.878	0.19
−3.719	0.0001	−0.842	0.20
−3.540	0.0002	−0.806	0.21
−3.432	0.0003	−0.772	0.22
−3.290	0.0005	−0.739	0.23
−3.239	0.0006	−0.706	0.24
−3.195	0.0007	−0.674	0.25
−3.156	0.0008	−0.643	0.26
−3.121	0.0009	−0.613	0.27
−3.090	0.001	−0.583	0.28
−2.878	0.002	−0.553	0.29
−2.748	0.003	−0.524	0.30
−2.652	0.004	−0.496	0.31
−2.576	0.005	−0.468	0.32
−2.326	0.01	−0.440	0.33
−2.054	0.02	−0.412	0.34
−1.960	0.025	−0.385	0.35
−1.881	0.03	−0.358	0.36
−1.751	0.04	−0.332	0.37
−1.645	0.05	−0.305	0.38
−1.555	0.06	−0.279	0.39
−1.476	0.07	−0.253	0.40
−1.405	0.08	−0.228	0.41
−1.341	0.09	−0.202	0.42
−1.282	0.10	−0.176	0.43
−1.227	0.11	−0.151	0.44
−1.175	0.12	−0.126	0.45
−1.126	0.13	−0.100	0.46
−1.080	0.14	−0.075	0.47
−1.036	0.15	−0.050	0.48
−0.994	0.16	−0.025	0.49
−0.954	0.17	0.000	0.50

(cont.)

Z score	Cumulative p value	Z score	Cumulative p value
0.025	0.51	0.994	0.84
0.050	0.52	1.036	0.85
0.075	0.53	1.080	0.86
0.100	0.54	1.126	0.87
0.126	0.55	1.175	0.88
0.151	0.56	1.227	0.89
0.176	0.57	1.282	0.90
0.202	0.58	1.341	0.91
0.228	0.59	1.405	0.92
0.253	0.60	1.476	0.93
0.279	0.61	1.555	0.94
0.305	0.62	1.645	0.95
0.332	0.63	1.751	0.96
0.358	0.64	1.881	0.97
0.385	0.65	1.960	0.975
0.412	0.66	2.054	0.98
0.440	0.67	2.326	0.99
0.468	0.68	2.576	0.995
0.496	0.69	2.652	0.996
0.524	0.70	2.748	0.997
0.553	0.71	2.878	0.998
0.583	0.72	3.090	0.999
0.613	0.73	3.121	0.9991
0.643	0.74	3.156	0.9992
0.674	0.75	3.195	0.9993
0.706	0.76	3.239	0.9994
0.739	0.77	3.290	0.9995
0.772	0.78	3.353	0.9996
0.806	0.79	3.432	0.9997
0.842	0.80	3.540	0.9998
0.878	0.81	3.719	0.9999
0.915	0.82	4.265	0.99999
0.954	0.83	4.768	0.999999

The values entered in this table were computed by the authors.

Notes

3 Using variance to test hypotheses

1 Strictly speaking, this is not quite true. More accurately, we need to say that: as the within-group variance *approaches* zero, F will *approach* infinity.

6 Following up a one-factor between-subjects ANOVA

1 It is also possible to compare overall means between combinations of groups, for example the performance of one group with the overall performance of two or more other groups. Thus, I could have compared the mean of the LCAL-group with the combined means of the other two groups. With this study, it would be inadvisable. Suppose the L-group was much worse than the LCAL-group and the LT-group was much better than the LCAL-group, overall these properties of the L-group and the LT-group would cancel each other out and, when combined, their means would appear to be identical to the LCAL-group. These more complicated analyses that may be performed will be discussed later in the chapter.

2 *Post-hoc* tests are also used when there is no intention to compare specific pairs of means, and instead every mean is to be compared with every other mean. They may also be used instead of *t*-tests with the Bonferroni adjustment if you intend to make many planned comparisons.

3 There are other Tukey tests that are not described here that you might encounter.

4 Technically, the word *focused* refers to statistical tests based upon one degree of freedom.

7 Calculating *F* ratios for one-factor within-subjects designs

1 Sometimes different subjects may be matched in pairs or triplets (e.g. on the basis of intelligence). If the scores on the dependent variable of the members of the pairs or triplets are related to each other, i.e. they are

correlated, then these data can also be analysed by using a within-subjects design.

2 In theory, an even more stringent assumption, known as *compound symmetry*, should be applied, but in practice this assumption is too stringent and so the sphericity is accepted as the assumption instead.

8 An introduction to factorial designs and interactions

1 This study is not an experiment in the strict sense of the word, the experimenter has not randomly manipulated expertise level, instead subjects have been *classified* according to their expertise level.

2 These differences would normally be tested for significance, and you will be shown how to do this in Chapters 10 and 11.

10 Following up a two-factor between-subjects ANOVA

1 If you have an experimental hypothesis in which not every simple main effect needs to be tested, then you should be making planned comparisons. In this case, as long as the comparisons were designated before any analysis was performed, and as long as the number of comparisons is one less than the number of cells, and is less than five in any case, then the analysis may proceed even if none of the F values is significant. If five or more planned comparisons are intended, then the Bonferroni adjustment should be applied, but the F ratio still need not be significant.

References

Cohen, J. (1988) *Statistical Power Analysis for the Behavioral Sciences* (2nd edn.), Hillsdale: Erlbaum.

Gaito, J. (1965) 'Unequal intervals and unequal *n* in trend analyses', *Psychological Bulletin* 63: 125–127.

Greenhouse, S. W. and Geisser, S. (1991) 'On methods in the analysis of profile data', *Psychometrika* 24: 95–112.

Howell, D. C. (1997) *Statistical Methods for Psychology* (4th edn.), Belmont, CA: Duxbury Press.

Keppel, G., Saufley, W. H., Jr. and Tokunaga, H. (1992) *Introduction to Design & Analysis: A Student's Handbook* (2nd edn.), New York: Freeman.

Kirk, R. E. (1982) *Experimental Design: Procedures for the Behavioral Science* (2nd edn.), Pacific Grove, CA: Brooks/Cole.

Maxwell, S. E. and Delaney, H. D. (1990) *Designing Experiments and Analyzing Data*, Pacific Grove, CA: Brooks/Cole.

Neave, H. R. and Worthington, P. L. (1988) *Distribution-Free Tests*, London: Unwin Hyman.

Rosenthal, R. and Rosnow, R. L. (1991) *Essential of Behavioral Research: Methods and Data Analysis* (2nd edn.), New York: McGraw-Hill.

Siegel, S. and Castellan, N. J., Jr. (1988) *Nonparametric Statistics for the Behavioral Sciences* (2nd edn.), New York: McGraw-Hill.

Wickens, T. D. (1995) *The Geometry of Multivariate Statistics*, Hillsdale: Erlbaum.

Index

analysis of covariance (ANCOVA) 231

analysis of variance (ANOVA): first principles of 31–40, 62, 112; limitations of 40; multivariate 231; non-parametric 72, 73–5, 132; *see also* assumptions; between-subjects designs; three-factor designs; two-factor designs; within-subjects designs

ANOVA tables 55–7, 61, 127–8, 165–7, 185, 204, 215, 220–1

arithmetic mean 10; *see also* cells; group means; means; population means; sample means

assumptions underlying analysis of variance 63, 69–75, 129–32

averages 10

basic ratios 58–61, 124, 159, 176, 207–9

between-subjects designs 3–4, 29, 42–4, 116, 133–6, 149, 153–7, 173–4, 188, 195; examples of 31–2, 102, 183–6

bias 4–5

bimodal data 11–13, 70–1

Bonferroni adjustment 88, 90, 93, 107, 181–2, 186, 188, 191, 207, 217, 223–9 *passim*, 258; with small sample size 218

Castellan, N. J. Jr. 72, 75

ceiling effects 5, 72, 75, 191–3

cells, cell means and cell sizes 136–7, 151, 228

central limit theorem 16, 62–5

classification variables 3, 70

Cohen, J. 28

compound symmetry 259

computer packages, use of 170–1, 196–7, 204, 227–8, 231–2

condition 30

confidence 6, 20, 28

contrast analysis *see* linear contrast analysis

counterbalancing 4, 109

degrees of freedom 14, 21, 39, 44, 52–6, 123–4, 127, 131, 161, 176, 201; definition of 52; for interactions 164–5; reporting of 57, 97, 234; residual 118–19, 125–6

Delaney, H. D. 120–30, 131, 197, 210

deletion of data, criteria for 80–1

dependent variables 2–3

design of experiments 3–4

deviation scores 14

dispersion 10; *see also* variability

distribution-free tests 7; *see also* non-parametric tests

distributions 10–13

diversity 35, 119; *see also* variability

equally sized groups 43, 47, 69–70,

94, 149; *see also* unbalanced designs
error 4, 31; *see also* experimental error; measurement error; random error; 'Type I' and 'Type II' errors
error rates, distributions of 72
error terms 37, 44, 57, 94–5, 116–19, 122, 127, 129, 161–2, 165, 188, 201, 204, 206, 223; multiple 195–6, 202, 218; reporting of 234; *see also* pooled error terms
experimental conditions 2–3, 33
experimental error 34–8, 44, 70, 111, 117, 157, 161
experiments, nature of 1–2, 259
extreme values: in data 78–81; of *F* ratio 38–9

F ratio 37–8, 42, 62–3, 153–71; calculation of 56–7, 64, 99–100, 110–33; extreme values of 38–9; meaning of a significant value 82–3; table of critical values 245–51
factorial designs 134–8, 148, 150–61, 165–6, 173–8, 182–3, 191, 224, 229; optimum complexity of 150–1; planning of 148–51
factors 30, 41
familywise Type I error 84–90 *passim*, 93, 106, 150, 180–1, 188, 217, 225
fatigue effects 4, 150
flat data 140–1
floor effects 5, 72, 75, 191–3
focused inferences and tests 98–9, 258
follow-up tests 82–5, 128–9, 150, 167, 172–93, 202, 223; summary of 224–7
Friedman One-Way Analysis of Variance by Ranks 132

Gaito, J. 109
Games–Howell correction 94
general linear model approach *see* unbalanced designs

graphs: three-dimensional 213; use in reports 236, 241; *see also* interaction plots
Greenhouse and Geisser correction 131–2, 210
group means, comparison of 22

histograms 10–13
homogeneity of variance assumption 63–4, 72–7, 129, 161, 242
Howell, D. C. 76, 92, 94, 128, 197, 210
Huynh–Feldt correction 131
hypotheses 5, 27; *see also* one-tailed tests; research hypotheses; statistical hypotheses; two-tailed tests

'independent-samples' *t*-test *see* *t*-test: between-subjects type
'independent subjects' design 3; *see also* between-subjects design
independent variables 2–3, 7, 30 *see also* factors
individual difference variability 114
individual differences 33–4, 37–8, 111
interaction 135, 139–51, 154–6, 172; analysis of simple designs 173–4; 'concealed' 148–50, 193; 'significant' 146–8, 151–2; with three or more levels 188, 199, 204, 211, 223, 225–6; with two or more factors 150–1; three-way 150–51, 211–12, 222, 226, 241
interaction plots 139–42, 197, 205, 217; with non-parallel lines 146, 185; reporting of 179, 236–7; scaling of 146–7, 151, 217; three levels in one factor 187, 191; for unusual types of interaction 155–6, 181–2
interpretation of results: in complex cases 228–9; problems and pitfalls in 70, 191–3; trade-off with complexity of design 150–1; for unbalanced

designs 170; for within-subjects
designs 128, 133
intuitive statistics 22

Keppel, G. 87
Kirk, R. E. 75, 102, 128, 130, 170,
197, 210
Kolmogorov–Smirnov test 72
Kruskal–Wallace One-Way
Analysis of Variance by Ranks 75

laboratory reports, preparation of
5, 233–43
level 30, 41
linear contrast analysis 83, 92,
98–107, 128, 182, 199, 204, 212,
223, 226, 234; directional
hypotheses in 108
linear trends 101, 103–4, 107–8
logarithmic transformation of data
77, 242

main effects 137–43, 151–4, 166, 172,
195; in complex cases 212, 223,
226; see also simple main effects
Mann–Whitney test 8, 75
Maxwell, S. E. 128–30, 131, 197, 210
Mean Square 55–6, 64–8;
appropriateness of using 69, 71,
229, 233; comparison of 28,
36–7, 43, 62, 92–100, 229;
weighted and unweighted
168–70; see also arithmetic
mean; pairwise comparisons;
variance: of sample means
measurement error 4, 34, 63
median 10, 72
mixed designs 194–9 passim, 210
mode 10
multiple comparisons, problem of
and adjustment for 31, 84–5, 87,
90, 92, 180, 207, 212, 238
multivariate analysis of variance
(MANOVA) 231

Neave, H. R. 8, 32, 75
Newman–Keuls test 93–4, 97–8,
225–6
non-parametric tests 7–8; see also

analysis of variance: non-
parametric
normal distribution 11–12, 24,
63–4, 70–1
null hypotheses 5–6, 18, 26–7, 62–3,
67–8, 92
number of subjects tested 28–9, 39;
see also equally sized groups

one-tailed tests 23–7, 108, 229
order effects 4, 70, 110
ordinal scales 76
orthogonal polynomial trend
contrasts, weights for 254
orthogonality 168–9
outliers in data 78–1
overlap between groups 32–3

p values 57, 131–2
'paired-means' t-test see t-test:
within-subjects type
pairwise comparisons 82–5, 93,
98–9, 103–5, 132, 134, 152–3,
173–4, 180–2, 188–91, 212–13,
223, 225, 234
parametric tests 7–8, 11, 69
Pearson's r correlation 8, 11
per-comparison significance level
188, 191
per-comparison Type 1 Error 84
planned comparisons 84–93, 98,
107, 128, 152, 182, 186–90, 199,
204, 206, 225–6, 231, 236, 259;
reporting of 234; see also
pairwise comparisons
pooled error terms 129–30, 197,
199, 213, 230–1
population means 16
populations 3, 14, 16
post-hoc tests 84–5, 90–7 passim,
128, 152, 188, 199, 204, 231,
234–5, 258; see also
Newman–Keuls test; Tukey test
practice effects 4
'protected' testing 88, 180–3

q tables 255
quadratic trends 101–7
quasi-experiments 2

r correlation 8, 11
random allocation of subjects 70 1
random error 4, 34, 37–8, 63–4, 111–12, 121
random error variance 115; *see also* residual variance
reaction times, data on 72, 78
reciprocal transformation of data 78–9
'related-means' *t*-test *see t*-test: within-subjects type
'related-samples' *t*-test *see t*-test: within-subjects type
'repeated measures' design 3; *see also* within-subjects design
reporting of results 170, 179, 186; *see also* writing up results
'research' hypotheses 5, 27
residual error *see* random error
residual variance 115–18, 121, 127, 194–5
robustness of tests 8, 69
rogue data 75
Rosenthal, R. 28
Rosnow, R. L. 28

sample means 16
sample size 149–50, 232
sampling 14, 17
Saufley, W. H. Jr. 87
Scheffé test 90–2
Siegel, S. 72, 75
significance levels 6, 21–2, 24, 88, 167, 180; choice of 230; as distinct from importance 28; exact 57; *see also* per-comparison significance level
simple main effects 143–4, 147, 152–6, 173–5, 180, 186–7, 197–201 *passim*, 204–6, 226
simple simple main effects 212–17, 226
skewness 11–12, 70–2, 78–9
Spearman correlation 8
sphericity 129–32, 210, 259
splitting of data 218–19, 222, 226
spurious results 36, 192
square root transformation of data 77

standard deviation 13–17, 23, 36, 44, 233
standard error 16–18
statistical hypotheses 5, 27
statistical power, concept of 27–9, 110, 149, 225
Stroop effect 120, 183
studentized range statistic 95, 206; tables of 255
Sum of Squares (SS) 14–15, 44–7, 51, 55–6, 58–60, 118–23 *passim*, 126, 161–4, 174–8, 201
summarising data 9–10
systematic errors 4

t table 21, 252–3
t-test 8, 11, 17–22, 134, 173, 182, 186, 188, 197, 223, 225–6; between-subjects type 20–2; one-sample type 18–19, 21; use and limitations of 30–1, 37; use in planned comparisons 85–90, 93, 98, 104, 128; within-subjects type 19, 21
tails of distributions 11, 78; *see also* one-tailed tests; two-tailed tests
three-factor designs 211–23, 226; reporting of 240–3
Tokunaga, H. 87
transformation of data 72, 74–81, 241–2; reporting of 79–80, 241–3
treatment of data, reporting of 233
treatment effects 33–4, 36, 38, 111–12, 117, 157, 161
treatment variables 2
trend, consistency in 112–18
trend analysis 100–9; with unequally-spaced intervals 109
Tukey test 93–5, 98, 128, 182–3, 188, 190, 199, 206, 223, 225–6, 258; *see also* studentized range statistic
two-factor designs 194–210; reporting of 236–40
two-tailed tests 23–7
'Type I' and 'Type II' errors 6–7, 20–1, 69, 71–2, 84, 93, 99, 131–2, 149; *see also* familywise Type I error

unbalanced designs 168–70
unfocused ANOVA *see* focused
  inferences and tests
'unpaired means' *t*-test *see* *t*-test:
  between-subjects type
'unprotected' tests *see* 'protected'
  testing
'unrelated-means' *t*-test *see* *t*-tests:
  between-subjects type

variability: of data 13–15, 32–3, 43;
  as distinct from variance 37, 43;
  see also dispersion; diversity
variance 13–14, 37–8, 43–4, 55–6;
  between-subjects 114;
  calculation with more than two
  levels 55; general equations for
  calculation of 60; of sample
  means 63, 65; within and
  between groups 38, 44–52, 62–4,
73–4, 111–17, 122–5, 157, 161–5,
  173–5; *see also* homogeneity of
  variance; residual variance
visual inspection of data 139,
  151–2, 172–3

Wickens, T. D. 52
Wilcoxon test 8, 132
within-subjects designs 3–4, 29,
  115–18, 122, 127, 136–7, 195,
  207; difficulties in interpreting
  128, 133; underlying
  assumptions of 129–32
Worthington, P. L. 8, 32, 75
writing up results 233–43; *see also*
  reporting

Yerkes–Dodson law 100

Z table 256–7